Joey Green's AMAZING Kitchen Cures

Also by Joey Green

Hellbent on Insanity
The Unofficial Gilligan's Island Handbook
The Get Smart Handbook
The Partridge Family Album
Polish Your Furniture with Panty Hose
Hi Bob!
Selling Out
Paint Your House with Powdered Milk
Wash Your Hair with Whipped Cream
The Bubble Wrap Book
Joey Green's Encyclopedia
The Zen of Oz
The Warning Label Book
Monica Speaks
You Know You've Reached Middle Age If . . .
The Official Slinky Book
The Mad Scientist Handbook
Clean Your Clothes with Cheez Whiz
The Road to Success Is Paved with Failure
Clean It! Fix It! Eat It!
Joey Green's Magic Brands
Jesus and Moses: The Parallel Sayings
The Mad Scientist Handbook 2
Senior Moments
Jesus and Muhammad: The Parallel Sayings

Joey Green's AMAZING Kitchen Cures

1,150 Ways to Prevent and Cure Common Ailments with Brand-Name Products

By Joey Green
Author of *Polish Your Furniture with Panty Hose*

BRISTOL PARK BOOKS / NEW YORK

First Bristol Park Books edition published in 2008.

Published by Bristol Park Books
252 W. 38th Street
NYC, NY 10018

Bristol Park Books is a registered trademark of
Bristol Park Books, Inc.

Published by arrangement with Rodale, Inc.

Library of Congress Catalog Number: 2002011483

ISBN 10: 0-88486-431-6
ISBN 13: 978-0-88486-431-8

Cover and interior design by Tara A. Long
Cover Illustrations by CSA Images
Cover photograph by Mitch Mandel/Rodale Images (woman with soda)
Cover photograph by Plastock/Photonica (refrigerator)

Printed in the United States of America.

To the amazing cure for whatever ails me:

Ingredients

But First, a Word from Our Sponsor xi

Acne	1	Broken Bones	51
Air Fresheners	5	Bruises	54
Allergies	8	Burns	56
Arthritis	11	Bursitis	60
Asthma	13	Calluses	62
Athlete's Foot	15	Canker Sores	65
Babies	18	Chafing	67
Backache	20	Chapped Lips	69
Bad Breath	23	Chicken Pox	71
Bathing	26	Cholesterol	73
Bed-Wetting	30	Cold Sores	76
Bee and Wasp Stings	32	Colds	78
Black Eyes	37	Constipation	83
Blisters	40	Contact Lenses	85
Body Odor	42	Corns	87
Boils	46	Cough	90
Breastfeeding	48	Cuts and Scrapes	92

Dandruff	96	Hair Coloring	173
Dehydration	99	Hair Gel	177
Dentures and Retainers	102	Hand Cleanser	179
Diaper Rash	104	Hangover	182
Diarrhea	108	Headache	184
Dry Hair	112	Heartburn	187
Dry Shampoo	116	Hemorrhoids	189
Dry Skin and Windburn	118	Herpes	192
Earache	123	Hiccups	194
Earwax	126	Hives	196
Eczema	129	Ice Packs	198
Eyeglasses	131	Indigestion	201
Eyes	134	Insect Bites	204
Facials	136	Insect Repellent	208
Fingernails and Toenails	140	Insomnia	210
Flatulence	146	Jellyfish Stings	213
Fleas	149	Kidney Stones	215
Flu	151	Knee Pain	217
Food Poisoning	156	Lactose Intolerance	219
Foot Ache	158	Lice	221
Foot Odor	161	Makeup	224
Freckles and Sunspots	164	Marital Relations	226
Green Hair	166	Memory Loss	231
Gum in Hair	169	Menopause	233

Menstruation	235	Stress	296
Muscle Pain	239	Stuck Ring	298
Nausea	242	Sunburn	302
Neck Pain	245	Swimmer's Ear	306
Nicotine Withdrawal	247	Tartar and Plaque	308
Nosebleed	249	Toothache	312
Pet Problems	251	Ulcer	315
Pizza Burn	258	Urinary Tract Infection	317
Poison Ivy	261	Varicose Veins	320
Pregnancy	265	Vomiting	322
Psoriasis	268	Warts	326
Rash	271	Wrinkles	329
Runny Nose	273	Yeast Infection	331
Shampoo	276		
Shaving	279	Acknowledgments	335
Shingles	284	The Fine Print	337
Skunk Odor	286	Trademark Information	341
Snoring	288	Index	349
Sore Throat	290	About the Author	369
Splinters	294	Bonus Section	371

But First, a Word from Our Sponsor

If necessity is the mother of invention, who is the father? Dumb luck? Desperation? Sheer panic?

When faced with a difficult problem, we human beings devise the most ingenious solutions.

During World War II, American soldiers—provided with packs of Wrigley's Spearmint Gum in their ration kits—used the chewed-up gum to patch Jeep tires, gas tanks, life rafts, and parts of airplanes.

During the Gulf War, American soldiers saturated Pampers disposable diapers with water to give themselves showers, treat heat exhaustion, and avoid dehydration in the blistering hot deserts of Saudi Arabia.

On April 30, 1998, a tanker truck flipped over on Interstate 74 in Cincinnati, Ohio, spilling four tons of inedible industrial animal fat. After workers tried unsuccessfully to clean up the spill with several industrial solvents, Cincinnati-based Procter & Gamble donated a tanker truck filled with Dawn dishwashing liquid to be sprayed over the oil slick and scrubbed with road sweeper brushes—in the largest demonstration of how well Dawn cuts through grease.

Ingenuity is everywhere. Nine out of ten Americans have a box of Arm & Hammer Baking Soda sitting in their refrigerator this very moment. Baking soda was not made to deodorize refrigerators. Baking soda was made for baking—explaining why the product was named "baking soda" in the first place. Most people know that Arm & Hammer Baking Soda can also be used to soothe insect bites, relieve poison ivy, and brush your teeth. It just goes to show that we all use brand-name products in unusual ways. In fact, most Americans drink

Coca-Cola to refresh their thirst—unaware that Coke was originally invented by an Atlanta pharmacist as an elixir and was advertised as a "brain tonic."

It got me wondering. How many ways are there to use brand-name products we've already got around the kitchen, bathroom, and garage to cure everyday aches and pains? To find out, I locked myself in the public library and dug through reference books and collections of home remedies. I obtained secret files from manufacturers. And I sifted through hundreds of e-mails I receive through my Web site, www.wackyuses.com, where devotees of offbeat uses for brand-name products share their discoveries with me.

Along the way, I unearthed some remarkable remedies and clever cures. Elmer's Glue-All removes blackheads and exfoliates the skin. Eating York Peppermint Patties soothes nausea. Soaking your feet in Jell-O deodorizes smelly feet. Vicks VapoRub foils toenail fungus. Lay's Potato Chips relieve the symptoms of premenstrual syndrome. Phillips' Milk of Magnesia doubles as hair gel. Colgate Toothpaste soothes burns. But I had to know more. Who invented Vicks VapoRub? Exactly who were the Smith Brothers? How did Pepto-Bismol get its name? What does the "Q" in Q-Tips stand for? And most importantly, aren't you glad you use Dial?

This book is the result of my obsessive quest to figure out how to avoid running to the drugstore in the middle of the night during a blizzard. So, now, if you're confronted with a sore throat, a splinter, a toothache, or a loved one telling you "Not tonight, I have a headache," you can take comfort knowing that an unusual yet useful solution lies right here at your fingertips.

How do people come up with these unconventional kitchen cures? Perhaps novelist Christopher Morely explained American ingenuity best when he wrote, "High heels were invented by a woman who had been kissed on the forehead."

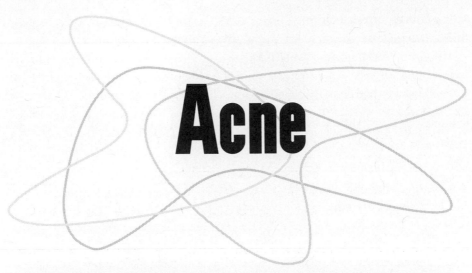

Acne

- **Arm & Hammer Baking Soda.** Pour a small amount of Arm & Hammer Baking Soda into the cupped palm of your hand and add a little water to make a paste. Put a small dab of the paste on any blemishes and let sit for a few minutes. Gently scrub your face with more of the paste. The baking soda cleans your skin thoroughly, exfoliates dead skin cells, loosens blackheads, and leaves your skin feeling wonderfully smooth.

- **Colgate Toothpaste.** Apply a dab of Colgate Regular Toothpaste on the pimples. The toothpaste dries up pimples quickly. Just be sure to use the regular flavor—not the tartar-control kind, which contains harsher chemicals.

- **Cortaid.** Applying a dab of Cortaid on your pimples reduces the swelling and tenderness.

- **Crest Toothpaste** and **Band-Aid Bandages.** Apply a dab of Crest Regular Toothpaste to the pimple, cover with a Band-Aid bandage before going to bed, and the swelling should dissipate by morning.

- **Dickinson's Witch Hazel.** Use a cotton ball to clean oil from the skin with this cooling astringent.

- **Elmer's Glue-All.** Rather than using Bioré strips to remove oil and blackheads, coat your face with a thin layer of Elmer's Glue-All (avoiding your eyes). Let the glue dry, then gently peel it off, exfoliating a thin layer of skin. Elmer's Glue-All is water soluble, so you can always wash it off with warm water should it stick to your eyebrows.

- **Epsom Salt.** To remove blackheads, add one teaspoon Epsom Salt and three drops iodine to one-half cup boiling water. Let the solution cool, dampen strips of cotton in it, and apply the strips to the clogged pores. Repeat three or four times, reheating the solution if necessary. Gently unclog your pores, then apply an alcohol-based astringent.

- **Heinz White Vinegar.** Mix equal parts Heinz White Vinegar and water, and use a cotton ball to clean your face with the astringent solution, to readjust your skin to the proper pH.

- **Hydrogen Peroxide.** Put a small amount of hydrogen peroxide on a cotton ball and rub it on your face, cleansing your pores with this mild astringent.

- **Kingsford's Corn Starch and ReaLemon.** When you break out in pimples, mix one teaspoon Kingsford's Corn Starch with one teaspoon ReaLemon lemon juice to make a paste. Apply to the affected areas and let dry. This acne treatment eliminates the redness and helps pimples dry up faster.

- **Kiwi White Liquid Shoe Polish.** Apply a few dabs of Kiwi White Liquid Shoe Polish over the pimples. The pipe clay and zinc oxide in the shoe polish dry the pimples and help bring them to a head.

- **Lipton Tea Bags.** To bring a pimple to a head quickly, dampen a Lipton Tea Bag with hot water (do not squeeze out the water) and apply as a compress.

- **Listerine.** Wash your face with warm water and soap, rinse, then saturate a cotton ball with Listerine and use the antiseptic mouthwash to cleanse your pores. Then dab the Listerine on blemishes. Leave the Listerine on your face for ten minutes or until you can no longer feel the tingling sensation. Then rinse your face with warm water to wash off all the Listerine and splash with cold water to close your pores again. Just be sure to use original flavor Listerine, not Cool Mint Listerine (which contains sugar).

- **Neosporin.** Dab a little Neosporin on pimples and blemishes. The antibiotic helps clear up acne.

- **Phillips' Milk of Magnesia.** Using Phillips' Milk of Magnesia as a facial mask helps dry up the excess oils from your face, and dabbing it on pimples reduces redness and speeds up healing.

- **Preparation H.** Applying a dab of Preparation H reduces the swelling of acne pimples.

- **Quaker Oats.** Make a bowl of oatmeal according to the directions on the back of the canister, let cool, and apply the oatmeal to your face. Cover with a washcloth dampened with warm water. Let sit for fifteen minutes, then wash clean. Repeat daily for one week, or whenever acne flares up. Oatmeal is a natural astringent that dries the skin.

- **ReaLemon.** Rub ReaLemon lemon juice over blackheads before going to bed. In the morning, wash off the juice with cool water. Repeat for several nights, and you should see a huge improvement in the skin. Also, dab ReaLemon on any blemish a few times during the day.

- **SueBee Honey** and **Band-Aid Bandages.** To bring an embedded pimple to a head, cover the blemish with a dab of SueBee Honey and place a Band-Aid bandage over it before you go to bed. Honey kills bacteria, keeps the pimple sterile, and speeds healing, bringing the pimple to the surface overnight.

- **Vicks VapoRub.** To dry up pimples, put a little dab of Vicks VapoRub on the blemishes, and the pimples will soon vanish.

- **Visine.** Applying a few drops of Visine to pimples and blemishes reduces the redness. Visine is a fast-acting vasoconstrictor. (If you intend to use the eyedrops in your eyes, do not let the tip of the bottle touch your skin.)

STRANGE FACTS

- ◆ During adolescence, the body begins producing large amounts of the hormone androgen, which causes the sebaceous glands in the skin to overproduce oil. When the excess oil gets trapped in the passageways under the skin, pimples form.

- ◆ A boy's body produces ten times more androgen than a girl's body does, meaning boys are ten times more likely than girls to get acne.

- ◆ Attempting to cover up heavy acne with makeup makes it worse.

- ◆ Despite folklore to the contrary, chocolate does not cause acne.

- ◆ In many episodes of the 1970s television series *The Partridge Family*, teen heartthrob David Cassidy has pimples on his face.

- General Manuel Antonio Noriega, former dictator of Panama, whose complexion was scarred by acne, was nicknamed "Pineapple Face" by his opponents.

- In the 1989 movie *How to Get Ahead in Advertising*, produced by former Beatle George Harrison, a British advertising executive planning a sales campaign for a new pimple cream suddenly develops a boil on his neck that turns into a second talking head.

- Bill Murray, Ray Liotta, Tommy Lee Jones, Edward James Olmos, Dennis Franz, Richard Belzer, James Woods, Richard Burton, Elizabeth Hurley, and Rene Russo can be seen in movies and on television with acne scars.

Air Fresheners

- **Arm & Hammer Baking Soda.** Add two teaspoons Arm & Hammer Baking Soda to two cups water in a sixteen-ounce trigger-spray bottle. Shake well, and spray the air of any room to banish bad odors. To deodorize a closet, place an open box of Arm & Hammer Baking Soda on a shelf.

- **Bounce.** Tape a Bounce dryer sheet to the front of a fan or inside an air conditioning vent, so the fan or air conditioner will blow fragrant air throughout the house. You can also place Bounce dryer sheets under sofas and carpets, in drawers, or suspended from a hanger in a closet—especially if you're about to close up a house for the winter.

- **Car-Freshner Pine Trees.** Hang a scented Car-Freshner Pine Tree on the window blinds, from an air conditioner vent, or from the pull string of a ceiling fan. Run the air conditioner or fan for two minutes. The fresh scent should last up to two hours. Keep the Car-Freshner Pine Tree in a Ziploc Storage Bag for another day.

- **Downy.** Add one tablespoon Downy liquid fabric softener to a sixteen-ounce trigger-spray bottle filled with water, shake well, and spray as an air freshener.

- **Heinz White Vinegar.** Remove odors from cooking, paint fumes, or cigarette smoke from a room by placing a small bowl of Heinz White Vinegar in the room. Heinz White Vinegar can also be used as a natural air freshener when sprayed full strength in a room.

- **Kingsford Charcoal Briquets.** Placing a clean, used coffee can filled with charcoal briquets (without any lighter fluid) in a closet or chest will absorb odors.

- **Maxwell House Coffee.** Fill a bowl with fresh grounds of Maxwell House Coffee as a room deodorizer and air freshener.

- **McCormick Vanilla Extract.** Saturate a cotton ball with vanilla extract and place it in your vacuum cleaner bag before cleaning to perfume the air.

- **Mennen Speed Stick.** Remove the lid from a Mennen Speed Stick and place the deodorant stick in a clothes drawer, linen closet, under a sofa, or under the seat of your car. You can also use a knife to slice the deodorant stick into chunks and place them around the house.

- **Nestea, ReaLemon,** and **Mr. Coffee Filter.** Mix one quart of Nestea according to the directions and add four tablespoons ReaLemon lemon juice. Strain through a paper coffee filter. Pour into empty trigger-spray bottles. Tea is a natural deodorizer.

STRANGE FACTS

- ◆ Before buying an air freshener in a grocery store, most shoppers pick a can off the shelf, remove the cap, and spray the air or their fingers, and breathe deep to test whether they like the fragrance. Air fresheners contain chemicals that no one in their right mind should be inhaling.

- ◆ Air is composed of 21 percent oxygen, 78 percent nitrogen, and 1 percent trace elements.

- ◆ To human beings, air is invisible, odorless, and tasteless.

- ◆ Your right lung takes in more air than your left lung does.

- ◆ People have lived more than a month without food and more than a week without water, but people cannot live more than a few minutes without air.

- ◆ If you are locked in a completely sealed room, you will die of carbon dioxide poisoning before you will die of oxygen deprivation.

◆ Air contains aerosols, which are invisible solid particles measuring roughly 0.1 micrometer in diameter. These aerosols include dust, sand, volcano and meteor ash, car exhaust, factory smoke, pollen, ocean salt, and microbes. Rain and snow wash many of these aerosols from the air.

◆ Humans live in the troposphere, which ends an average of approximately eight miles above the earth's surface (about ten miles above the equator, and roughly six miles above the North and South Poles). Beyond the troposphere, the air is too thin to support life as we know it.

Allergies

- **Altoids Peppermints.** Chewing two curiously strong Altoids Peppermints may clear up a stuffed-up nose. Peppermint relieves congestion.

- **Dannon Yogurt.** According to the *International Journal of Immunotherapy*, eating yogurt with active cultures enhances the body's immune system by increasing the production of gamma interferons, which play a key role in fighting certain allergies and viral infections.

- **Endust.** As fan blades turn through the air, they create static electricity, which attracts dust to the edges of the blades. Spraying Endust on the blades of overhead ceiling fans and oscillating fans and wiping them clean lubricates the blades, preventing dust from settling on them.

- **Glad Trash Bags** and **Scotch Packaging Tape.** Cut open the sides of several Glad Trash Bags, wrap your mattress and pillow in the plastic, and tape it in place to prevent dust mites from burrowing into the mattress.

- **Maybelline Crystal Clear Nail Polish.** If you are allergic to nickel or other metals, paint the backs of the fly buttons on jeans and the posts on earrings with clear nail polish and let dry to prevent skin irritations.

- **Mr. Coffee Filters.** In a pinch, you can use a Mr. Coffee Filter as a dust mask by simply placing it over your nose and mouth and breathing normally.

- **Scotch Packaging Tape.** Remove fuzz, lint, and pet hair from clothing by wrapping a strip of Scotch Packaging Tape around your hand, adhesive side out, and patting your clothes.

NOTHING TO SNEEZE AT

In 1872, John Kimberly, Charles Clark, Havilah Babcock, and Frank Shattuck founded Kimberly, Clark & Company in Neenah, Wisconsin, to manufacture newsprint from rags. In 1889, the company built a pulp and paper plant on the Fox River and, in 1914, developed Cellucotton, a cotton substitute used by the United States Army as surgical cotton during World War I. After the war, Kimberly-Clark, eager to find a commercial market for Cellucotton, introduced Kleenex Kerchiefs as a disposable facial towel to remove makeup. Army nurses had used Cellucotton pads as disposable sanitary napkins, prompting Kimberly-Clark to introduce Kotex, the first disposable feminine hygiene product, in 1920. The following year, Chicago inventor Andrew Olsen designed Serv-a-Tissue, a pop-up tissue box that Kimberly-Clark soon produced for its Kleenex Kerchiefs.

Housewives soon discovered that their husbands were using their Kleenex Kerchiefs as disposable handkerchiefs, and the subsequent letters of praise to Kimberly-Clark prompted the company to test-market the two possible uses for the product. In 1930, sixty percent of consumers in Peoria, Illinois, who were offered two different coupons redeemable for a free box of the tissues, chose the offer describing the product as a disposable handkerchief. And that's the way Kimberly-Clark has marketed Kleenex Tissues ever since.

DURING WORLD WAR II, soldiers used a more absorbent version of Cellucotton as air filters in gas masks.

IN 1936, Kimberly-Clark inserted a list of forty-eight alternative uses for the product into every box of Kleenex Tissues, including polishing furniture, cleaning pots and pans, and cleaning car windshields.

THE TRADEMARKED BRAND NAME KLEENEX appears as an entry in *Webster's Tenth New Collegiate Dictionary*, which clearly recognizes "Kleenex" as a protected trademark.

- **York Peppermint Pattie.** Eating a York Peppermint Pattie should quickly clear up a stuffed-up nose, because peppermint relieves congestion.

STRANGE FACTS

- ◆ Eighty percent of house dust is dead skin cells.

- ◆ When you sneeze, all bodily functions stop, including your heart.

- Between 25 and 33 percent of the population sneeze when they are exposed to light. The nerve endings in the nose are connected to the nerves in the eyes.

- Particles expelled by a sneeze have been recorded traveling at 103.6 miles per hour.

- *Gesundheit* is German for "good health." The word for sneeze in German is *niesen*.

- The Old English word for sneeze is *fneosan*.

- Roughly 15 percent of Americans have an allergy requiring repeated medical treatment.

- Allergies are caused by house dust, mold spores, pollen, and the dandruff or hair of household pets.

- The existence of airborne bacteria was discovered in 1861 by French bacteriologist Louis Pasteur.

- The sneezewort, a plant that grows in America, Europe, and Asia, got its name from the fact that its odor makes people sneeze.

Arthritis

- **Bubble Wrap** and **Scotch Packaging Tape.** If you have difficulty holding pens, silverware, brooms, mops, and rakes, cut a strip of Bubble Wrap, wrap it around the body of the instrument or utensil, and secure it in place with a piece of Scotch Packaging Tape, creating a more convenient grip.

- **French's Mustard.** Rub French's Mustard over the afflicted joints or empty a bottle of French's Mustard into a bathtub filled with hot water, mix well, and soak in the mustard bath for fifteen minutes.

- **Heinz Apple Cider Vinegar.** Before each meal, drink a glass of water containing two teaspoons Heinz Apple Cider Vinegar. Give this folk remedy at least three weeks to start relieving arthritis pain and joint immobility.

- **McCormick Bay Leaves, Star Olive Oil**, and **Mr. Coffee Filters.** Place three bay leaves and four teaspoons Star Olive Oil in a saucepan and warm over a low heat without letting the oil burn or smoke. Let cool, then strain through a Mr. Coffee Filter. Apply to the affected area.

- **Quaker Oats.** Mix two cups Quaker Oats and one cup water in a bowl and then warm it in the microwave oven. Cool slightly. Apply the warm mixture to your hands to soothe arthritis pain.

- **Tabasco Pepper Sauce.** Spread the hot sauce on achy joints. Tabasco Pepper Sauce is made from a variety of pepper called *Capsicum frutescens*, which contains the alkaloid capsaicin, a spicy compound proven to numb pain when applied topically. Capsaicin enters nerves and temporarily depletes them of the neurotransmitter that sends pain signals to the brain. If you feel a burning sensation on the skin, apply a thin coat of Colgate Toothpaste over the dried Tabasco Pepper Sauce. The glycerin in the toothpaste will reduce the burning discomfort, and may also enhance the pain relief from the capsaicin. Do not apply Tabasco Pepper Sauce to an open wound.

- **Wilson Tennis Balls.** If you have difficulty holding silverware or a toothbrush, ask someone to use a razor blade to carefully slice small slits in opposite sides of a Wilson Tennis Ball. Slip the handle of the utensil through the tennis ball, creating a handy grip.

Strange Facts

- ◆ While scores of people swear that rubbing WD-40 into aching joints relieves arthritis pain, the WD-40 Company refuses to condone using WD-40, a product made from petroleum distillates, to ease arthritis.

- ◆ A new case of arthritis is diagnosed every thirty-three seconds.

- ◆ More than 31 million Americans suffer from arthritis. That's one out of every seven people.

- ◆ There is no cure for arthritis.

- ◆ In osteoarthritis, the cartilage between the bones in a joint disintegrates, causing the bones to rub against each other.

- ◆ In rheumatoid arthritis (better known as rheumatism), inflamed tissue around a joint causes the cartilage and bones to disintegrate. Doctors do not know what causes rheumatism or how to cure it.

- ◆ Other forms of arthritis include gout (painful swelling caused by too much uric acid in the blood), ankylosing spondylitis (inflamed spinal joints leading to a stooped back), and septic arthritis (bacterial infection of a joint).

- ◆ In the 1956 movie *Bigger Than Life*, James Mason plays a small-town schoolteacher who, given cortisone to treat a severe case of arthritis, turns into a scheming megalomaniac.

- ◆ Norma Wickwire, an American suffering from rheumatoid arthritis, had both hips, both knees, both shoulders, and both elbows replaced—achieving the world record for artificial joints.

Asthma

- **Coca-Cola.** If you feel the onset of an asthma attack and you don't have your inhaler with you, drink two cans of Coke. The caffeine can help thwart an asthma attack in an emergency until you can get to your medicine or inhaler.

- **Glad Trash Bags** and **Scotch Packaging Tape.** Cut open the sides of several Glad Trash Bags, wrap your mattress and pillow in the plastic, and tape in place to prevent dust mites from using them as a home.

- **Gold's Horseradish.** Eating Gold's Horseradish on a cracker or a stalk of celery decongests bronchial tubes.

- **Heinz Apple Cider Vinegar.** If you start to feel congested and about to wheeze, taking a teaspoon of Heinz Apple Cider Vinegar may stop the onset of a full-blown asthma attack.

- **Maxwell House Coffee.** In an emergency, drink two cups of black coffee to thwart an asthma attack. The caffeine helps dilate the bronchial passages.

- **Tabasco Pepper Sauce** and **Campbell's Tomato Juice.** Mix ten to twenty drops Tabasco Pepper Sauce in a glass of Campbell's Tomato Juice. Drink several of these decongestant tonics daily to help relieve congestion in the nose, sinuses, and lungs.

> Don't let asthma take your breath away. Get emergency care if walking or talking becomes difficult, your fingernails or lips turn blue, breathing is labored, and your nostrils flare.

Strange Facts

◆ Research sponsored by the National Heart, Lung, and Blood Institute reveals that adults with asthma who drink coffee regularly suffer 33 percent fewer symptoms than non-coffee-drinking adult asthmatics.

◆ Approximately nine million Americans suffer from asthma. That's roughly one out of every twenty-nine people.

◆ In most cases, asthma is an allergic reaction to pollen, house dust, or foods.

◆ Asthmatic wheezing can be triggered by a whiff of cologne or a perfume sample in the pages of a magazine.

◆ Many people with asthma are allergic to aspirin.

◆ In the short story "The Norwood Builder" by Sir Arthur Conan Doyle, renowned sleuth Sherlock Holmes reveals his astute observation skills when he tells a perfect stranger, "You mentioned your name as if I should recognize it, but I assure you that, beyond the obvious facts that you are a bachelor, a solicitor, a Freemason, and an asthmatic, I know nothing whatever about you."

◆ Composer Ludwig van Beethoven, author Charles Dickens, president Woodrow Wilson, actress Elizabeth Taylor, rock star Alice Cooper, film director Martin Scorsese, and basketball player Dennis Rodman have all suffered from asthma.

Athlete's Foot

- **Arm & Hammer Baking Soda.** Add a little water to baking soda to make a paste. Rub the paste between your toes and over the affected area, let sit for five minutes, then rinse clean and dry.

- **Clorox.** Mix one-half cup Clorox bleach in a gallon of water, and soak your feet in the solution for fifteen minutes twice a day until the affliction disappears. Many people say that chlorine bleach kills athlete's foot fungus.

- **ConAir Pro Style 1600 Hairdryer.** Before putting on socks and shoes, make sure your feet are completely dry by holding a hair dryer a few inches from your toes.

- **Dr. Bronner's Peppermint Soap.** Soap up your feet with Dr. Bronner's Peppermint Soap, dry your feet, then apply a dash of the soap as a lotion to your dry feet.

- **Heinz White Vinegar.** Soak your feet in Heinz White Vinegar for ten minutes four times daily for several weeks. Vinegar is acidic and kills bacteria and fungi.

- **Kingsford's Corn Starch.** Sprinkle Kingsford's Corn Starch on your feet and in your shoes to absorb moisture and reduce friction.

- **Listerine.** Washing your lesions with Listerine will sting and burn like the dickens, but the antiseptic seems to kill the foot fungus.

SIDE EFFECTS
SMELLY SHOES AND SOCKS

ARM & HAMMER BAKING SODA
In the evening, sprinkle Arm & Hammer Baking Soda inside shoes to kill odors. Shake out the powder in the morning.

BABY MAGIC BABY POWDER
To keep shoes and sneakers dry and comfortable, dust the insides with Baby Magic Baby Powder.

BOUNCE
Place a sheet of Bounce inside your shoes and sneakers, let sit overnight, and by morning your shoes will smell fresh.

CONAIR PRO STYLE 1600 HAIRDRYER
If your shoes, boots, or sneakers get wet from rain or excessive perspiration, insert the nozzle of a ConAir Pro Style 1600 Hairdryer into the footwear and use on a low setting for five minutes.

DIAL SOAP
Place a wrapped bar of Dial Soap in your shoes or sneakers overnight so they'll smell great in the morning.

FEBREZE
Spraying Febreze in smelly shoes and sneakers eliminates the offensive odor.

HEINZ WHITE VINEGAR
Add one-half cup Heinz White Vinegar to your laundry during the rinse cycle, eliminating the need for harsh chemicals.

KINGSFORD'S CORN STARCH
Dust the insides of your shoes and sneakers with Kingsford's Corn Starch to keep them dry and comfortable. Cornstarch absorbs moisture.

LISTERINE
Add one cup Listerine to your regular wash to kill the bacteria and fungi.

LYSOL
Spray the inside of your shoes with Lysol disinfectant spray to kill the fungus spores living inside.

MAXWELL HOUSE COFFEE
Sprinkle a pinch of unused Maxwell House Coffee in each shoe every other day or so. The coffee absorbs excess moisture and deodorizes the footwear.

PLAYTEX GENTLE GLIDE ODOR ABSORBING TAMPONS
Place a Playtex Gentle Glide Odor Absorbing Tampon inside each shoe overnight. By morning, odors vanish.

TIDY CATS and L'EGGS SHEER ENERGY PANTY HOSE
Cut off the feet from a pair of clean, used L'eggs Sheer Energy Panty Hose, fill each foot with unused Tidy Cats, tie the ends, and place inside shoes or sneakers overnight. The cat box filler absorbs moisture and odors.

20 MULE TEAM BORAX
Sprinkle 20 Mule Team Borax into shoes or sneakers, let sit overnight, and empty the borax from the shoes in the morning. The vile smell and perspiration will be absorbed by the borax.

USA TODAY
Crumple up pages from *USA Today* and shove into smelly footwear. Let sit overnight to absorb moisture and odors.

- **Morton Salt.** Dissolve eight teaspoons salt in one quart warm water and soak your feet in the solution for five to ten minutes daily until the problem disappears. The salt creates an inhospitable environment for the fungus.

- **Pine-Sol.** Mix one-quarter cup Pine-Sol into a bowl of warm water and soak your feet in the pine solution for ten to fifteen minutes. Repeat every few days until the athlete's foot disappears.

- **Preparation H.** Coat your feet with Preparation H to soothe athlete's foot and relieve itchy toes.

- **Ziploc Storage Bags.** To avoid powdering the floor, fill a gallon-size Ziploc Storage Bag with cornstarch and dip your feet in the bag.

STRANGE FACTS

- ◆ Athlete's foot is a fungus from the ringworm family called *Tinea pedis*.

- ◆ Athlete's foot is not limited to athletes or feet. Athlete's foot fungus can spread to your hands or groin—at which point it becomes known as ringworm.

- ◆ Dr. William Scholl, founder of Dr. Scholl's foot care products, lived by his own credo: "Early to bed, early to rise, work like hell and advertise."

- ◆ In Eskimo tradition, a woman having difficulty conceiving a child carries a piece of an old shoe with her at all times to boost her fertility.

- ◆ Like fingerprints, no two footprints are alike.

- ◆ In a 1939 radio address, President Franklin D. Roosevelt said, "A radical is a man with both feet firmly planted—in the air."

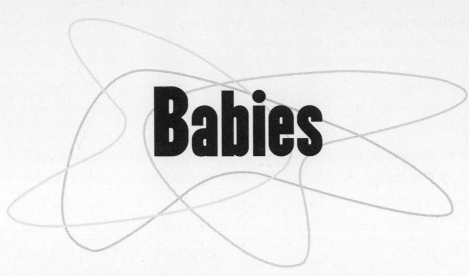

Babies

- **CoverGirl NailSlicks Classic Red.** If you have identical twins and have difficulty telling them apart, paint one infant's fingernail or toenail with CoverGirl NailSlicks Classic Red to tell the children apart.

- **Johnson's Baby Shampoo, Johnson's Baby Oil, Smirnoff Vodka, and Bounty Paper Towels.** To make your own baby wipes, mix three teaspoons Johnson's Baby Shampoo, two teaspoons Johnson's Baby Oil, one tablespoon Smirnoff Vodka, and two cups water. Tear off twenty individual sheets of Bounty paper towels. Cut each square in half, and fold each half into thirds (like a baby wipe). Place all the folded sheets in a pan. Drizzle the mixture over the paper towels, allowing the towels to absorb the liquid. Stack the towels in an airtight container.

- **Lipton Tea Bags.** Relieve a baby from the pain of an inoculation by dampening a Lipton Tea bag in warm water and applying to the sore spot. The tannic acid in the tea soothes the soreness.

- **Mott's Apple Sauce.** If your children have difficulty swallowing pills, empty the contents of the capsule into some applesauce, stir, and have them eat the applesauce.

- **Stayfree Maxi Pads and Scotch Packaging Tape.** Protect your infant or toddler from sharp corners on coffee tables, end tables, cabinets, dining room tables, and other pieces of furniture by taping Stayfree Maxi Pads over the corners.

- **Wilson Tennis Balls** and **Scotch Packaging Tape.** Cut old Wilson Tennis Balls in half or in quarters, and use Scotch Packaging Tape to tape the sections over sharp corners of furniture, which might be dangerous to a baby.

STRANGE FACTS

- ◆ Kids eat more Play-Doh than crayons, finger paint, and white paste *combined*.

- ◆ Baby oil is made primarily from mineral oil, a clear, colorless, oily liquid with little odor or taste. Distilled from petroleum, mineral oil is used medicinally as a lubricant and laxative, as an oil base in cosmetics and hair tonics, and as an ingredient of paints and varnishes.

- ◆ A baby oyster is called a spat.

- ◆ Harry S. Truman said, "I have found that the best way to give advice to your children is to find out what they want and then advise them to do it."

- ◆ Gerber Foods started selling baby food in Africa, using the same packaging as in the United States—the Gerber baby on the label. Unfortunately, in Africa, where illiteracy runs rampant, companies label jars and bottles of food with pictures of the ingredients.

- ◆ In 1974, to promote toy safety at Christmastime, the Consumer Product Safety Commission printed up 80,000 buttons that read "For Kids' Sakes, Think Toy Safety." The buttons—made with sharp edges, lead-based paint, and pins that came off easily and could be swallowed by a child—were immediately recalled.

- ◆ Italian Renaissance artist Leonardo da Vinci, United States treasury secretary Alexander Hamilton, French Impressionist Paul Cézanne, American novelist Jack London, and actress Sophia Loren were all born to unmarried parents.

- ◆ On November 7, 1996, sixty-three-year-old Arceli Keh of Highland, California, gave birth to a baby girl at Loma Linda University Medical Center, making her the world's oldest new mother.

Backache

- **Adolph's Meat Tenderizer.** Make a paste from meat tenderizer and water, then rub the mixture into your back as a liniment. The meat tenderizer helps ease the pain in your back.

- **Bayer Aspirin.** Bayer Aspirin is an anti-inflammatory, and taking one aspirin a day can help eliminate inflammation around the site of the back pain. Do not try this if you are allergic to aspirin.

- **Bubble Wrap.** Cut rectangular sheets of Bubble Wrap and stuff them into an empty pillowcase or a gallon-size Ziploc Freezer Bag. Place the Bubble Wrap pillow behind the small of your back when sitting in an office chair, when driving the car, or on long airplane flights.

- **Flex Free Horse Liniment.** Rub a teaspoon of Flex Free Horse Liniment into your back and neck for instant relief from back pain and a stiff neck. (After using the horse liniment on your skin, you may experience a slight garlicky aftertaste in your mouth.)

- **French's Mustard.** Rub French's Mustard over your back, or empty a bottle of French's Mustard into a bathtub filled with hot water, mix well, and soak in the mustard bath for fifteen minutes.

- **McCormick Bay Leaves, Star Olive Oil**, and **Mr. Coffee Filters.** Place three bay leaves and four teaspoons of Star Olive Oil in a saucepan and warm over a low heat without letting the oil burn or smoke. Let cool, then strain through a Mr. Coffee Filter. Apply this potent herbal remedy to the affected area.

- **Smirnoff Vodka** and **Mr. Coffee Filters.** Fill a clean, used mayonnaise jar with freshly picked lavender flowers, fill the jar with Smirnoff Vodka, seal the lid tightly, and set the jar in a window in the sun for three days. Strain the lavender liquid through a Mr. Coffee Filter, then use a cotton ball to apply the tincture to your back, reapplying as needed.

- **Tabasco Pepper Sauce.** Spread the hot sauce on your back. The alkaloid capsaicin in Tabasco Pepper Sauce deadens pain when applied topically. Capsaicin enters nerves and temporarily depletes them of the neurotransmitter that sends pain signals to the brain. If you feel any burning, apply some Colgate Toothpaste over the dried Tabasco Pepper Sauce. The glycerin in the toothpaste minimizes the sting and may also boost the capsaicin's pain-killing properties. Do not apply Tabasco Pepper Sauce to an open wound.

- **Uncle Ben's Converted Brand Rice.** Pour two cups Uncle Ben's Converted Brand Rice into a microwave-safe container and heat in the microwave for one minute. Carefully pour or spoon the hot rice into a sock (not too compactly), tie a knot in the end, and place the warm sock on the spot where your back hurts for ten minutes to relieve the pain. The sock conforms wherever applied.

- **Wilson Tennis Balls.** Fill a sock with three or four Wilson Tennis Balls and tie a knot in the end of the sock. Have a partner roll the sock over your back. This technique is frequently used by labor coaches to massage the back of a pregnant woman in labor.

- **Ziploc Freezer Bags.** A gallon-size Ziploc Freezer Bag makes an excellent inflatable portable travel pillow. Simply seal the bag securely, leaving a half-inch opening at one end of the "zipper." Inflate the bag and quickly seal the remaining half-inch. Place behind the small of your back when sitting in an office chair, when driving the car, or on long airplane flights. Deflate and flatten for easy storage.

- **Ziploc Freezer Bags.** Heat relieves a backache. Fill a gallon-size Ziploc Freezer Bag with hot (not scalding) water, seal it securely, wrap it in a paper towel, and place it on your back, letting the flexible hot water bottle conform to the shape of your body.

- **Ziploc Freezer Bags.** Placing an ice pack on your back for ten minutes relieves back pain. Fill a Ziploc Freezer Bag with water and freeze it or fill it with ice cubes to make an ice pack. Wrap the ice pack in a paper towel before applying. For other ways to make and apply an ice pack, see page 198.

STRANGE FACTS

- In Greek mythology, according to the Greek poet in the *Theogony*, Zeus condemns Apollo "to bear on his back forever the cruel strength of the crushing world and the vault of the sky."

- In 1972, the O'Jays—Eddie Levert, Walter Williams, and William Powell—recorded the hit song "Backstabbers," earning the trio a gold record.

- According to the Vermont Back Research Center at the University of Vermont in Burlington, at this very moment, one out of every ten adults in the United States is experiencing back pain.

- "Breaking your back" means doing whatever it takes to accomplish a task.

- "Going behind someone's back" means to circumvent someone.

- "Talking behind someone's back" means to speak treacherously.

- "Falling flat on your back" means to fail utterly.

- "Breaking someone's back" means to cause someone to fail.

- "Getting off someone's back" means to stop nagging or criticizing someone.

- "Backing someone into a corner" means pressuring someone by limiting their options.

- "Patting someone on the back" means giving praise.

- "Stabbing someone in the back" means betraying someone with an act of treachery.

- "Turning your back on someone" means intentionally neglecting someone.

- "Backing down" means to retreat, "backing out" means withdrawing from a commitment, and "backing up" means to give your support.

Bad Breath

- **Alka-Seltzer.** Dissolve two Alka-Seltzer tablets in a glass of warm water and use as a mouthwash. The baking soda in the Alka-Seltzer lowers the pH level in your mouth, killing odor-producing bacteria.

- **Arm & Hammer Baking Soda.** Add one teaspoon Arm & Hammer Baking Soda to one-half glass warm water, and swish through your teeth for a refreshing mouthwash. The baking soda solution raises the acid level in your mouth, inhibiting odors.

- **Country Time Lemonade.** Put one teaspoon Country Time Lemonade powdered drink mix in your mouth, swish around, and swallow. The citric acid in Country Time Lemonade stimulates saliva production and impedes the odor-producing enzymes in your mouth, while the powdered mix makes your breath lemon fresh.

- **Dr. Bronner's Peppermint Soap.** Add two drops of Dr. Bronner's Peppermint Soap to a cup of water, rinse your mouth, and spit out. Dr. Bronner's Peppermint Soap is made from 100 percent vegetable oil and will kill the bacteria in your mouth.

- **Heinz Apple Cider Vinegar.** Mix equal parts Heinz Apple Cider Vinegar and water in a drinking glass for a potent mouth rinse. The acetic acid in the vinegar lowers the pH level in your mouth, killing odor-producing bacteria.

- **MasterCard.** Scrape your tongue with the edge of a credit card to remove all the tongue grunge, removing armies of odor-producing bacteria from your mouth.

- **McCormick Ground Cinnamon, Smirnoff Vodka,** and **Mr. Coffee Filters.** Mix nine tablespoons powdered cinnamon and one cup vodka. Seal in an airtight container and let sit for two weeks, shaking the contents twice a day. Strain the liquid through a Mr. Coffee Filter. Use one tablespoon of the resulting tincture mixed in a glass of warm water to rinse your mouth.

- **ReaLemon.** If you're all out of mouthwash or just hate that harsh sting, squirt a few drops of ReaLemon lemon juice into your mouth, swish it around, and swallow to make your breath lemon fresh. The citric acid alters the pH level in your mouth, killing bacteria.

- **Tang.** Put a teaspoon of Tang powdered drink mix in your mouth, swish it around, and swallow. The citric acid in Tang stimulates saliva production and impedes the odor-producing enzymes in your mouth. The orange taste of the Tang also freshens your breath.

STRANGE FACTS

- The scientific term for bad breath is *halitosis*.

- It is impossible to kill yourself by simply holding your breath.

- Syphilis can cause bad breath.

- Bacteria making their home on your gums and tongue, where they convert food particles into sulfuric gases, are the major cause of bad breath.

- Ancient Greek courtesans (mistresses of wealthy men) perfumed their breath with an aromatic oil that they swished around their mouths and then spat out.

- The Bible contains the poetic verse "May the fragrance of your breath be like apples" (Song of Songs 7:8).

- Forty-five percent of Americans use mouthwash every day.

- In the 1960s, television commercials for Scope Mouthwash showed nervous coworkers in an office building trying to determine which one of them would tell the boss he had bad breath.

- In 1971, the rock group Jethro Tull released the album *Aqualung*, containing the song "Locomotive Breath."

HOLY LIFE SAVERS!

In the early 1900s, Cleveland-based chocolate maker Clarence A. Crane came up with the idea for white-circle mints with a hole in the center—as something different. He had a pharmaceutical manufacturer produce them on his pill machine, and named the mints Life Savers because they resembled the flotation devices. Crane created a label depicting an old sailor tossing a life preserver to a beautiful lady swimmer. The type read "Crane's Peppermint Life Savers—5¢—For That Stormy Breath." The original package was a small cardboard tube with paper caps on each end.

In 1913, New York advertising salesman Edward John Noble tried to convince Crane to let him advertise the product. Instead, Crane sold the rights to Life Savers to Noble and his boyhood friend, J. Roy Allen, for $2,900. Realizing that the mints soon lost their flavor and absorbed the odor of the cardboard package, Noble switched to the tinfoil wrapping and paper band label still used to this day. He paid six women five dollars a week each to hand-wrap the mints, refusing to quit his advertising job until the Life Savers business took off. Noble told his customers to place the rolls of Life Savers next to the cash register with a big five-cent price card, and then to make sure all customers received a nickel with their change. Within a few years, Noble's company had made a quarter of a million dollars from sales of the minty impulse item.

THE MOST POPULAR FLAVOR of Life Savers is Pep-O-Mint.

IN 1913, the company had costumed women hand out Life Savers for free on streets and in office building lobbies.

EDWARD NOBLE designed a cardboard display rack to be placed next to the register to hold Life Savers and other manufacturers' chewing gum and candy bars.

AN ESTIMATED 75 PERCENT of Life Savers are purchased by people who did not plan to buy them until they saw the display.

ADVERTISEMENTS FOR LIFE SAVERS have included the corny puns *hole-some, enjoy-mint, refresh-mint,* and *content-mint.*

THE WORLD RECORD for keeping a Life Saver in the mouth with the hole intact is 7 hours, 10 minutes.

IF YOU BITE INTO a Wint-O-Green Life Saver in a dark room, a quick burst of bluish-green light flashes the moment the wintergreen candy is crushed. Crushing a crystalline substance, in this case the synthetic wintergreen (methyl salicylate), emits light. This phenomenon is called *triboluminescence.*

IN A LETTER PUBLISHED in the *New England Journal of Medicine*, two Illinois physicians, Dr. Howard Edward Jr. and Dr. Donald Edward, warned that biting a Wint-O-Green Life Saver while in an oxygen tent, operating room, or space capsule could be life threatening. The *Journal* declared Wint-O-Green Life Savers safe for oxygen tents and gas stations.

Bathing

- **Arm & Hammer Baking Soda.** Dissolve one-half cup Arm & Hammer Baking Soda in a bathtub filled with warm water for soft, smooth skin and a relaxing bath.

- **Carnation NonFat Dry Milk.** For a luxurious milk bath, add a handful of Nestlé Carnation NonFat Dry Milk powder to warm running bathwater. The lactic acid in the milk softens the skin.

- **Clairol Herbal Essences Shampoo.** Add a capful of Clairol Herbal Essences Shampoo to running bathwater for a luxurious, aromatic, relaxing, and 99 percent all-natural bubble bath.

- **Coppertone.** Add two tablespoons Coppertone to a warm bath as a moisturizing bath oil.

- **French's Mustard** and **Epsom Salt.** Add six tablespoons French's Mustard and a handful of Epsom Salt to the bathtub as it fills for a soothing, rejuvenating mustard bath that will ease the kinks and stiffness in your muscles.

- **Huggies Baby Wipes.** If you're unable to shower or bathe, give yourself a sponge bath with Huggies Baby Wipes.

- **Johnson's Baby Oil.** Add a few drops of Johnson's Baby Oil to your bathwater as a lavish bath oil that will moisturize your skin.

- **L'eggs Sheer Energy Panty Hose.** Cut off one leg from a pair of clean, used L'eggs Sheer Energy Panty Hose, fill the foot with the herb of your choice (lavender, mint, orange peel, rosemary), and hang it from the faucet in the bathtub under running bathwater.

- **L'eggs Sheer Energy Panty Hose.** Cut off the leg of a pair of clean, used L'eggs Sheer Energy Panty Hose, stick a bar of soap inside at the knee, tie a knot around both ends, and use the panty hose to wash your back in the bath or shower.

- **Maxwell House Coffee.** For an invigorating coffee bath, take freshly used Maxwell House Coffee grounds, get into an empty bathtub, and rub the warm grounds all over your body from the neck down. Wait ten minutes, then fill the tub with warm water and soak for an instant spa treatment that would cost you hundreds of dollars in Beverly Hills. (Put a plastic strainer over the drain to prevent it from clogging with coffee grounds.)

- **Noxzema.** Add two tablespoons Noxzema skin cream to a warm bath as a moisturizing bath oil to soothe your skin.

- **Pampers.** To give yourself a rejuvenating sponge bath, saturate a Pampers disposable diaper with water (you'll be amazed at how much liquid it holds) and use it to wipe down your body. During the Gulf War, United States soldiers used disposable diapers (sent from home) to give themselves showers in the desert.

- **Skin-So-Soft.** For a soothing bath, add two tablespoons Skin-So-Soft to a warm bath as a bath oil.

- **Ziploc Freezer Bags.** To make a waterproof pillow for the bathtub, seal a Ziploc Freezer Bag securely, leaving a half-inch opening at one end of the "zipper." Inflate the bag and quickly seal the remaining half-inch, and place the pillow under your head.

- **Ziploc Storage Bags.** If you've lost the plug for the bathtub drain, fill a Ziploc Storage Bag with water, and without sealing it, place it over the drain hole. The suction from the drain will hold the plastic bag in place, corking the drain.

STRANGE FACTS

◆ By 3000 B.C.E., Pakistanis had private bathtubs in their homes with taps and terra-cotta pipes.

- As early as 2000 B.C.E., royal families living in the Minoan palace at Knossos on the island of Crete had bathtubs with stone pipes to carry cold and hot water, which were eventually replaced with fitted pipes made of glazed pottery.

- In ancient Egypt, priests bathed in cold water four times a day.

- While her husband Agamemnon, a Greek hero who had just returned from fighting in the Trojan War, was relaxing in the bathtub, Clytemnestra killed him with two strokes of an ax.

- While taking a bath, Greek scientist Archimedes realized that his body, immersed in water, lost weight equal to the weight of the water it displaced. This law of physics is known as the Archimedean principle.

- In the second century B.C.E., the Romans built extensive public bath houses, complete with libraries, exercise rooms, shops, gardens, and a wide variety of hedonistic spa treatments.

- The Ancient Egyptian queen Cleopatra luxuriated in milk baths.

- Since full-body bathing required nudity, the Church in the Middle Ages labeled the activity as sinful, banning the temptation of the flesh and putting an end to regular bathing throughout Europe. Without good hygiene, diseases like the Black Plague spread like wildfire, killing thousands.

- On July 13, 1793, Charlotte Corday stabbed Jean-Paul Marat, an advocate of violence during the French Revolution, while he was taking a bath.

- French playwright Edmond Rostand wrote his 1898 play *Cyrano de Bergerac* while sitting in a bathtub.

- William Howard Taft, who weighed three hundred pounds, was the only United States president to get stuck in the White House bathtub.

- In 1964, astronaut John Glenn fell in the bathtub, forcing him to withdraw from his race for senator from Ohio. Glenn was elected to the senate in 1974.

SIDE EFFECTS
BATHTUB RINGS

CASCADE
Fill the bathtub with warm water, add two tablespoons Cascade, let stand for about ten minutes, then use a sponge to scrub the tub, then rinse with water. Cascade contains 7.5 percent phosphates. Phosphates contain the element phosphorus, one of many nutrients essential to water plants and algae. But since phosphorus also contributes to accelerated eutrophication—the excessively rapid growth of aquatic plant life in water bodies—many state governments have banned the sale of detergents with phosphates.

CLAIROL HERBAL ESSENCES SHAMPOO
Pour Clairol Herbal Essences Shampoo on a sponge and scrub the soap scum in the tub, let sit overnight, then rinse clean.

CLEAN SHOWER
Spray the tub with Clean Shower, scrub gently with a sponge, and rinse clean.

COCA-COLA
To get rid of rust in a bathtub, saturate a sponge with Coca-Cola and scrub the rust stain. The phosphoric acid in the Coke removes rust.

EASY-OFF OVEN CLEANER
To clean stubborn bathtub rings, spray Easy-Off Oven Cleaner on the tub (making sure the room is well-ventilated), let sit for thirty minutes, then rinse thoroughly with dishwashing liquid and water.

HEINZ WHITE VINEGAR
Fill the bathtub with hot water, pour in two cups Heinz White Vinegar, and let sit for three hours to soften calcium deposits and other hard-water stains, making them easier to scrub clean.

MCCORMICK CREAM OF TARTAR and HYDROGEN PEROXIDE
To clean rust stains from a bathtub, make a paste from Cream of Tartar and hydrogen peroxide, scrub with a brush, and rinse thoroughly.

SKIN-SO-SOFT
Fill the bathtub with hot water, add two capfuls Skin-So-Soft, and use a sponge to wipe grease stains clean.

SMIRNOFF VODKA
To clean the caulking around bathtubs and showers, fill a trigger-spray bottle with Smirnoff Vodka, spray the caulking, let sit five minutes, and wash clean. The alcohol in the vodka kills the mold and mildew.

TURTLE WAX
After cleaning your bathtub, rub Turtle Wax Car Polish into the tub and immediately polish with a soft cloth, giving it a great shine and protecting the tub from future stains.

20 MULE TEAM BORAX and REALEMON
Make a paste from 20 Mule Team Borax and ReaLemon lemon juice, and using an abrasive sponge, scrub rust stains for easy removal.

Bed-Wetting

- **Glad Trash Bags.** To improvise a plastic sheet to waterproof a mattress, cut a Glad Trash Bag down the sides and place it under the sheets. Or wrap the mattress in several Glad Trash Bags and secure them in place with Scotch Packaging Tape.

- **Krispy Original Saltine Crackers.** Have the child eat a dozen saltine crackers before going to bed. Saltine crackers absorb the excess liquid in the stomach.

- **Scotchgard.** Protect the mattress from a bed wetter by spraying it with Scotchgard to make it waterproof.

- **SueBee Honey.** A teaspoon of honey at bedtime will attract and retain fluid in a child's body during the hours of sleeping. Honey is hygroscopic and absorbs liquid. (Honey should not be fed to infants under one year of age.)

STRANGE FACTS

- ◆ One out of every seven children wets the bed.

- ◆ Approximately 60 percent of all bed wetters are boys.

- ◆ At age eighteen, 1 percent of boys still wet the bed.

- ◆ The scientific term for bed-wetting is *enuresis*.

- As early as 77 B.C.E., the Roman scholar Pliny the Elder suggested as a cure adding "boiled mice" to the food of children who wet the bed.

- An ancient Byzantine remedy for bed-wetting was a wine made from the testicles of a hare.

- As a child, novelist George Orwell, author of *1984* and *Animal Farm*, was a bed wetter.

- Birds do not urinate in their nests.

SIDE EFFECTS
URINE TROUBLE

ARM & HAMMER BAKING SODA
After blotting up the urine and cleaning with club soda (see below), let the spot dry completely, then cover with Arm & Hammer Baking Soda. Let it sit for one hour, then vacuum up. The baking soda will remove the smell of urine.

CANADA DRY CLUB SODA
After blotting up as much urine as possible, pour Canada Dry Club Soda over the stained area and immediately blot up.

HEINZ WHITE VINEGAR
Blot up urine, flush area several times with lukewarm water, then apply a mixture of equal parts Heinz White Vinegar and cool water. Blot up, rinse, and let dry. The vinegar will remove the smell of the urine.

HEINZ WHITE VINEGAR
Deodorize urine-stained sheets and clothes by adding a cup of Heinz White Vinegar to the laundry water.

PAMPERS
Place a Pampers disposable diaper over the stain, set several heavy books on top of the diaper to keep it pressed flat against the stain, and let sit for one hour. The absorbent diaper will soak up most of the urine.

20 MULE TEAM BORAX
To neutralize urine odors in mattresses and mattress covers, dampen the spot with water, rub in 20 Mule Team Borax, let dry, then vacuum or brush clean.

Bee and Wasp Stings

- **Adolph's Meat Tenderizer.** To relieve bee and wasp stings, mix Adolph's Meat Tenderizer with water to make a paste and apply to the sting, making sure you have removed the stinger. The enzymes in meat tenderizer break down the proteins in bee venom.

- **Arm & Hammer Baking Soda** and **Band-Aid Bandages.** Make a paste from Arm & Hammer Pure Baking Soda and water, apply it to the sting, making sure you have removed the stinger, and cover with a Band-Aid bandage. The baking soda draws out the venom and neutralizes the sting.

- **Ban Deodorant.** Apply Ban Deodorant directly on a bee or wasp sting to stop the pain and swelling immediately.

- **Bayer Aspirin.** Wet the skin and rub a Bayer Aspirin tablet over the sting, making sure you have removed the stinger, to help control inflammation (unless you are allergic to aspirin).

- **ConAir Pro Style 1600 Hairdryer.** Set a hair dryer on warm and aim at the insect sting, making sure you have first removed the stinger, to let the heat neutralize one of the chemicals in the venom of a bee or wasp sting.

- **Domino Sugar.** Make a paste from a teaspoon of Domino Sugar and water, and rub the sticky mixture over the sting for a few minutes, making sure you have first removed the stinger. The sugar neutralizes the poison from the sting.

- **Heinz White Vinegar.** Use a cotton ball to apply Heinz White Vinegar to a bee or wasp sting to neutralize the venom and relieve the stinging pain.

- **Lipton Tea Bag.** Place a dampened Lipton Tea Bag over the sting and hold it in place for ten minutes. The tannic acid in the tea relieves the stinging sensation and also draws the stinger to the surface of the skin, making it easier to remove.

- **Listerine.** Dabbing Listerine on bee or wasp stings relieves the pain instantly. The antiseptic kills the proteins in the bee venom and disinfects the sting.

- **MasterCard.** Remove the stinger and venom sac from a bee sting by using the MasterCard to lightly scrape the skin and flick it away.

- **Mrs. Stewart's Liquid Bluing.** Luther Ford & Company, the maker of Mrs. Stewart's Liquid Bluing, has received countless letters over the years reporting that a dab of bluing immediately relieves a bee sting.

- **Orajel.** Applying a dab of Orajel to a bee or wasp sting numbs the pain immediately.

- **Parsons' Ammonia.** Use a cotton ball to dab Parsons' Ammonia on the sting, making sure you have first removed the stinger. Ammonia seems to neutralize the acids in bee venom, relieving the pain quickly.

- **Pepto-Bismol.** To soothe itching after being stung, slather on Pepto-Bismol.

- **Popsicle.** Scrape the stinger out with the exposed end of the Popsicle stick, then apply the icy Popsicle to the sting to relieve the pain.

- **Preparation H.** Applying a liberal coat of Preparation H to the sting helps remove the stinger (by reducing swelling) and provides immediate relief from the stinging pain.

- **SueBee Honey.** Applying SueBee Honey to a bee sting, making sure you have first removed the stinger, reduces the swelling and eases the pain. Honey is a disinfectant, an antibacterial, and an antiseptic.

- **Tabasco Pepper Sauce.** Dab Tabasco Pepper Sauce on the sting, making sure you have first removed the stinger, to relieve the pain and disinfect the sting. *Capsicum frutescens*, the variety of pepper used to make Tabasco Pepper Sauce, contains the alkaloid capsaicin, a spicy compound proven to anesthetize pain when applied topically. The vinegar in the Tabasco Pepper Sauce disinfects the sting and provides relief as well.

- **Windex.** Spray Windex on bee stings to lessen the pain. The ammonia in Windex neutralizes the bee venom, reducing the swelling, and the mild soaps in the window cleaner disinfect the sting.

- **Ziploc Freezer Bags.** Fill a Ziploc Freezer Bag with water and freeze it or fill it with ice cubes to make an ice pack. Applying an ice pack to a bee or wasp sting constricts the blood vessels, slowing the venom, relieving the swelling, and easing the pain. Wrap the ice pack in a paper towel before applying. For other ways to make and apply an ice pack, see page 198.

Make a beeline to the hospital or call your local emergency medical number if you show signs of an allergic reaction or have been badly stung by a large number of bees. If you notice red streaks, drainage, or crusting around the sting, or you've had pain and swelling for more than seventy-two hours, see your doctor.

STRANGE FACTS

◆ In the 1950s, Brazilian geneticist Warwick Kerr imported twenty-six killer bee queens from Africa to São Paulo in the hope of cross-breeding them with Brazilian bees to create more prolific honey producers. Unfortunately, the killer bees escaped from Kerr's laboratory and reproduced in the wild, spreading across South America and into Mexico and the United States.

◆ Utah is known as the beehive state, despite the fact that North Dakota leads the nation in honey production.

◆ Honeybees have hair on their eyes.

◆ The ratel, a weasel also known as the honey badger because of its fondness for honey and bees, can withstand hundreds of bee stings, protected by its long, loose fur.

◆ Bees have five eyes—two compound eyes (made up of thousands of single eyes) on the sides of the head and three simple eyes in a triangle on the top of the head.

SIDE EFFECTS

KILLING BEES AND WASPS

AUNT JEMIMA ORIGINAL SYRUP

Coat a few small pieces of cardboard with Aunt Jemima Original Syrup and place around the perimeter of the yard. Stinging insects, like wasps, bees, and yellow jackets, will be attracted to the syrup and get stuck in it.

AQUA NET HAIRSPRAY

Spray the stinging insects with Aqua Net Hairspray. The hair spray stiffens the insect's wings, bringing the pest spiraling to the ground—immobilized and encapsulated.

BUDWEISER and ORAL-B MINT WAXED FLOSS

Tie a loop of Oral-B Mint Waxed Floss through the flip-top lid of a can of Budweiser, and hang the open beer can from a fence post or tree branch near the plants where the bees are busy. Bees love beer. They fly into the can, drink the beer, get drunk, and drown—which, if you're a bee, probably isn't a bad way to go. Also, hanging beer cans around the backyard is a nice decorative touch that is sure to make the neighbors sit up and take notice.

DAWN

Add one teaspoon Dawn dishwashing liquid to a sixteen-ounce trigger-spray bottle filled with water, shake well, and spray the pests. The soap dries up the insects. They die instantly.

FORMULA 409

Spray bees, wasps, hornets, and yellow jackets with Formula 409 All-Purpose Cleaner. They drop to the ground instantly, and the cleaning liquid kills them within seconds.

MOUNTAIN DEW and DAWN

Add two teaspoons Dawn dishwashing liquid to an open can of Mountain Dew, and place the can near bees. The sugary soda attracts the insects, which fly into the can, drink the mixture, and die.

PARSONS' AMMONIA

Fill a sixteen-ounce trigger-spray bottle with Parsons' Ammonia and spray bees, wasps, or hornets.

SMIRNOFF VODKA

Fill a sixteen-ounce trigger-spray bottle with Smirnoff Vodka and spray the bees. This not only kills the bees but gives them an interesting buzz first.

WD-40

Spraying a beehive or wasp nest with WD-40 kills all the inhabitants, so the nest can be knocked down.

WINDEX

People say spraying bees or wasps with Windex kills them immediately, and, if you happen to be cleaning the windows at the same time, kills two birds with one stone.

- Rock musician Sting got his nickname for wearing a yellow-and-black striped shirt until it literally fell apart. His real name is Gordon Sumner.

- You are more likely to get stung by a bee on a windy day that in any other kind of weather.

- A worker honeybee usually loses its stinger when it attacks and dies a few hours later. A bumblebee retains its stinger, enabling it to sting repeatedly.

- Bees have stingers for self-defense. Wasps (including hornets and yellow jackets) use their stingers to hunt insects, spiders, and caterpillars to feed their larvae.

- Bees fly twelve miles per hour.

- When a bee injects its stinger into flesh, muscles still active in the stinger force it deeper into the wound, while other muscles continue pumping venom.

- In an episode of *Gilligan's Island*, a rock 'n roll group called the Mosquitoes visits the island, prompting Ginger, Mary Ann, and Mrs. Howell to form their own girl group called the Honeybees.

Black Eyes

- **Green Giant Sweet Peas.** Ice reduces the swelling, eases the pain, and constricts the blood vessels to prevent discoloration. Use a plastic bag of frozen Green Giant Sweet Peas as an ice pack around your eye for ten minutes. If the bag of peas feels too cold, place a paper towel between your skin and the bag. The sack of peas conforms to the shape of your face, and you can refreeze the peas for future ice-pack use. (If you want to eat the peas, cook them after the first time they thaw, never after refreezing.)

- **Jell-O** and **Ziploc Freezer Bags.** Prepare Jell-O according to the directions on the box, and let it cool enough to pour into a Ziploc Freezer Bag until the bag is three-quarters full. Seal the bag shut securely, freeze, and you have a homemade, flexible ice pack. When the Jell-O melts, simply refreeze. Place around your eye for ten minutes to relieve the pain, reduce the swelling, and constrict the blood vessels to prevent discoloration. Wrap the ice pack in a paper towel before applying.

- **Playtex Living Gloves.** Fill a Playtex Living Glove with ice, tie the cuff securely to prevent leaks, and apply to the area around your eye for ten minutes to relieve the pain.

- **Smirnoff Vodka, Ziploc Freezer Bags**, and **McCormick Food Coloring.** Pour one-half cup Smirnoff Vodka and one-half cup water into a Ziploc Freezer Bag (add five drops blue food coloring for easy identification) and freeze. The alcohol doesn't freeze, but the water does—giving you a slushy, re-freezable ice pack that you can apply to the area around your eye to soothe the pain. Wrap the ice pack in a paper towel before applying.

THE RISE OF GREEN GIANT

In 1903, the Minnesota Valley Canning Company was founded in Le Sueur, Minnesota, selling roughly 11,750 cases of white cream-style corn in its first year. In 1907, the company introduced Canned Early June Peas, followed in 1925 by an unusually large pea bred to be more flavorful, more tender, and sweeter than Early June Peas—giving birth to the name Green Giant to describe the new peas. The company's trademark attorney, Warwick Keegin, insisting that the descriptive name could not be trademarked, suggested adding a picture of a giant to the label so the name—referring to the giant, not the peas—could be trademarked.

A drawing of a wild-haired, nongreen giant wearing an animal skin helped the company secure a trademark for the brand name and first appeared in advertising in 1928. Keegin later argued for a truly green giant, and in 1935, Leo Burnett, a young, aspiring Chicago advertising man, revised the giant—adding green skin, a leaf cloak, and a smile.

In 1929, the Minnesota Valley Canning Company, investing twice as much money into research than the food industry average, developed corn with longer, more tender kernels, and introduced Niblets Brand Whole Kernel corn, the first vacuum-packed corn. The company soon had six canneries in Minnesota, and the Green Giant came to symbolize the entire company, not merely the large pea. In 1950, Minnesota Valley Canning Company changed its name to Green Giant Company. In 1979, Green Giant merged with the Pillsbury Company.

THE GREEN GIANT COMPANY introduced the world's first yellow corn, the world's first "Green Giant" pea, and the first mushrooms in a glass jar.

IN 1933, researchers at the Green Giant Company discovered that tender peas float when placed in a liquid of a certain density. Using these gravity separators, the company began measuring the nuances of pea quality, separating peas into ten distinct grades.

IN 1961, the Green Giant Company developed vegetables frozen in butter sauce and sealed in a plastic, airtight bag. Boil-in-bag vegetables are Green Giant's best-known innovation.

IN 1969, Green Giant introduced the world's first frozen corn on the cob.

THE JOLLY GREEN GIANT lives in the Valley of the Jolly Green Giant, and is best known for his catchphrase, "Ho ho ho!"

IN 1972, the Green Giant Company introduced Sprout—a walking, talking Brussels sprout—as the Green Giant's sidekick.

IN 2000, the Green Giant celebrated his seventy-fifth birthday with the slogan "Give Peas a Chance."

STRANGE FACTS

- English poet John Milton, British war hero Horatio Nelson, American movie director John Ford, actor Rex Harrison, Israeli minister of defense Moshe Dayan, and American entertainer Sammy Davis Jr. all had one eye.

- The black-eyed Susan, scientifically classified as *Rudbeckia hirta*, is a perennial daisy with orange-yellow petals and a purplish black center.

- The black-eyed pea, also known as the cowpea, is cultivated in the United States, particularly in the South, as both fodder for cattle and a popular food eaten shelled as a side dish or cooked in soups and stews.

- The phrase "giving a black eye" also means tarnishing someone's reputation.

- The medical term for the bleeding into the tissue around the eye that causes a black eye is *ecchymosis*.

- Slang words for a black eye are "shiner" and "mouse."

- The 1974 Warner Brothers blaxploitation movie *Black Eye* stars Fred Williamson as a black private eye.

- In 2000, the rock group Pinetop Seven released a CD titled *Bringing Home the Last Great Strike*, which includes the song "A Black Eye to Be Proud Of."

Blisters

HEALING:

- **Fruit of the Earth Aloe Vera Gel.** Rub Fruit of the Earth Aloe Vera Gel over the blister. Aloe is an analgesic that will soothe the burning sensation.

- **Listerine.** To disinfect a broken blister, dab on Listerine, a powerful anti-septic.

- **Preparation H.** Applying this hemorrhoid ointment to a blister soothes the inflammation and lubricates the skin, preventing further rubbing.

- **Smirnoff Vodka.** If a blister bursts open, pour Smirnoff Vodka over the raw skin as a local anesthetic that also disinfects the exposed dermis.

- **Stayfree Ultra Thin Maxi Pads.** Using a pair of scissors, cut a Stayfree Ultra Thin Maxi Pad into a doughnut shape and place over the blister, leaving the hole over the blister and letting the adhesive strip adhere to the skin. The maxi pad will protect the blister while it heals.

- **Vaseline Petroleum Jelly.** After washing the blister with soap and water, apply Vaseline Petroleum Jelly to lubricate the skin and prevent more friction.

PREVENTING:

- **Kingsford's Corn Starch.** Powder your feet with Kingsford's Corn Starch before putting on your socks so the socks better glide over your feet, preventing blisters.

- **Lipton Tea Bags.** Apply wet Lipton Tea Bags to blister-prone areas on your feet twice a day. The tannic acid in tea toughens the skin.

- **Stayfree Ultra Thin Maxi Pads.** Use a pair of scissors to cut a pair of Stayfree Ultra Thin Maxi Pads to make shoe insert pads, which will prevent your ankle and heel from rubbing against the top edge of the shoes. The ultra thin maxi pads are the perfect thickness, and also contain deodorants to prevent smelly feet.

- **Vaseline Petroleum Jelly.** Apply Vaseline Petroleum Jelly liberally on your feet wherever you feel friction from your shoes.

STRANGE FACTS

- ◆ At the end of the song "Helter Skelter" on the Beatles' *White Album*, John Lennon yells, "I've got blisters on my fingers."

- ◆ Blisters can be caused by friction, burns, sunburn, poison ivy, allergies, herpes, or shingles—among other things.

- ◆ Until the discovery of a vaccine in 1796, smallpox epidemics killed thousands of people and left thousands more permanently scarred from blisters, often disfiguring facial features.

- ◆ Blister beetles produce a secretion capable of blistering the skin.

- ◆ In chemical warfare, blister gas burns or blisters the tissues of the body.

- ◆ White pine trees are prone to blister rust, a disease caused by a rust fungus that leaves blisters on the stems of the tree.

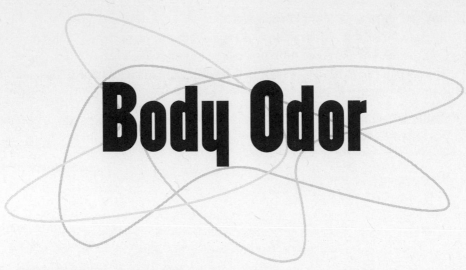

Body Odor

- **Arm & Hammer Baking Soda.** Dust Arm & Hammer Baking Soda into your armpits. Baking soda absorbs odors and kills odor-causing bacteria.

- **Dial Soap.** The simplest way to get rid of body odor is to kill the bacteria that thrive in the moist areas of your body, and the easiest way to do that is by frequently scrubbing your entire body—most notably your armpits and groin—with an antibacterial soap like Dial.

- **Dr. Bronner's Peppermint Soap.** Wet your hands and apply a drop of Dr. Bronner's Peppermint Soap under your arms (unless you just shaved your underarms). According to the label, "Peppermint is nature's own unsurpassed fragrant deodorant!"

- **Kingsford's Corn Starch.** Dust Kingsford's Corn Starch under your arms to absorb odors and kill odor-causing bacteria.

- **Listerine.** Use a cotton ball to dab Listerine under your arms (unless you just shaved your underarms). The antiseptic in Listerine helps kill the bacteria that cause perspiration odor.

- **Morton Salt.** If you forget to use deodorant before leaving the house, rub a pinch of Morton Salt in each armpit (unless you recently shaved your underarms). The salt absorbs perspiration, keeping your underarms dry—an inhospitable environment for bacteria.

- **Purell.** Rub a dollop of Purell into your underarms. Purell kills the existing bacteria and prevents new bacteria from populating your armpits, where they die, decompose, and emit foul smells.

SIDE EFFECTS

SMELLY CLOTHES

ARM & HAMMER BAKING SODA

Sprinkle Arm & Hammer Baking Soda in your laundry basket over each layer of added clothes. The baking soda absorbs the nasty odors, and when the white powder goes through the washing machine, it helps soften and freshen the garments.

BOUNCE

Place a sheet of Bounce in the bottom of a laundry bag or hamper to mask the pungent smells.

DIAL SOAP

Cover up odors in dirty laundry by placing a wrapped bar of Dial Soap at the bottom of a laundry bag or hamper.

EFFERDENT

To clean yellow stains from the underarms of white shirts, drop two Efferdent tablets in a glass of water, wait until the bubbling stops, then pour the liquid over the stain. Let sit for five minutes, then launder as usual.

HEINZ WHITE VINEGAR

Remove body odor from laundry by adding one cup Heinz White Vinegar to your regular wash while the machine fills with water. For intense perspiration smells, add one cup vinegar to a bucket of water and soak the garments in the mixture for one hour, then launder as usual.

PARSONS' AMMONIA and ORAL-B TOOTHBRUSH

To remove sweat stains from the underarms of white shirts, mix equal parts Parsons' Ammonia and water, and scrub the stain with a clean, used Oral-B Toothbrush.

SCOTCHGARD

If you tend to perspire profusely, spray the underarms of your dress shirts with Scotchgard to waterproof the fabric. The Scotchgard prevents sweat from wetting the shirt. Wear an undershirt to absorb the perspiration.

STAYFREE MAXI PADS

Prevent perspiration stains on the headband inside of a baseball cap or hat by peeling the adhesive strip from a Stayfree Maxi Pad and sticking the pad inside the hat along the headband for your forehead. Replace the maxi pad as necessary.

STAYFREE MAXI PADS

If your underarms sweat excessively, peel the adhesive strip from Stayfree Maxi Pads and attach the pads inside the armpits of your clothing. The maxi pads will absorb the perspiration, putting an end to wetness and stains in the underarms of your clothes.

20 MULE TEAM BORAX and HEINZ WHITE VINEGAR

To clean sweat stains from clothes, make a paste of 20 Mule Team Borax and Heinz White Vinegar and apply to the stain. Let sit for one hour, then rinse in hot water.

STRANGE FACTS

◆ The ancient Egyptians developed underarm deodorants made from citrus and cinnamon. They also discovered that shaving underarm hair minimized body odor—although they did not know why.

◆ In extreme heat, humans have been known to sweat up to three gallons of perspiration in twenty-four hours.

◆ Heat and physical activity cause the eccrine glands to release odorless perspiration. Stress, however, causes the apocrine glands concentrated in your underarms, groin, and perineum (the flesh betwen the anus and genitals) to release a musky perfume. Bacteria thrive in these warm, moist regions, making the odor worse.

◆ In a love letter to his Empress Joséphine, Napoleon Bonaparte wrote, "See you next Thursday. Please don't bathe in the meantime!"

◆ The year 1888 marked the introduction of the world's first antiperspi-rant, aptly named Mum.

◆ Deodorants kill the bacteria that thrive on apocrine fluid. Antiperspi-rants temporarily seal up the sweat gland pores, preventing the body from secreting perspiration.

◆ In the 1987 movie *Broadcast News*, Albert Brooks plays a news re-porter who, when he gets the chance to read the news on television, sweats profusely, ending his chances of ever becoming an on-air personality.

THE DIRT ON DIAL SOAP

In 1948, just after World War II, scientists at the Armour Soap Company began analyzing the cause of perspiration odor to develop an effective deodorant soap. Armour chemists determined that perspiration odor resulted when bacteria mingle with perspiration. Realizing that perspiration odor could be eliminated by controlling the bacteria, Armour scientists went to work developing an odorless, non-irritating bactericide that would remain effective when combined with soap.

Hexachlorophene, a chemical offered to soap manufacturers a few years earlier, seemed to fit the bill. Armour scientists made up sample bars of soap with a 2 percent concentration of hexachlorophene, and laboratory technicians systematically used the sample bar of soap to wash under one arm each morning, while using ordinary soap to wash under the other. Convinced they had developed an effective deodorant soap, the company hired outside research laboratories. All confirmed the soap stopped perspiration odor before it could start. Armour named the chemical AT-7. Meanwhile, Armour scientists conducted experiments to find the right perfume for the soap—eventually selecting a light clover fragrance made up of some fourteen different oils.

Armour executives decided to test-market the soap in 1948. Dial was introduced at a price of twenty-five cents a bar—or twice the price of competing brands. Sales were so brisk that before the thirteen-week test period was over, the company was preparing to introduce the product in Chicago, followed by New York, Washington, and Philadelphia. National advertising began in 1949, and by 1953 (the year Dial introduced its advertising slogan "Aren't you glad you use Dial? Don't you wish everybody did?") Dial was the number one soap in dollar volume. Armour eventually changed its name to the Dial Corporation.

AN ARMOUR EMPLOYEE suggested the name *Dial* because the soap offers around-the-clock protection. The Armour advertising department developed the design of the clock's dial and the slogan "Keep Fresh around the Clock," later changed to "Round the Clock Protection."

THE BRIGHT YELLOW MONUMENT wall at the entrance to the Dial Corporation building in Scottsdale, Arizona, looks like a bar of Dial soap.

A BAR OF DIAL SOAP can be found in one out of three American homes.

DIAL SOAP, America's number one antibacterial soap, sells nearly one million bars a day.

LIQUID DIAL is the second-best-selling antibacterial soap in the world.

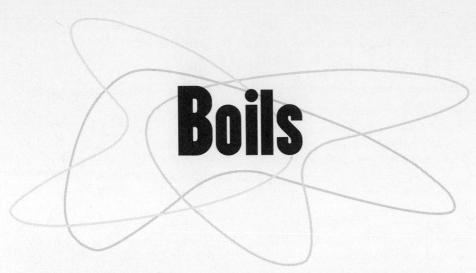

Boils

- **Arm & Hammer Baking Soda.** Make a paste of Arm & Hammer Baking Soda and water, apply to the boil, and cover with a washcloth dampened with hot water as a compress to relieve the pain and bring the boil to a head.

- **Hunt's Tomato Paste.** Cover the boil with Hunt's Tomato Paste as a compress. The acids from the tomatoes will soothe the pain and help bring the boil to a head.

- **Lipton Tea Bags.** To drain a boil, dampen a Lipton Tea Bag with hot—but not scalding—water (do not squeeze out the water), and cover the boil with it overnight. The boil should burst by the following morning.

- **Quaker Oats** and **Band-Aid Bandages.** Cook up a cup of oatmeal according to the directions, let it cool slightly, cover the boil with a dollop of the warm oatmeal, and hold in place with a Band-Aid bandage. The boil should burst within a few hours.

- **Wonder Bread.** Soak a piece of Wonder Bread in warm milk and apply as a poultice to bring the boil to a head.

STRANGE FACTS

- ◆ A boil with two or more heads is called a carbuncle.

- ◆ A boil with one head is also known as a furuncle.

- When *Staphylococcus* bacteria infect a hair follicle, the body responds by filling the hair follicle with pus—creating a boil.

- In the biblical Book of Exodus, the sixth plague God sends against the Egyptians is festering boils.

- In the biblical Book of Job, God afflicts Job with boils.

- In 1999, The Boils, a punk-rock band from Philadelphia, released their first CD, titled *World Poison*.

- In his play *King Lear*, William Shakespeare wrote, "Thou art a boil, a plague sore, an unbossed carbuncle."

- In his 2001 novel, *Boils: Tales of Tainted Mothers Milk*, author Carkan Moil tells the story of a Vietnam veteran covered with gigantic boils that hatch into miniature clones of himself.

Breastfeeding

- **Bag Balm.** To soothe nipples made sore from breastfeeding, simply rub on a dab of Bag Balm. Developed to soothe sore cow teats, Bag Balm also soothes human nipples. Wash off the Bag Balm before breastfeeding.

- **Castor Oil.** To relieve breast inflammation or help heal minor breast infections, fold a wool flannel cloth in quarters. Saturate the cloth with cold-pressed castor oil, place on the breast, cover with a piece of Saran Wrap, and then apply a heating pad set on moderate (increasing the temperature to the hottest you can handle). Let sit for an hour. Repeat for three to seven days. Cold-pressed castor oil helps increase T11 lymphocyte function, which will help speed the healing of the infection. Wash off the castor oil before breastfeeding.

- **ChapStick.** Use cherry-flavored ChapStick on sore nipples to prevent cracking from breastfeeding. ChapStick is safe for babies, so nursing mothers don't have to wash off the ChapStick before feeding the baby. Babies also seem to like the cherry taste and tend to latch on quicker.

- **Kleenex Tissues.** Nursing mothers can fold a Kleenex Tissue in quarters and secure it inside a bra as an impromptu absorbent pad.

- **Lipton Tea Bags.** To soothe nipples made sore from breastfeeding, saturate a Lipton Tea Bag with hot (not scalding) water, then place the tea bag on your sore nipple and cover with a nursing pad under your bra for about five minutes. The tannic acid in the tea helps soothe and heal the nipple.

- **McCormick Garlic Powder.** Spice your meals with garlic. Eating garlic produces an odor in breast milk that prompts infants to suck longer, rather than playing with the nipples. (The garlic in your diet will not harm the baby's digestion.)

- **Pampers.** If you run out of nursing pads and can't get to the store to buy more, cut two circles from a Pampers disposable diaper and use them for nursing pads.

- **Stayfree Maxi Pads.** A Stayfree Maxi Pad makes an excellent substitute for nursing pads. Cut two circles from the pad, and use the adhesive strip to adhere the absorbent pads inside the bra cups.

- **Ziploc Freezer Bags.** If you have very engorged and painful breasts, apply an ice pack. Fill a Ziploc Freezer Bag with water and freeze it or fill it with ice cubes. Wrap the ice pack in a paper towel before applying. For other ways to make and apply an ice pack, see page 198.

STRANGE FACTS

- In ancient Egypt, women tipped their bare nipples with gold paint.

- Hunt-Wesson introduced its Big John products in French Canada as Gros Jos, unaware that in Quebec the slang phrase means "big breasts."

- When the American Dairy Association expanded its "Got Milk?" advertising campaign to Mexico, the Spanish translation read "Are you lactating?"

- In 1975, a Holstein cow in Indiana produced 195.5 pounds of milk in one day. That's enough to provide one hundred people with nearly a quart of milk each.

- Cow's milk is 87 percent water.

- A cow has to eat grass to produce milk.

- If Barbie were life size, her measurements would be 39-23-33.

- In many states across America, breastfeeding in public is outlawed as a form of indecent exposure.

◆ On January 28, 2002, United States Attorney General John Ashcroft announced that he had spent eight thousand dollars of the taxpayers' money for drapes to veil the exposed breast of *The Spirit of Justice*, an eighteen-foot-tall aluminum statue of a woman that stands in the Department of Justice's Hall of Justice. Ashcroft insisted that he had ordered the drapes so that a large breast would not appear behind him during press conferences. Critics insisted that despite the draped statue, photographers and television cameras would still be focused on a big boob.

SIDE EFFECTS
CRYING OVER SPILT MILK

BAR KEEPERS FRIEND
To remove yellow stains from clothes, soak the garments in Bar Keepers Friend overnight.

COCA-COLA
Saturate the milk stains with a can of Coca-Cola, let the garment sit for five minutes, then launder in your regular wash.

CASCADE
Mix one-quarter cup Cascade in a bucket of very hot water, soak the yellowing white garment in the solution overnight, then launder as usual.

DAWN and ORAL-B TOOTHBRUSH
Squirt a dab of Dawn dishwashing liquid on the stain, scrub with a clean, used Oral-B Toothbrush, then toss the garment in your regular wash.

EASY-OFF OVEN CLEANER
To remove yellow milk stains from clothes, carefully spray Easy-Off Oven Cleaner on the spot (in a well-ventilated area), let sit for thirty minutes, then launder in hot water. Stubborn stains may require two treatments.

HUGGIES BABY WIPES
The moment the baby spits up on your clothes, clean the spot with a Huggies Baby Wipe to prevent staining.

MURPHY'S OIL SOAP
Pour Murphy's Oil Soap on the stain, let sit for ten minutes, then launder as usual.

PINE-SOL and ORAL-B TOOTHBRUSH
Pour some Pine-Sol on the stain, brush with a clean, used Oral-B Toothbrush, then launder with your regular wash.

RESOLVE
Spray Resolve Carpet Cleaner on infant spittle stains on clothes, let sit for ten minutes, then launder as usual.

WINDEX
Immediately spray Windex on the stain on your clothes, then blot with a sponge.

Broken Bones

- **Baby Magic Baby Powder** and **ConAir Pro Style 1600 Hairdryer.** To relieve itching inside a cast, sprinkle some Baby Magic Baby Powder inside the cast, and then use a blow-dryer set on low to gently blow the powder deep down inside the cast.

- **Bubble Wrap** and **Scotch Packaging Tape.** In an emergency, immobilize the broken bone by wrapping Bubble Wrap around the injured arm or leg several times and securing it in place in with Scotch Packaging Tape, then head for the emergency room. Once the broken limb has been set in a cast, you can avoid damaging the cast by wrapping it with Bubble Wrap (bubble side in, to resist the temptation to pop the bubbles) held in place with Scotch Packaging Tape.

- **Glad Trash Bags.** Place the cast inside a Glad Trash Bag to avoid getting the cast wet when taking a shower or bath.

- **L'eggs Sheer Energy Panty Hose.** Cut off a section of the leg from a pair of panty hose, and slip your cast through the panty hose leg. The panty hose will help your cast glide through clothes more readily.

- **Ziploc Freezer Bags.** Fill a Ziploc Freezer Bag with water and freeze it or fill it with ice cubes to make an ice pack. Applying an ice pack to a broken bone for ten-minute intervals can help ease the swelling and pain until you can get to a doctor. Wrap the ice pack in a paper kitchen towel before applying. For other ways to make and apply an ice pack, see page 198.

Make no bones about it! If you suspect that you have a fracture, have a doctor check it out immediately.

STRANGE FACTS

◆ Humans are born with 300 bones but have only 206 bones after reaching adulthood.

◆ The longest bone in the human body is the thigh bone, which averages 19.75 inches in a six-foot man.

◆ The word *bones* is slang for "dice," which were originally carved from bones.

◆ In the Bible, the prophet Ezekiel envisions a valley filled with dry human bones baking in the hot sun. At God's command, he orders the bones to live again. The bones join together, grow flesh, and come to life as a huge gathering of people (Ezekiel 37:1–14).

◆ Two days before he broke the sound barrier on October 14, 1947, Chuck Yeager broke two ribs.

◆ On *Star Trek*, Captain James T. Kirk calls Dr. McCoy by the nickname "Bones."

◆ In 1982, rock band George Thorogood and the Destroyers released their album *Bad to the Bone*, which features the hit song of the same name.

◆ In June 1999, while walking along a road in Maine, novelist Stephen King was hit by a car, resulting in broken bones in his legs, broken ribs, a punctured lung, and a head injury.

◆ The word *boneyard* is slang for "cemetery."

POPPING IN ON BUBBLE WRAP

In 1957, American inventor Alfred Fielding and his partner, Swiss inventor Marc Chavannes, working in Saddle Brook, New Jersey, failed at their attempt to develop a plastic wallpaper with a paper backing. Instead, they decided to use the resulting sheets of bubbles encased in plastic as packaging material—naming their invention AirCap material. Two years later, having raised $9,000 to develop the product, Fielding and Chavannes built a crude six-inch-wide pilot machine that could make AirCap material continuously. They formed Sealed Air Corporation, raised $85,000, and began full-scale production in 1960.

Unfortunately, the AirCap bubbles leaked, slowly deflating. By 1965, Fielding and Chavannes developed a machine that would apply a special coating on the outside of the bubbles to prevent them from losing air. In 1970, the company added a barrier coating on the inside of the bubbles.

In 1971, Fielding and Chavannes recruited T. J. Dermot Dunphy, a graduate of Oxford University and Harvard Business School, to head the Sealed Air Corporation. Under Dunphy's direction, annual sales went from five million dollars to five hundred million dollars by 1994. Today, Sealed Air sells many protective packaging materials, including Jiffy Padded Mailers, polyethylene foams, and Instapak, a machine that sprays a polyurethane liquid that expands into foam cushioning.

THE SEALED AIR CORPORATION developed the Solar Pool Blanket pool cover, an energy conservation product that is transparent, permitting the rays of the sun to penetrate the blanket and heat the water, thus saving heating costs while reducing the water and chemical loss through evaporation.

IN 1993, the New Jersey Inventors Hall of Fame inducted Bubble Wrap inventors Alfred Fielding and Marc Chavannes.

AMONG JOURNALISTS, "Bubble Wrap" is slang for a superficial news story or magazine article filled with fluff or padded material.

PEOPLE WEEKLY is nicknamed *"Bubble Wrap Weekly."*

IN JAPAN, building contractors use Bubble Wrap brand products as insulation in the construction of homes to sound-proof paper-thin walls and prevent beams from creaking.

IN THE SONG "STEAM" on his album *Us*, Peter Gabriel sings the praises of Bubble Wrap.

FIFTY-YEAR-OLD FARRAH FAWCETT, who starred for one season on *Charlie's Angels*, appeared on the cover of the July 1997 issue of *Playboy*, enveloped in Bubble Wrap.

Bruises

- **Dickinson's Witch Hazel.** Apply Dickinson's Witch Hazel to the bruise to cool and heal the skin.

- **French's Mustard** and **SueBee Honey.** Combine three parts French's Mustard, one part SueBee Honey, and one part finely chopped onion, apply to the affected area, and cover with a bandage or handkerchief.

- **Heinz White Vinegar.** Soak a cotton ball in Heinz White Vinegar and apply to the bruise for one hour. The vinegar reduces the blueness and hastens healing.

- **Orajel.** Rub a dollop of Orajel into the skin on and around the bruise. The numbing ointment helps stop the blood vessels from constricting, sometimes preventing discoloration.

- **Preparation H.** Rubbing Preparation H into the skin helps heal bruises, making them disappear faster.

- **Star Olive Oil.** To prevent a bruise from appearing, immediately rub Star Olive Oil on the sensitive spot.

- **Tabasco Pepper Sauce.** Applying Tabasco Pepper Sauce to the tender area anesthetizes the pain. Tabasco sauce contains the alkaloid capsaicin, a spicy compound proven to numb pain when applied topically. Do not apply Tabasco Pepper Sauce to an open wound.

- **Vaseline Petroleum Jelly.** Upon bumping yourself, immediately rub some Vaseline Petroleum Jelly on the spot to minimize the swelling and prevent discoloration.

- **Ziploc Freezer Bags.** Immediately placing an ice pack made from a Ziploc Freezer Bag over the injury can prevent a bruise from developing. To make the ice pack, fill the freezer bag with water and freeze it or fill it with ice cubes. Wrap the ice pack in a paper towel before applying. For other ways to make and apply an ice pack, see page 198.

STRANGE FACTS

♦ In the Bible, God punishes the serpent in the Garden of Eden by putting enmity between all of the serpent's descendants and all of Eve's descendants. "They shall bruise thy head," God tells the serpent, "and thou shalt bruise their heel" (Genesis 3:15).

♦ When Eleanor Roosevelt, wife of President Franklin Delano Roosevelt, fell ill at the age of seventy-eight and began bleeding and bruising at the slightest touch, her doctors incorrectly diagnosed that she was suffering from a fatal blood disease. The former First Lady actually had tuberculosis. Rather than giving Roosevelt an open bone marrow biopsy to confirm their diagnosis, the doctors began treating her with prednisone—a drug that fights blood diseases. Unfortunately, prednisone also lowers the body's resistance to infection, enabling the undiagnosed tuberculosis to spread faster, killing Eleanor Roosevelt.

♦ The phrase "cruisin' for a bruisin'" means to live dangerously.

♦ In 1977, Air Supply—the easy-listening Australian male pop duo—released their debut album, titled *Love & Other Bruises*, which included the song "Bruises."

♦ In 1993, the Clinicas de Salud del Pueblo in Brawley, California, banned employees from coming to work with visible hickeys on their necks. Employees who refused to cover up the amorous bruises would be sent home and docked pay.

♦ According to *Juggler's World*, a survey revealed that the number one reported injury among professional jugglers is bruising.

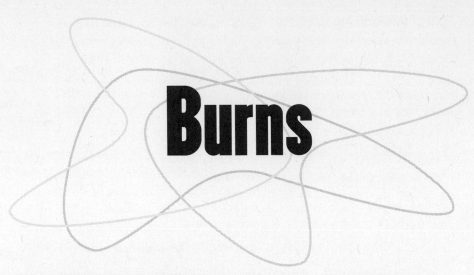

Burns

- **Arm & Hammer Baking Soda.** Make a thick paste of Arm & Hammer Baking Soda and water, apply to the burn, and cover with wet gauze for ten minutes.

- **Aunt Jemima Original Syrup** and **Gold Medal Flour.** Make a paste from equal parts Aunt Jemima Original Syrup and Gold Medal Flour. Apply the mixture to the burn and cover with wet gauze for ten minutes to alleviate the burning sensation.

- **Betty Crocker Potato Buds.** Mix Betty Crocker Potato Buds with enough water to make a thick paste, and apply to the burn.

- **Carnation Condensed Milk.** Saturate a washcloth or sponge with Carnation Condensed Milk, and apply it to the burn as a compress to relieve the pain and prevent blistering.

- **Colgate Toothpaste.** Spread a dollop of Colgate Regular Flavor Toothpaste on the skin immediately after burning, let dry, and leave on for several hours to prevent blistering and speed up healing. The toothpaste protects the skin from exposure to oxygen (lessening the burning pain almost immediately) and dries the skin (preventing liquid from building up under the skin).

- **Cool Whip.** To treat minor burns, apply Cool Whip on the burn. Let sit for fifteen minutes, then wash off with cool water.

- **Desitin.** Relieve first-degree burns by applying Desitin to the affected area. The diaper-rash ointment soothes burning pain.

- **Fruit of the Earth Aloe Vera Gel.** Apply Fruit of the Earth Aloe Vera Gel over the burned skin. Aloe is an analgesic that helps soothe the burning sensation.

- **Heinz White Vinegar.** Applying Heinz White Vinegar to a burn soothes the pain.

- **Kikkoman Soy Sauce.** To relieve a burn, pour Kikkoman Soy Sauce over the affected area.

- **Lipton Tea Bags.** Apply wet Lipton Tea Bags directly to the burn, or secure in place with gauze. The tannic acid in the tea may relieve the burning sensation.

- **McCormick Vanilla Extract.** If you burn yourself while cooking in the kitchen, apply McCormick Vanilla Extract on the burn. It immediately relieves the pain.

- **Nestea.** Following the directions on the back of the jar, mix up enough Nestea to soak whatever part of your body has been burned. The tannic acid relieves burns.

- **Noxzema.** Applying a dab of Noxzema skin cream to the burn soothes the pain and prevents the skin from blistering.

- **Orajel.** If used immediately, Orajel helps numb the pain of small burns and prevent blistering.

- **Preparation H.** To relieve burning pain and prevent blistering, apply Preparation H to the burn and cover with a fresh sterile bandage every day.

- **Smucker's Concord Grape Jelly.** Applying Smucker's Concord Grape Jelly on a mild burn relieves the pain. The jelly moisturizes and cools the skin, while the tannin from the grapes soothes the burning pain.

- **SueBee Honey.** Applying SueBee Honey on burns speeds healing. Honey is hygroscopic and absorbs water, preventing blistering and creating an environment in which disease-producing microorganisms, deprived of moisture, cannot live.

- **Vaseline Petroleum Jelly.** In 1859, Brooklyn chemist Robert Augustus Chesebrough learned from oil-drilling workers in Titusville, Pennsylvania, that the jelly residue that gunked up oil-drilling rods quickened healing when rubbed on a burn. Chesebrough purified the jelly gunk and called it Vaseline Petroleum Jelly.

- **Vicks VapoRub.** To prevent a burn from blistering, immediately apply Vicks VapoRub to the burn. The ointment makes the burning pain subside in just minutes.

A burn is too hot for you to handle on your own when it is larger than the palm of your hand, extremely painful, swollen and blistered, or producing a yellow discharge. Head for the doctor's office or emergency room.

STRANGE FACTS

◆ When spaghetti is cooked in a pot of boiling water, organic materials leach out from the cooking pasta and weaken the surface tension of the water in the pot. This makes it easier for bubbles and foam to form, often causing the water to boil over. Adding a drop of vegetable oil to a pot of boiling water before adding the spaghetti strengthens the surface tension of the water and prevents it from boiling over.

◆ Doctors advise against using butter on a burn. They claim that butter is an ideal medium for bacteria (which can infect the burn) and the salt in most butter can further damage burned skin.

◆ In 1680, British physicist Robert Boyle coated a piece of paper with the element phosphorus and coated the tip of a small stick of wood with sulfur, creating the first chemical matches. Phosphorus, however, was a rare and costly element, making the wide-scale production of matches economically infeasible.

◆ As early as the seventeenth century, British children played a game in which a lit candle was placed in the middle of a room and the players tried to jump over it without extinguishing the flame. The game inspired the nursery rhyme "Jack be nimble, Jack be quick, Jack jump over the candlestick."

◆ In 1826, British pharmacist John Walker, attempting to invent a new explosive, invented the first friction match by accident. When a glob of one of his chemical solutions dried on the end of his mixing stick, he tried to remove it by rubbing the coated end of the stick against the stone floor. The tip immediately burst into flame. The solution was a mixture of antimony sulfide, potassium chlorate, gum, and starch. Walker never patented his invention.

♦ The first commercial matches, manufactured by Samuel Jones in London, England, in the late 1820s, were called Lucifers and boosted the popularity of smoking tobacco.

♦ In 1830, French chemist Charles Sauria developed phosphorus matches, inadvertently giving rise to "phossy jaw," a fatal disease technically known as *phosphorus necrosis* and primarily affecting factory workers. Highly poisonous, phosphorus essentially causes bones to disintegrate and deform. The phosphorus scraped from the heads of a pack of matches could also be used to commit suicide or murder.

♦ Mice chewing on phosphorus match heads at night frequently caused kitchen fires.

♦ In 1892, Joshua Pusey, a lawyer from Lima, Pennsylvania, invented the matchbook—foolishly placing the striking surface inside the front cover, enabling the slightest friction to cause the entire matchbook to go up in flames.

♦ In 1896, a brewery ordered more than 50,000 matchbooks from the Diamond Match Company, originating the idea of advertisements on the covers of matchbooks and creating the demand for machinery to mass-produce matches.

♦ On December 1, 1903, the Iroquois Theater opened in Chicago, Illinois, billed as the world's first fireproof theater. That same month, a blue stage light blew out and set fire to the scenery, burning the "fireproof" theater to the ground.

♦ In 1911, the Diamond Match Company introduced the first nontoxic match, waiving the right to a patent so other companies could produce the matches as well, eliminating the scourge of "phossy jaw."

♦ During World War II, the United States military airdropped millions of matchbooks printed with propaganda messages behind enemy lines to boost the morale of people living in countries occupied by the Axis powers.

Bursitis

- **Castor Oil.** When the acute pain of bursitis subsides after four or five days, spread castor oil over the afflicted joint, place a piece of cotton or wool flannel over it, and apply a heating pad to relieve lingering pain.

- **L'eggs Sheer Energy Panty Hose.** Cut off the calf section from a pair of panty hose and wear it over your knee or other affected area as a brace to soothe the pain.

- **Star Olive Oil.** Warm Star Olive Oil and massage it into the shoulder or upper arm daily to relieve bursitis pain.

- **Stayfree Maxi Pads.** Peel off the adhesive strip and stick a Stayfree Maxi Pad to each knee or elbow for a comfortable, disposable set of knee pads or elbow pads.

- **Uncle Ben's Converted Brand Rice.** Pour two cups Uncle Ben's Converted Brand Rice into a microwave-safe container and heat in the microwave for one minute. Carefully pour or spoon the hot rice into a sock (not too compactly), tie a knot in the end, and place the warm sock over the afflicted area for ten minutes to relieve the pain. The sock conforms wherever applied.

- **Ziploc Freezer Bags.** Heat helps bursitis. Fill a gallon-size Ziploc Freezer Bag with hot (not scalding) water, seal it securely, wrap it in a paper towel, and place it over the aching joint, letting the flexible hot water bottle conform to the shape of your body.

- **Ziploc Freezer Bags.** Applying an ice pack to bursitis relieves the pain. Fill a Ziploc Freezer Bag with water and freeze it or fill it with ice cubes. Wrap the ice pack in a paper towel before applying. For other ways to make and apply an ice pack, see page 198.

STRANGE FACTS

- ◆ Bursitis is an aching pain in a joint caused when the bursae (sacs filled with synovial fluid to reduce friction) become inflamed.

- ◆ The human body contains up to 156 bursae—including eleven around each knee and eight around each shoulder.

- ◆ Bursitis of the elbow is called miner's elbow, bursitis of the knee is called housemaid's knee, and bursitis of the buttocks is called weaver's bottom.

- ◆ Raffi, the popular children's singer whose hit songs include "Baby Beluga" and "Joshua Giraffe," suffers from bursitis.

- ◆ Tennis elbow is not bursitis. The medical term for tennis elbow is *lateral epicondylitis*. Tennis elbow is actually tendinitis of a muscle.

Calluses

- **Bayer Aspirin, ReaLemon,** and **Saran Wrap.** Crush six Bayer Aspirin tablets into a powder using a mortar and pestle. Add one-half teaspoon ReaLemon lemon juice and one-half teaspoon water and mix into a paste. Apply to your feet, then wrap Saran Wrap around each foot and wrap in a warm towel for ten minutes, allowing the paste to penetrate the skin. Then unwrap each foot and scrub with a pumice stone. If you are allergic or sensitive to aspirin, do not use aspirin on your skin to avoid the remote possibility of a reaction.

- **Castor Oil.** Applying castor oil to your calluses will help them disappear.

- **Heinz White Vinegar** and **Star Olive Oil.** Mix one teaspoon Heinz White Vinegar and two tablespoons Star Olive Oil, and rub the mixture into your calluses. The oil softens them, and the vinegar kills any bacteria.

- **Krazy Glue.** If you're a guitar player, you can prevent calluses on your fingers from splitting open by using Krazy Glue to hold calluses together. Avoid getting calluses in the first place by applying small dabs of Krazy Glue on your fingertips to form protective shields for playing the guitar.

- **Nestea.** Soak your calluses in warm Nestea for a half-hour each day to soothe and soften the toughened skin. The tannic acid in the tea gently dissolves calluses.

- **Vicks VapoRub** and **Band-Aid Bandages.** Coat calluses with Vicks VapoRub and cover with a Band-Aid bandage. Repeat for several days until the calluses disappear.

A QUICK WRAP-UP ON BAND-AIDS

In 1867, Brooklyn pharmacist Robert Wood Johnson formed a partnership with George J. Seabury to make and sell Belson's Capcine Porous Plasters (the predecessor of the Band-Aid bandage).

At the time, surgeons used dressings pressed from the sawdust waste collected from the floors of wood mills. Johnson personally disinfected every bandage he used, soaking them in a carbolic acid solution. After hearing Dr. Joseph Lister explain his theory that germs cause disease at the 1876 Philadelphia Medical Congress, Johnson convinced his two brothers—James Johnson and Edward Mead Johnson—to help him attempt to develop a prepackaged, antiseptic surgical dressing.

In 1885, James Johnson and Edward Mead Johnson founded Johnson & Johnson in New Brunswick, New Jersey, launching Quiniform pills and Carapin (for "Dyspepsia, Indigestion, and Diphtheria"). The following year, Robert Wood Johnson joined the family company to make and sell his own antiseptic surgical dressings from cotton and gauze. Each Johnson's Capcine Plaster was individually sealed in its own germ-resistant wrapper.

In 1920, James Johnson discovered that his one of his employees, newlywed Earle Dickson, had invented a small homemade bandage for his accident-prone bride by placing a small wad of sterile cotton and gauze in the center of an adhesive strip. Tired of making his own bandages, Dickson demonstrated his homemade bandage for James Johnson in the hopes of having them mass-produced using crinoline fabric to cover the sticky parts. W. Johnson Kenyon, a superintendent at the New Brunswick factory, suggested the name Band-Aid.

INITIALLY, JOHNSON & JOHNSON workers made Band-Aid bandages by hand.

TO PROMOTE THE NEW PRODUCT in the 1920s, Johnson & Johnson gave away free Band-Aid bandages to Boy Scout troops across the country and local butchers.

THE FRAGRANCE OF Johnson & Johnson Baby Powder is one of the most recognized scents in the world.

IN 1928, Johnson & Johnson added aeration holes in the crinoline fabric over the Band-Aid gauze pad to give the wound air and speed healing.

SINCE 1888, Johnson & Johnson has used the same red Greek cross that the International Committee of the Red Cross has used since 1863. In 1905, United States law gave the American Red Cross exclusive use of the symbol, but vigorous lobbying by Johnson & Johnson and other companies resulted in an amendment in 1910 allowing companies that had used the trademark prior to 1905 to continue doing so. The Geneva Convention of 1929 forbids use of the trademark by any group other than the International Committee of the Red Cross.

THE TRADEMARKED WORD *BAND-AID* can be found in the dictionary.

STRANGE FACTS

- ◆ Pumice, a natural glass that comes from lava, is widely used to remove calluses.

- ◆ When a broken bone starts to mend, a substance called callus forms around the fracture. Unlike a skin callus, which is simply hardened and thickened skin, the callus around a bone is composed of cartilage and new bone.

- ◆ The word *callous* means "hardened, insensitive" and, while spelled differently, stems from the word *callus*.

- ◆ Soprano Maria Callas became one of the world's best-known opera singers due to her feisty disposition and remarkable voice.

Canker Sores

- **Arm & Hammer Baking Soda.** Moisten the end of your finger, dip it in Arm & Hammer Baking Soda, and rub the powder on the canker sore. Or add one teaspoon baking soda to half a glass of water and rinse your mouth with the solution. The baking soda neutralizes the bacteria in the sore, helping it heal faster.

- **Dannon Yogurt.** Eat two servings of Dannon yogurt a day until the sores clear. The active cultures of *Lactobacillus acidophilus* in yogurt fight the bacteria that cause canker sores.

- **Fruit of the Earth Aloe Vera Gel.** Mix one teaspoon of Fruit of the Earth Aloe Vera Gel in a glass of water, rinse your mouth with the liquid, and spit it out. The aloe kills the bacteria in your mouth, disinfecting the canker sore.

- **Hydrogen Peroxide.** Mix one teaspoon of Hydrogen Peroxide in a glass of water and rinse your mouth with the mixture to disinfect the canker sore and hasten healing.

- **Lipton Tea Bags.** Apply a wet Lipton Tea Bag to the canker sore. Tannin is an astringent that relieves pain.

- **Listerine.** Rinse your mouth with this strong antiseptic mouthwash to kill the bacteria that irritate the canker sore and to speed healing.

- **McCormick Alum.** Moisten the end of your finger, dip it in McCormick Alum, and rub the powder on the canker sore. Alum is both a pain reliever and an antiseptic that can prevent the infection from getting worse.

- **Phillips' Milk of Magnesia.** Swish Phillips' Milk of Magnesia around your mouth to coat the canker sore. Milk of magnesia counteracts the acid environment in which the bacteria thrive.

- **Vegemite.** Apply a dab of this Australian icon on the canker sore to soothe the pesky mouth ulcer.

STRANGE FACTS

- A canker sore is an ulcer inside the mouth that looks like a small crater.

- Doctors do not know what causes canker sores.

- The word *canker* stems from the Latin word *cancer*, meaning "crab" (like the constellation) or "gangrene."

- In Sonnet 35, William Shakespeare wrote:
    Roses have thorns, and silver fountains mud;
    Clouds and eclipses stain both moon and sun,
    And loathsome canker lives in sweetest bud.
    All men make faults.

- Eating canker lettuce, also known as consumption weed, was once believed to cure canker.

- The word *cankered* means "ill-natured," "bad-tempered," or "morally corrupt."

- The cankerworm, a striped green caterpillar, feeds on the foliage of fruit trees and shade trees, frequently causing extensive damage, to the point where the trees are described as being cankered.

Chafing

- **Alberto VO5 Conditioning Hairdressing.** Rub a dab of this soothing mixture of five organic emollients over the area being chafed to prevent your thighs from rubbing together and creating more painful friction.

- **Band-Aid Bandages.** Putting a Band-Aid bandage over the irritated spot protects the sensitive skin from further rubbing.

- **ChapStick.** Rub ChapStick over the chafed skin, coating the area liberally. The waxes in the lip balm eliminate the friction causing the problem, and the medicinal ingredients promote healing.

- **Crisco All-Vegetable Shortening.** Smear a dab of Crisco All-Vegetable Shortening over the spot being chafed to lubricate the skin and prevent further rubbing.

- **Kingsford's Corn Starch, Stayfree Maxi Pads,** and **Ziploc Storage Bags.** Fill a gallon-size Ziploc Storage Bag with Kingsford's Corn Starch, and use a Stayfree Maxi Pad as if it were a powder puff to apply the cornstarch between your thighs, or wherever your skin is rubbing against itself. The cornstarch lubricates the skin.

- **Pam Cooking Spray.** Spray Pam Cooking Spray between your thighs, or wherever your skin is rubbing against itself, to reduce the friction and simultaneously moisturize the chafed skin.

- **Vaseline Petroleum Jelly.** Smear a dab of Vaseline Petroleum Jelly on the parts of your thighs that rub against each other to prevent chafing and moisturize the irritated skin.

STRANGE FACTS

◆ A chafing dish is a covered pan with legs that sits over a can of liquid heat.

◆ Chafing occurs when electrical wiring is improperly routed over sharp edges or a vibrating part that cuts or wears down the plastic coating over the wire, leading to a short circuit and possibly fire.

◆ Cowboys wear chaps, leather shields worn over pants, to protect their inner thighs from chafing and saddle sores while riding horses.

◆ Ralph Lauren markets a men's cologne called Chaps.

Chapped Lips

- **Alberto VO5 Conditioning Hairdressing.** Soothe chapped lips by rubbing in a small amount of Alberto VO5 Conditioning Hairdressing. *VO5* stands for the five *v*ital *o*rganic emollients in the hairdressing.

- **Bag Balm.** Soothe chapped lips by rubbing on a dab of Bag Balm, the salve created to relieve cracking in cow udders. It keeps lips moist.

- **Crisco All-Vegetable Shortening** and **Kool-Aid.** Place three tablespoons Crisco All-Vegetable Shortening in a ceramic coffee cup and heat in a microwave oven for one minute (or until the shortening liquefies). Empty a packet of your favorite flavor Kool-Aid into the cup of melted shortening and stir well until dissolved. Carefully pour the colored liquid into a clean, empty Kodak 35mm film canister, cap tightly, and refrigerate overnight. In the morning, you've got tasty homemade lip gloss that moisturizes chapped lips.

- **Gatorade.** Keeping your body well-hydrated keeps your lips naturally moist, giving your chapped lips the moisture they need to heal themselves.

- **Johnson's Baby Oil.** Use a drop of Johnson's Baby Oil to moisturize your chapped lips.

- **Maybelline Moisture Whip Lipstick.** Wearing an opaque lipstick helps shelter the lips from the sun.

- **Noxzema.** To soothe and heal chapped lips, apply a dab of Noxzema Original Skin Cream. The cream moisturizes your lips, and the sharp taste will prevent you from licking your lips further.

- **Vaseline Petroleum Jelly.** Apply a dab of Vaseline Petroleum Jelly to your lips. It works just like ChapStick.

STRANGE FACTS

- ◆ The fact that a large percent of American women wear lipstick may explain why women get a significantly lower percentage of cases of lip cancer than men do.

- ◆ ChapStick lip balms come in five flavors: Regular, Cherry, Mint, Orange, and Strawberry.

- ◆ In *M*A*S*H*—the novel by Richard Hooker, the 1970 movie starring Donald Sutherland, and the television series starring Alan Alda— Major Margaret Houlihan is nicknamed "Hot Lips."

- ◆ Pop artist Andy Warhol designed the Rolling Stones' logo of a tongue sticking out from between a pair of thick lips. The logo first appeared on the cover of the Rolling Stones' 1971 album *Sticky Fingers*, which was also designed by Warhol.

- ◆ The 1975 cult movie *The Rocky Horror Picture Show* begins with a close-up of a pair of lips singing the opening song.

- ◆ "Giving someone lip service" means insincerely professing concern, dedication, or loyalty.

- ◆ "Biting your lip" means to refrain from expressing your feelings, "buttoning your lips" or "zippering your lips" means to keep information secret, and "keeping a stiff upper lip" means to face adversity courageously.

Chicken Pox

- **Arm & Hammer Baking Soda.** Dissolve one cup Arm & Hammer Baking Soda in a bathtub filled with warm water for a soothing bath to relieve the itching.

- **Cheerios.** Pour two cups Cheerios in a blender and blend into a fine powder on medium-high speed. Put the powdered Cheerios into a warm bath and soak in the oats for thirty minutes. (Use a plastic or mesh drain cover to prevent the Cheerios from clogging your drain.) The comforting oatmeal relieves the itching from chicken pox.

- **Fruit of the Earth Aloe Vera Gel.** Smooth Fruit of the Earth Aloe Vera Gel over the chicken pox spots to let the analgesic soothe the itching.

- **Kingsford's Corn Starch** and **Johnson's Baby Oil.** Mix cornstarch and baby oil with a little water to make a paste, and apply to the skin to relieve the itching.

- **Phillips' Milk of Magnesia.** Use a cotton ball to apply Phillips' Milk of Magnesia like lotion to soothe chicken pox.

- **Quaker Oats** and **L'eggs Sheer Energy Panty Hose.** Pour one cup Quaker Oats in a blender and blend into a powder. Cut off the foot from a clean, used pair of L'eggs Sheer Energy Panty Hose and fill with the powdered Quaker Oats. Tie a knot in the nylon, hang it from the tub's spigot, and fill the tub with warm water. Soak in the tub for thirty minutes for an inexpensive and soothing oatmeal bath. Use the oatmeal sack as a washcloth.

STRANGE FACTS

◆ Chicken pox is caused by a herpes virus called *Varicella zoster* virus—not to be confused with the sexually transmitted herpes simplex 2 virus.

◆ With chicken pox, red blotches appear on the skin, turn into pimples after a few hours, then become enlarged blisters which, after a few days, dry up into scabs.

◆ While someone who has suffered through chicken pox will rarely get the itchy disease again, the *Varicella zoster* virus remains in the body and may emerge in later life, causing shingles.

◆ The chicken pox vaccine, made available in 1995, does not always prevent the disease, but does lessen its severity.

◆ Getting chicken pox as an adult is more painful than getting chicken pox as a child.

◆ Chicken pox gets its name because people used to say that this childhood disease was mild enough for a chicken—not from the fact that the itchy blisters make the sufferer want to scratch like a hen.

Cholesterol

- **Cheerios.** Beta-glucan—a soluble bran-based fiber found in whole oats, oat bran, and oat flour—can reduce serum cholesterol, a major risk factor in heart disease. A one-cup bowl of the traditional version of Cheerios in the bright yellow box contains at least 0.75 grams of beta-glucan, no more than three grams of fat, and no more than one gram of saturated fat—as required by the Food and Drug Administration to make the claim that eating Cheerios, in conjunction with a diet low in saturated fats and cholesterol, can reduce the risk of heart disease. Data suggests very strongly that you need between three and four grams of beta-glucan a day to see a significant cholesterol-lowering effect. That's equal to four to six cups of Cheerios every day. (A diet high in fat can negate any benefits from the oats.)

- **Dannon Yogurt.** In 1979, the *American Journal of Clinical Nutrition* reported that subjects with normal blood cholesterol levels who ate three cups of yogurt in a week saw their blood cholesterol levels drop 5 to 10 percent, while the helpful HDL cholesterol levels rose.

- **Lipton Tea Bags.** Drinking tea may actually help control cholesterol. The tannins in tea seem to help the body maintain normal blood cholesterol levels.

- **Quaker Oats.** Eating one cup of Quaker Oats oatmeal a day for approximately three weeks lowers harmful LDL cholesterol by about 20 percent and raises helpful HDL cholesterol by roughly 15 percent—in most people who do not suffer from hypercholesteremia (a disorder that causes high cholesterol levels).

- **Star Olive Oil.** Supplement a strict low-fat diet with two or three table-spoons Star Olive Oil every day. Olive oil is high in monounsaturated fat, which may lower cholesterol. Research has shown that a diet high in monounsaturated fat actually lowers total cholesterol levels—better than a low-fat diet would.

STRANGE FACTS

- In 1988, when nutritionists claimed that oat bran reduced cholesterol, sales for the Quaker Oats Company jumped 600 percent. In July 1992, a major report in the *Journal of the American Medical Association*, sponsored by the Quaker Oats Company, concluded that oat bran lowers blood cholesterol by an average of just 2 to 3 percent. On the bright side, the report claimed that a 1 percent reduction in cholesterol nationwide could lead to a 2 percent decrease in deaths from heart disease.

- For the body to work at its best, according to the National Cholesterol Education Program, your total blood cholesterol level should remain below 200—with your LDL cholesterol below 130 and your HDL level above 65.

- More than half of all American adults have cholesterol levels over 200 milligrams per deciliter of blood. Twenty percent have cholesterol levels of 240 or above.

- Low-density lipoprotein (LDL) cholesterol, found in meats, milk, eggs, and butter, oxidizes in the bloodstream, prompting immune cells to ingest them. Once full, these immune cells adhere to the walls of arteries, forming plaque and eventually clogging the arteries.

- A clogged artery to the heart causes a heart attack. A clogged artery to the brain causes a stroke.

- High-density lipoprotein (HDL) cholesterol absorbs LDL cholesterol from the bloodstream and carries it to the liver to be excreted from the body. If the LDL level rises too high, the HDL cholesterol cannot do its job fast enough, leaving excess LDL cholesterol in the bloodstream.

♦ The liver produces cholesterol to make sex hormones, cell membranes, vitamin D, and bile acids.

♦ As fiber travels through the digestive tract, it absorbs water, making stools larger and moving them through the system more quickly, taking harmful substances along with it.

♦ Every year roughly 500,000 Americans die from heart attacks, making heart disease the number one killer in the United States. Another one million Americans live through heart attacks each year.

♦ In China, the average cholesterol level is 127. In America, the average cholesterol level is 227.

♦ A diet low in saturated fats (the fats found in red meat, milk, eggs, cheese, and butter) significantly lowers the levels of LDL cholesterol in the bloodstream.

Cold Sores

- **Arm & Hammer Baking Soda** and **Colgate Toothpaste.** Mix a pinch of Arm & Hammer Baking Soda with a dollop of Colgate Regular Flavor Toothpaste and dab a little onto the cold sore, letting it dry. Repeat three to five times a day until the sore disappears.

- **Balmex.** Apply Balmex, the diaper rash ointment, to a cold sore the moment you feel it forming.

- **Barbasol Shaving Cream.** Rub a dab of Barbasol into the cold sore. The emollients in the shaving cream hasten healing.

- **Carnation Condensed Milk.** Saturate a cotton ball with condensed milk and apply to the cold sore for fifteen minutes to soothe the pain and expedite healing.

- **Cool Whip.** Place a compress of Cool Whip on the cold sore to speed healing, then rinse with cool water.

- **Coppertone.** If you're prone to cold sores, wear sun screen with a sun protection factor (SPF) of 15 or more to protect your lips and face from ultraviolet rays, which trigger one out of every four cases of cold sores.

- **Dannon Yogurt.** Putting plain yogurt on a cold sore helps dry it up. The acidophilus bacteria in yogurt kill the bacteria infecting the cold sore.

- **Dickinson's Witch Hazel.** Gently break open the cold sore, and using a Q-Tips Cotton Swab, apply Dickinson's Witch Hazel to the cold sore to help it dry.

- **Fruit of the Earth Aloe Vera Gel.** Apply a dab of Fruit of the Earth Aloe Vera Gel to the cold sore.

- **Heinz White Vinegar.** With a cotton ball, apply Heinz White Vinegar liberally to the cold sore. The vinegar kills bacteria, dries up the cold sore, and eases the swelling and pain.

- **Lipton Tea Bags.** When you feel a cold sore forming, dampen a Lipton Tea Bag with warm water and place it over the cold sore. When the tea bag cools, wet it with warm water again and again. The tannin in the tea dries the cold sore and soothes the pain.

- **Phillips' Milk of Magnesia.** Using a cotton ball, dab the cold sore with Phillips' Milk of Magnesia. This antacid dries up the acid in the lesion.

- **Preparation H.** The moment you feel a cold sore forming on your lips, dab Preparation H on the spot to stop the swelling.

- **Purell.** Put a dab of Purell anti-bacterial hand gel on the sore to disinfect it and speed healing.

- **Smirnoff Vodka.** Using a Q-Tips Cotton Swab, apply Smirnoff Vodka to the cold sore to help it dry out.

- **Vaseline Petroleum Jelly.** Apply a dab of Vaseline Petroleum Jelly over the cold sore to protect it from further contamination.

STRANGE FACTS

- ◆ Cold sores are caused by a virus known as herpes simplex 1—not to be confused with genital herpes, the sexually transmitted disease caused by herpes simplex 2.

- ◆ Cold sores can be transmitted from one person to another by kissing or sharing a drinking glass.

- ◆ A cold sore and a fever blister are the same thing.

- ◆ In the 1984 movie *This Is Spinal Tap*, directed by Rob Reiner, the members of the fictional heavy metal band are interviewed in one scene with cold sores on their lips—apparently contracted from groupies.

- ◆ In the 1987 movie *The Witches of Eastwick*, Jack Nicholson afflicts Michelle Pfeiffer with a fever that produces cold sores on her lips.

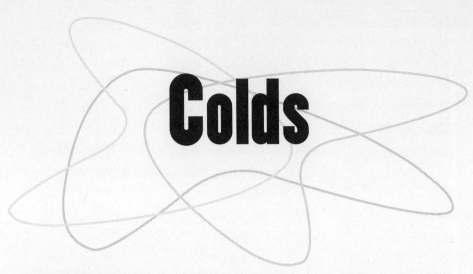

Colds

- **Altoids Peppermints.** Chewing two Altoids Peppermints helps clear up a stuffy nose. Peppermint relieves congestion.

- **Campbell's Chicken Noodle Soup.** Sipping a bowl of hot chicken soup actually helps decongest nasal passages while simultaneously rehydrating and reenergizing the body with essential salts. Long considered a folk remedy, chicken soup as a cure for the common cold is now considered a proven fact—thanks to research conducted by the Mount Sinai Medical Center in Miami Beach, Florida.

- **ChapStick.** If your nose gets red and sore from being blown too often, rub unflavored ChapStick on the tender spots to heal the irritation.

- **Dial Soap.** Washing your hands frequently with Dial antibacterial soap may help you avoid contracting a cold from a sick family member by killing any germs you may have inadvertently picked up.

- **French's Mustard.** Rub a generous amount of French's Mustard on your chest. Cover with a washcloth dampened with warm water and wrung out, making an old-fashioned mustard plaster to relieve congestion.

- **Gatorade.** Drinking a quart of liquids daily replaces vital bodily fluids, flushes impurities from your system, and helps speed healing. Gatorade replaces electrolytes (the potassium and salt lost through fever and perspiration).

- **Gold's Horseradish.** Gold's Horseradish is a natural cure for a congested nose. Simply eat some horseradish on a cracker.

- **Heinz Apple Cider Vinegar** and **SueBee Honey.** Mix one-quarter cup Heinz Apple Cider Vinegar with one-quarter cup SueBee Honey. Take one tablespoon six times daily. The vinegar kills bacteria and the honey soothes your throat. (Honey should not be fed to infants under one year of age.)

- **Life Savers.** Sucking on hard candy helps your body create more saliva to moisturize and soothe your dry, scratchy throat.

- **Lipton Tea Bags.** Drinking hot tea replaces vital bodily fluids, flushes impurities from your system, and helps soothe your throat and decongest your sinuses.

- **Maxwell House Coffee** and **Glad Flexible Straws.** Sipping a cup of hot, black coffee through a plastic straw helps relieve chest congestion.

- **McCormick Garlic Powder.** Spice a bowl of chicken soup with McCormick Garlic Powder. Garlic is a natural antibiotic.

- **Morton Salt.** Dissolve one teaspoon salt in a glass of warm water and gargle with the solution three times a day to relieve your throat and loosen phlegm.

- **Morton Salt** and **Glad Flexible Straws.** To clear congested sinuses, dissolve one-half teaspoon Morton Salt in one cup warm water. Insert a Glad Flexible Straw into the liquid, cover the open end of the straw with your finger, insert the straw into your nostril, release your finger from the straw, and inhale the liquid. Repeat several times, then blow your nose thoroughly.

- **Mott's Apple Sauce.** When you have the energy to eat, applesauce makes a great starter food that the body can easily digest.

- **Popsicle.** Sucking on a nice cold Popsicle brings instant relief to a sore throat, and the sugars help coat the throat and give you energy.

- **SueBee Honey.** To help yourself sleep at night, eat one teaspoon of SueBee Honey (or mix it into a cup of tea) before bedtime. (Do not feed honey to infants under one year of age.)

- **Tabasco Pepper Sauce** and **Campbell's Tomato Juice.** Mix ten to twenty drops Tabasco Pepper Sauce in a glass of Campbell's Tomato Juice. Drink several of these decongestant tonics daily to help relieve congestion in the nose, sinuses, and lungs. Or gargle with ten to twenty drops Tabasco Pepper Sauce mixed in a glass of water to clear out the respiratory tract.

- **Vaseline Petroleum Jelly.** When your nose gets sore from too much blowing, apply a thin coat of Vaseline Petroleum Jelly around your nostrils.

- **York Peppermint Pattie.** Eating a York Peppermint Pattie can clear up a stuffy nose. Peppermint relieves congestion.

- **Ziploc Storage Bags.** Keep a gallon-size Ziploc Storage Bag on hand so you can dispose of used tissues and seal the bag to avoid spreading germs.

STRANGE FACTS

- ◆ Chemical analysis shows that chicken soup contains chemicals similar to those found in medications that thin mucus secretions, providing quicker relief from coughing and sneezing.

SIDE EFFECTS
SMELLY HUMIDIFIER

CLOROX
Add two drops of Clorox Bleach per gallon of water when refilling your humidifier to prevent bacteria from growing in the water.

HEINZ WHITE VINEGAR
Add two teaspoons Heinz White Vinegar to the water to kill the bacteria.

LISTERINE
Mix one tablespoon Listerine per gallon of water when filling the humidifier. Listerine kills the germs that cause smelly humidifiers.

REALEMON
Eliminate odors in your humidifier by pouring three or four teaspoons ReaLemon lemon juice into the water. Lemon juice kills bacteria while giving the water a pleasant lemon scent.

20 MULE TEAM BORAX
Once or twice a year, dissolve one tablespoon 20 Mule Team Borax per gallon of water before filling up the humidifier. The borax deodorizes the unit.

DROP IN ON THE SMITH BROTHERS

In 1847, after candy maker James Smith moved his family from St. Armand, Quebec, to Poughkeepsie, New York, and opened a restaurant, a customer sold him the formula for a cough remedy for five dollars. Smith cleverly used the formula and his candy-making skills to create a cough lozenge. The lozenges, sold from a large glass bowl on drugstore counters, began to catch on as a remedy for cold symptoms, and in 1852, Smith ran his first advertisement for the cough drops in a Poughkeepsie newspaper.

Smith's two sons, William and Andrew, helped him mix the secret formula in his kitchen and sold the product in the streets of Poughkeepsie. When their father died in 1866, the two sons inherited the business, officially naming the company Smith Brothers. As sales grew throughout the Hudson Valley, a flurry of imitators jumped on the bandwagon, marketing cough lozenges called "Schmitt Brothers," "Smythe Sisters," and even creating another "Smith Brothers." To beat the competition, the real Smith Brothers decided to use their bearded faces as the company trademark on the glass bowls for counter displays and on the small envelopes shopkeepers used to package the Smith Brothers Cough Drops for their customers. In 1872, to stop drugstore owners from using the Smith Brothers bowls and envelopes to sell other companies' lozenges, Andrew and William Smith designed the first box of Smith Brothers cough drops, featuring their bearded faces. Those two faces appear on boxes of Smith Brothers cough drops to this very day.

ANDREW SMITH BECAME KNOWN as "Trade" and William Smith became known as "Mark" because the word *trade-mark* is split into two syllables on the cough drop box, one half of the word under each image.

ANDREW SMITH REFUSED TO ALLOW ginger ale in his house because, as a fervent prohibitionist, he objected to the alcoholic nature of its name.

THE FIRST NEWSPAPER ADVERTISE-MENT for Smith Brothers Cough Drops reads: "All afflicted with hoarseness, coughs, or colds should test its virtues, which can be done without the least risk."

A BOX OF SMITH BROTHERS COUGH DROPS was the first factory-filled candy package in the United States.

CONFECTIONER WILLIAM LUDEN, creator of Luden's Throat Drops in Reading, Pennsylvania, initiated the idea of lining a cough drop box with waxed paper to keep the candies fresh.

ANDREW SMITH DIED IN 1895, but William Smith continued as president of Smith Brothers almost up to his death in 1913. He was succeeded by his son, Arthur G. Smith.

IN 1922, Smith Brothers introduced Menthol Cough Drops, followed in 1948 by Wild Cherry Flavor.

- A runny nose, sore throat, and sneezing are common symptoms of a cold. A fever, headaches, hacking coughs, muscle aches, and extreme fatigue rarely accompany colds, but are symptoms of the flu. Unlike colds, the flu is never associated with sneezing.

- When tea was first introduced in the American colonies, many housewives, in their ignorance, served the tea leaves with sugar or syrup after throwing away the water in which they had been boiled.

- People do not get sick from cold weather. People actually get sick more often from being indoors than outdoors.

- The common cold is the most common contagious disease in the world.

- The scientific name for the common cold is acute nasopharyngitis.

- Americans spend an estimated 500 million dollars on nonprescription cold remedies every year.

- Colds make people more susceptible to bronchitis and pneumonia.

- On January 15, 2000, eighty-year-old George Crowley, inventor of the electric blanket, died of pneumonia.

Constipation

- **Coca-Cola.** Drinking a can of the real thing can have a laxative result.

- **Kellogg's Raisin Bran.** Eating one cup of Kellogg's Raisin Bran every morning adds seven grams of all-important fiber to your diet, helping your body produce soft bowel movements.

- **Maxwell House Coffee.** For many people, the caffeine in a cup of coffee triggers the muscular contractions in the intestines, immediately unclogging a backed-up digestive system.

- **Orville Redenbacher's Gourmet Popping Corn.** Eating thirty grams of fiber, such as popcorn, daily puts an end to constipation and keeps bowel movements regular.

- **Quaker Oats.** Eating one cup of Quaker Oats adds eight grams of fiber to your diet. Thirty grams of fiber daily puts an end to constipation and keeps bowel movements regular.

- **ReaLemon** and **SueBee Honey.** To make a natural laxative, mix four tablespoons ReaLemon lemon juice in one cup warm water and sweeten with SueBee Honey to taste. (Honey should not be fed to infants under one year of age.)

- **Star Olive Oil.** Taking one to three tablespoons Star Olive Oil works as a mild laxative.

- **Sun-Maid Raisins.** Eating thirty grams of fiber daily puts an end to constipation and keeps bowel movements regular. One cup of Sun-Maid Raisins contains eight grams of fiber.

Strange Facts

- Around 8000 B.C.E., Scots living in the Orkney Islands developed the first indoor plumbing to carry human waste from stone huts to streams.

- As early as 2500 B.C.E., Mesopotamians and Egyptians used castor oil as a laxative. Experts now caution against using castor oil as a laxative because it breaks down to form ricinoleic acid, frequently causing intense diarrhea, depleting the body of fluids and nutrients.

- As early as 2000 B.C.E., royal families living in the Minoan palace at Knossos on the island of Crete had the world's first known flush toilet.

- Hippocrates (circa 460–377 B.C.E.), considered the father of modern medicine, incorrectly claimed that north winds cause constipation.

- In 1596, Sir John Harrington devised and installed a flush toilet for his godmother Queen Elizabeth that emptied into a nearby cesspool.

- In 1775, British watchmaker Alexander Cumming invented the first flush toilet with a "sink trap," which created a buffer of water to block returning fumes from the cesspool. The sink trap is used to this very day in all toilets.

- Euphemisms for the rest room include the "powder room," "facilities," "water closet," "john," "crapper," "can," "lavatory," "comfort station," "necessary," "latrine," "chamber pot," "reading room," "throne," and "smallest room in the house."

- In 1905, upon immigrating to New York, Hungarian pharmacist Max Kiss combined chocolate with phenolphthalein to make a commercial laxative, which he named Ex-Lax—a contraction of the words *excellent* and *laxative*.

- Euphemisms for constipation include such peculiar phrases as having "clogged plumbing," "a logjam," "an impasse," "a plugged drain," "a corked spigot," and "an airtight bomb shelter."

Contact Lenses

- **Arm & Hammer Baking Soda.** To clean hard contact lenses, mix one-quarter teaspoon Arm & Hammer Baking Soda and your regular disinfectant solution to make a paste in the cupped palm of your hand. Dip each contact lens in the paste and rub with your finger. Baking soda is a mild abrasive. Never use Arm & Hammer Baking Soda to clean soft contact lenses.

- **Glad Flexible Straws, Johnson & Johnson Cotton Balls,** and **Scotch Transparent Tape.** If you accidentally drop a contact lens down the drain of the sink, use Scotch Transparent Tape to make a long stick from two or three Glad Flexible Straws and attach a cotton ball at one end. Stick it down the drain and fish for the contact lens. It will stick to the cotton.

- **L'eggs Sheer Energy Panty Hose.** If you lose a contact lens in the carpeting, cut off the toe from a clean, used pair of L'eggs Sheer Energy Panty Hose and use it to cover the end of a vacuum cleaner hose attachment (secure it in place with a few rubber bands). Vacuum an inch above the carpet, frequently checking the panty hose to see if you've sucked up the contact lens.

STRANGE FACTS

♦ In the sixteenth century, Italian Renaissance artist Leonardo da Vinci first proposed the idea of contact lenses. He suggested that a short tube filled with water and covered at one end with a flat lens be placed directly against the eyeball. Today, soft contact lenses—made from porous, liquid-absorbing plastic—contain a high percentage of water.

◆ In 1877, Swiss physician A. E. Fick developed the first practical hard contact lenses. These thick glass lenses covered the entire eyeball.

◆ In 1936, the German company I. G. Farben invented the first Plexiglas contact lenses, which covered the entire eyeball.

◆ In the 1940s, American opticians developed the corneal contact lens, which covered only the cornea of eye.

◆ In their 1969 book *The Peter Principle*, Laurence Peter and Raymond Hull wrote, "Competence, like truth, beauty, and contact lenses, is in the eye of the beholder."

◆ People who have had cataracts removed see better with contact lenses than with eyeglasses.

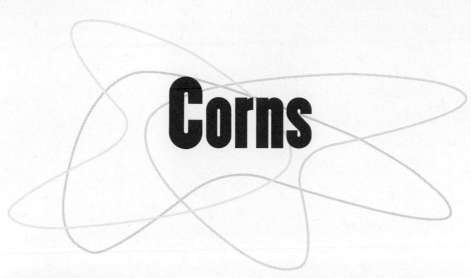

Corns

- **ChapStick.** Rub ChapStick on the corn to soften the hard, thickened skin and ease the pain.

- **Epsom Salt.** To relieve the pain from a corn temporarily, soak your feet in a solution of Epsom Salt and warm water. Doing so reduces the size of the bursa sac—a pocket of fluid between the corn and the bone.

- **Heinz White Vinegar** and **Wonder Bread.** Saturate a piece of Wonder Bread with one-quarter cup Heinz White Vinegar. Let sit for thirty minutes, then apply the poultice to the corn and cover with gauze or a handkerchief to keep in place overnight. By morning, the vinegar should have dissolved the thick skin, making the corn easier to peel off. If necessary, reapply the poultice for several nights.

- **Karo Corn Syrup.** Apply Karo Corn Syrup to the corn and wrap with gauze to soften the hard skin.

- **Nestea.** Soak the corn in warm Nestea for thirty minutes each day for a week or two until the tannic acid in the tea dissolves the corn.

- **Stayfree Maxi Pads.** Using a pair of scissors, cut a Stayfree Maxi Pad into a doughnut shape and place over the corn, positioning the hole over the corn and letting the adhesive strip adhere to the skin. The maxi pad will protect the corn while it heals.

- **Tide.** Add one capful Tide Liquid Detergent to a gallon of water, soak your feet in the soapy solution for thirty minutes to soften the hard skin, then rinse well with clean water.

• **Vaseline Petroleum Jelly.** Coat the corn with Vaseline Petroleum Jelly to moisturize and soften the hardened skin and promote healing.

STRANGE FACTS

◆ Corns throb before the onset of bad weather.

◆ The word *corn* is derived from the Latin word *cornu*, meaning "horn."

◆ In seventeenth-century England, doctors and surgeons considered cutting corns beneath their dignity, creating a window of opportunity for anyone willing to cut corns to earn a living. Corn cutters hawked their talent in the streets.

◆ In the second act of Ben Jonson's 1614 play *Bartholomew Fair*, a corn cutter enters the fairground with his cry.

◆ In Shakespeare's play *Romeo and Juliet*, Capulet declares: "Welcome gentlemen! ladies that have their toes unplagu'd with corns . . . which of you all now deny to dance? She that makes dainty, she, I'll swear hath corns."

◆ Author Charles Dickens based Mrs. Moucher in his novel *David Copperfield* on Mrs. Seymour Hill, a well-respected corn cutter in London.

◆ In the children's book *The Tin Man of Oz*, the twelfth book in the Wizard of Oz series, author L. Frank Baum introduces Tommy Kwikstep, a character with twenty legs, who complains that "a corn on one toe is not so bad, but when you have a hundred toes—as I have—and get corns on most of them, it is far from pleasant. Instead of running, I now painfully crawl."

◆ In Walt Disney's 1937 animated movie *Snow White and the Seven Dwarfs*, the seven dwarfs return home to discover the lights on. "Mark my words, there's trouble a-brewing!" predicts Grumpy. "Felt it comin' all day. Corns hurt!"

◆ In German, a corn is called a *Hühnerauge*.

IN THE FLOW WITH KARO

On May 13, 1902, the Corn Products Refining Company introduced Karo Light and Dark Corn Syrups, sold in "friction-top tins." Legend holds that the chemist who formulated the syrup named it Karo in honor of his wife Caroline. Another theory traces the name Karo back to an earlier table syrup named Kairomel. Before the advent of Karo corn syrups, American housewives carried a syrup jug to the grocery store to be refilled from the grocer's barrels of syrup.

In 1903, the Corn Products Refining Company placed a full-page advertisement in the *Ladies' Home Journal*, promoting the new Karo corn syrups as "The Great Spread for Daily Bread," offering eleven recipes and a free cookbook to anyone who wrote to the company. Seven years later, the company launched a $250,000 advertising campaign and published the second edition of the *Karo Cook Book*, compiled and written by Emma Churchman Hewitt, former associate editor of the *Ladies' Home Journal*. The fifty-page booklet offered "120 Practical Recipes for the Use of Karo Syrup." Karo published updated cookbooks in 1949 and 1981, featuring two hundred recipes using its syrups.

CORN SYRUP IS MADE by cooking cornstarch and water under pressure and adding enzymes to the mixture—turning it into glucose, maltose, and dextrin. Another enzyme can be added to turn some of the glucose into fructose.

KARO SYRUPS ARE THE ONLY nationally distributed corn syrup products in the United States.

CORN SYRUPS ARE USED AS TOPPINGS for French toast, pancakes, and waffles, and in recipes for pies, candies, glazes, sauces, beverages, and ice creams.

IN 1930, the wife of a corporate sales executive discovered a revolutionary new use for corn syrup. She baked a mixture of corn syrup, sugar, eggs, vanilla, and pecans in a pie shell, creating the pecan pie—destined to become an international favorite.

THE DIONNE QUINTUPLETS, five girls born in Callander, Ontario, in 1934, became spokespersons for Karo corn syrups throughout the 1940s.

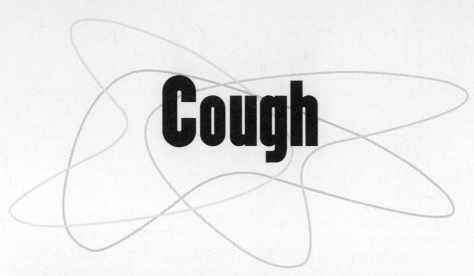

Cough

- **Altoids Peppermints.** Chewing two Altoids Peppermints helps alleviate a nagging cough. The peppermint clears phlegm and relieves congestion.

- **Heinz Apple Cider Vinegar, Tabasco Pepper Sauce**, and **SueBee Honey.** To relieve a nagging cough from a cold, mix one-half cup Heinz Apple Cider Vinegar, one-half cup water, one teaspoon Tabasco Pepper Sauce, and four teaspoons SueBee Honey. Take one tablespoon when your cough acts up. Take another tablespoon at bedtime. (Honey should not be fed to infants under one year of age.)

- **Life Savers.** Sucking on hard candy helps your body create more saliva to moisturize and soothe your dry, scratchy throat.

- **ReaLemon, Star Olive Oil**, and **SueBee Honey.** Mix four tablespoons ReaLemon lemon juice, one-half cup Star Olive Oil, and one cup SueBee Honey. Warm the mixure, then stir vigorously for two minutes. Take one teaspoon every two hours. (Honey should not be fed to infants under one year of age.)

- **SueBee Honey** and **ReaLemon.** Mix one tablespoon SueBee Honey and one tablespoon ReaLemon lemon juice in a small glass of warm water and sip the solution. For a stronger concoction, combine equal parts SueBee Honey and ReaLemon, and take one teaspoon at bedtime. Both mixtures help loosen phlegm. (Honey should not be fed to infants under one year of age.)

- **York Peppermint Pattie.** Eating a York Peppermint Pattie may help relieve a cough. The peppermint clears phlegm and congestion.

STRANGE FACTS

◆ Around 1000 B.C.E., Egyptian confectioners of the Twentieth Dynasty developed the world's first candy cough lozenges by mixing together honey, herbs, spices, and citrus fruits.

◆ In the nineteenth century, scientists developed drugs that suppressed the brain's cough reflex—most notably morphine, a derivative of opium.

◆ In 1898, Dr. Heinrich Dreser, head of the drug research laboratory at the Bayer Company in Germany, developed diacetylmorphine—a derivative of morphine with four to eight times the painkilling power. The Bayer Company marketed diacetylmorphine under the brandname Heroin (derived from the "heroic" state of mind the drug purportedly induced), and the new drug was used in cough syrups—until 1910, when doctors realized that heroin is far more addictive than morphine.

◆ Today, doctors commonly prescribe methylmorphine, a mild opium derivative, to suppress coughs. Methylmorphine is better known as codeine.

◆ Herbal remedies for soothing a cough include anise, elm bark, eucalyptus oil, hyssop, lavender, peppermint oil, and horehound.

◆ When a man goes to the doctor for a standard physical exam, the doctor gently squeezes the man's testicles and instructs him to cough. The cough causes the diaphragm to contract, pulling the testicles up slightly toward the body.

Cuts and Scrapes

- **Bag Balm.** Covering the abrasion with a dab of Bag Balm and a bandage keeps the scab soft and helps the wound heal faster.

- **ChapStick.** Heal paper cuts or shaving nicks by rubbing ChapStick on the wound. The lip balm stops the sharp pain caused by air hitting the nerves and helps the cut heal.

- **Dial Soap.** Washing a wound with soap and water works just like an antiseptic, particularly if you use an antibacterial soap like Dial.

- **Dickinson's Witch Hazel.** Apply Dickinson's Witch Hazel to the wound to disinfect it. Witch hazel is a mild astringent.

- **Huggies Baby Wipes.** To clean scrapes easily and effectively, use Huggies Baby Wipes.

- **Krazy Glue.** After disinfecting a paper cut with an antiseptic, glue it closed with Krazy Glue. The Krazy Glue deprives the nerve endings of air, instantly relieving the sharp pain. Physicians in Canada use n-Butyl Cyanoacrylate, an adhesive similar to Krazy Glue, instead of stitches.

- **Lipton Tea Bags.** To stop minor bleeding from a cut, dampen a Lipton Tea Bag with warm water and press the tea bag over the wound.

- **Listerine.** Pouring Listerine over a laceration or abrasion disinfects the cuts and scrapes. Listerine is an astringent.

- **Maalox.** Using a cotton ball, apply a few dabs of Maalox to open sores to speed healing.

- **McCormick Alum.** To stop the bleeding and disinfect a minor wound, dab McCormick Alum on the cut skin. Alum is both an antiseptic and a pain reliever. It clots the blood and helps prevent infection.

- **McCormick Ground (Cayenne) Red Pepper.** Applying cayenne pepper to a cut or nick may stop the bleeding.

- **Pampers.** Use a Pampers disposable diaper as a compress to stop a wound from bleeding.

- **Preparation H.** Apply a dab of Preparation H to cuts and scrapes to help them heal faster.

- **Purell.** Applying Purell Instant Hand Sanitizer to an open wound helps stop the bleeding and disinfects the wound.

- **ReaLemon.** Pouring ReaLemon lemon juice on a cut or applying it with a cotton ball disinfects the wound.

- **Scotch Packaging Tape.** In an emergency, provide first aid by bandaging wounds with torn bedsheets and Scotch Packaging Tape.

- **SueBee Honey.** Applying SueBee Honey to the injury as an ointment disinfects the wound, kills bacteria, and hastens healing. Honey is hygroscopic and absorbs water, creating an environment in which disease-producing microorganisms, deprived of moisture, cannot live.

- **Sure-Jell.** Sprinkling a little Sure-Jell powder on a wound stops the bleeding by clotting the blood.

- **Tampax Tampons.** Use a tampon as a compress for wounds or lacerations to control bleeding. You can hold the tampon in place with a piece of Scotch Packaging Tape.

- **Vaseline Petroleum Jelly.** Applying a dab of Vaseline to a cut speeds healing by preventing air from stinging exposed nerves and keeping the area moist so new skin cells can grow easily.

Don't cut corners! See your doctor if foreign material, like gravel or dirt, is embedded in the wound or if you see signs of infection such as pus or inflammation.

Strange Facts

- The ancient Greek physician Galen (circa 130–200 C.E.), considered the father of experimental physiology, mistakenly believed that the body is governed by four humors (blood, phlegm, black bile, and yellow bile) and that a disorder in any one of the four humors causes disease. He incorrectly claimed that diseases could be cured by bleeding the patient to remove the "corrupt humors." If a patient did not recover from a disease after a pint of blood was removed from the body, the physician would remove more blood—weakening the patient further and often hastening death. Galen's absurd remedy was widely practiced by physicians and barbers for the next 1,500 years, resulting in the deaths of millions of people—including the British poet Lord Byron and England's King Charles II.

- When President James A. Garfield was shot by Charles Guiteau on July 2, 1881, a doctor at the scene poured brandy and ammonia down Garfield's throat, causing the wounded president to vomit. Garfield was taken to the White House, where Dr. Willard Bliss inserted a "Nelaton Probe" into the wound to find the bullet slug, but only succeeded in damaging more tissue when the probe got stuck in the shattered fragments of Garfield's eleventh rib. Bliss inserted his unwashed finger in the wound, as did other doctors, infecting it. Inventor Alexander Graham Bell showed up with a telephone receiver wired to a metal detector to help locate the slug, but when doctors cut open the deep spot indicated by Bell, the slug was not there. Garfield died on September 19, 1881. The autopsy revealed that the slug had been enveloped by a protective cyst, four inches from Garfield's spine, and was relatively harmless.

- The average human body contains 60,000 miles of blood vessels.

- On *Star Trek*, Mr. Spock's blood type is T negative.

- In the Beatles' 1967 made-for-television movie *Magical Mystery Tour*, one of the passengers aboard the bus is named Buster Bloodvessel.

- In every episode of the television sitcom *WKRP in Cincinnati*, news reporter Les Nessman wore a Band-Aid bandage—on either his body, eyeglasses, or clothing.

- Curad bandage wrappers sparkle in the dark when they are ripped open. The adhesive used to seal the bandage wrappers contains an ultraviolet dye. The friction creating by tearing the wrapper electrifies the dye, making it sparkle.

- Surgeons treat an arterial venous fistula (an entangled cluster of arteries) by injecting liquid acrylic agents into the abnormal blood vessels to seal off the excessive flow of blood. The material used, n-Butyl Cyanoacrylate, is similar to Krazy Glue.

SIDE EFFECTS
PULLING OFF BANDAGES

ALBERTO VO5 CONDITIONING HAIRDRESSING
To remove adhesive bandages painlessly, rub a dab of Alberto VO5 Conditioning Hairdressing into the bandage wings, wait a few minutes, then peel off.

CONAIR PRO STYLE 1600 HAIRDRYER
Blowing warm air on the bandage with a Conair Pro Style 1600 Hairdryer will soften the adhesive so you can ease off the bandage.

HUGGIES BABY WIPES
After peeling off a bandage, use a Huggies Baby Wipe to remove the sticky adhesive left on the skin.

JIF PEANUT BUTTER
Coat the bandage with Jif Peanut Butter, let sit for five minutes, then peel off. The oils in the peanut butter dissolve the glues in the gum.

JOHNSON'S BABY OIL
Rub Johnson's Baby Oil around the bandage to dissolve the adhesive before pulling off the bandage.

SKIN-SO-SOFT
To clean the adhesive from skin after removing a bandage, apply a few drops of Skin-So-Soft, rub the lotion into the skin, then wipe clean with a dry cloth.

SMIRNOFF VODKA
To remove a bandage painlessly, saturate the bandage with Smirnoff Vodka. The solvent dissolves the adhesive.

Dandruff

- **Dannon Yogurt.** To treat dandruff and soothe an itchy scalp, apply a thick coat of Dannon Yogurt to your hair and wrap in a towel. Let set for twenty minutes, then rinse clean.

- **Heinz White Vinegar.** Rinsing your hair with Heinz White Vinegar kills bacteria, helps treat dandruff, and soothes the scalp.

- **Listerine.** Wash your hair with your regular shampoo, then rinse with Listerine. The label on the back of the Listerine bottle used to advertise that this antiseptic mouthwash also cures dandruff when applied to hair.

- **McCormick Bay Leaves** and **Mr. Coffee Filters.** Bring one quart of water to a boil, remove from heat, and add three teaspoons crumbled bay leaves. Cover and let steep for thirty minutes. Strain through a Mr. Coffee Filter and refrigerate the liquid. After shampooing and rinsing your hair, rinse your hair again with the bay leaf tea, massaging it into the scalp. Let set for one hour, then rinse clean. Use daily.

- **McCormick Thyme Leaves** and **Mr. Coffee Filters.** Add two heaping teaspoons McCormick Thyme Leaves to one cup water and bring the solution to a boil for ten minutes. Strain through a Mr. Coffee Filter and let cool. Gently pour the solution over clean damp hair, working well into the scalp. Let dry. Thyme is a mild antiseptic that helps reduce dandruff.

- **Morton Salt.** Dissolve three tablespoons Morton Salt in one cup warm water. Wet your hair with the salt water, massage gently into your scalp, then shampoo as usual. Salt helps reduce dandruff and kill any bacteria in your hair that might be causing your dry scalp.

- **ReaLemon.** Massage two tablespoons ReaLemon lemon juice into your scalp, rinse with water, then rinse your hair with one teaspoon ReaLemon stirred into one cup water. Repeat this treatment daily until dandruff disappears. The side benefit? Your hair will smell lemon fresh.

- **Smirnoff Vodka, McCormick Rosemary Leaves,** and **Mr. Coffee Filters.** Mix one cup Smirnoff Vodka with two teaspoons crushed rosemary, let sit for two days, then strain through a Mr. Coffee Filter. Massage the tincture into your scalp and let dry.

- **Star Olive Oil.** Warm some Star Olive Oil in the microwave oven, massage into the scalp, and let sit for twenty minutes. Then brush with a hard-bristle hairbrush to loosen dandruff scales. Repeat twice a week. The olive oil moisturizes the dry scalp.

STRANGE FACTS

- ◆ Dead skin cells flake from the scalp naturally, but when they become excessive, the result is called dandruff. The excessive flaking is sometimes caused by seborrhea, a bacterial disease, or a fungus called *Tinea capitis*, a relative of athlete's foot.

- ◆ Dandruff does not cause baldness.

- ◆ In his 1930 poem "The Tunnel," Hart Crane wrote:
  And why do I often meet your visage here, your eyes like agate
      lanterns—on and on
  Below the toothpaste and the dandruff ads?

- ◆ In the 1968 movie *Head*, starring the Monkees, Davy, Mike, Peter, and Micky find themselves dressed as flakes of dandruff in the head of Hollywood legend Victor Mature.

- ◆ In the 1970s, the Schlitz Brewing Company changed the formula of Schlitz ("the Beer That Made Milwaukee Famous" and, at the time, the second-best-selling brand in America), substituting corn syrup for barley and cutting fermentation time to one-third the original time, ruining the original taste. In 1976, the company added new chemicals to stabilize the foam, but wound up creating tiny flakes in the beer and having to recall and destroy an estimated ten million cans of Schlitz, killing sales and destroying the company. In 1981, the Stroh Brewery Company bought Schlitz and moved "the Beer That Made Milwaukee Famous" to Detroit.

◆ In the 1985 movie *The Breakfast Club*, directed by John Hughes, Ally Sheedy, playing the part of an aloof high school girl, scratches her hair so her dandruff falls like snowflakes over her drawing of a house in a snow scene.

◆ In French, the word for dandruff is *pellicules*.

Dehydration

- **Domino Sugar, Morton Salt**, and **ReaLemon.** To make your own rehydration solution, mix three teaspoons sugar, one teaspoon salt, and two teaspoons lemon juice in a tall glass of water. Drink the entire solution to replace the glucose, minerals, and vitamin C being flushed out of your body.

- **Gatorade.** Dehydration causes a rise in body temperature, which can result in loss of appetite, headache, dizziness, and sometimes nausea and vomiting. Drinking Gatorade replaces electrolytes (the potassium and salt lost through perspiration) and prevents heat exhaustion.

- **Pampers.** If you can't rehydrate your skin by taking a shower or jumping into a swimming pool, saturate a Pampers disposable diaper with water (you'll be amazed at how much liquid it holds), wipe down your body, then wear it on your head to cool you down.

- *USA Today*. Keep yourself cool by folding a paper fan from a section of *USA Today* and fanning yourself.

Strange Facts

◆ While more than 70 percent of the earth's surface is covered with water, only about 3 percent of the earth's water is fresh, and 75 percent of that is frozen in glaciers and ice caps.

- The average person drinks eight thousand gallons of water during his or her lifetime.

- Babe Ruth wore a cabbage leaf under his baseball cap to keep cool, changing the cabbage leaf every two innings.

- In the 1966 movie *Batman*, starring Adam West and Burt Ward, the Riddler, Joker, Catwoman, and Penguin team up to dehydrate members of the Security Council at the United World Building in Gotham City.

- Gatorade rehydrates the body 30 percent faster than water.

- The higher the percentage of carbohydrate in a fluid, the more slowly that fluid is absorbed by the body. Gatorade, containing 6 percent carbohydrate, is rapidly absorbed by the body. Beverages containing more than 7 percent carbohydrate (such as fruit juices, soft drinks, and some sports drinks) are not recommended beverages during exercise.

- The sodium and glucose in Gatorade (plus the taste of the beverage) stimulate people to drink more fluid voluntarily until the body is rehydrated.

- The sodium in Gatorade helps people maintain body fluids. Water, caffeinated beverages, and alcoholic beverages activate urine production, causing people to lose fluids.

- Consuming beverages that contain less than 7 percent carbohydrate during exercise enables a person to work out longer and harder and feel better. Carbohydrates provide the body with an easy-to-use energy source. Drinking thirty-two ounces of Gatorade (which contains approximately seven grams of carbohydrates) during each hour of exercise will spark an improvement in performance.

- Gatorade, developed at the University of Florida, was named in honor of the University of Florida Gators football team.

- When you feel thirsty, you are already in the early stages of dehydration.

- Taste preferences are different during exercise and at rest. Gatorade is formulated to taste best when people are hot, sweaty, and thirsty.

◆ Drinking carbonated beverages during exercise increases the risk of nausea. The carbonation also makes it difficult to ingest fluids quickly.

◆ In 1987, the New York Giants doused coach Bill Parcells with a vat of Gatorade near the end of every winning game, inspiring other teams to mimic the ceremony.

◆ Frogs do not drink water. They absorb water from their surroundings by osmosis.

◆ The animal that can last the longest without drinking water is the rat.

Dentures and Retainers

- **Arm & Hammer Baking Soda.** To clean dentures, wet a toothbrush, dip it into a box of Arm & Hammer Baking Soda to coat the brush with powder, and scrub the dentures. The abrasive baking soda will clean away stains while simultaneously deodorizing the false teeth.

- **Clorox.** To sterilize dentures and clean stains, mix one teaspoon Clorox Bleach in a glass of cold water and soak the dentures for ten minutes. Then rinse the dentures well and brush as usual. The bleach whitens the false teeth and makes the dentures sparkling clean, removing coffee stains.

- **Dr. Bronner's Peppermint Soap.** Stir a drop of Dr. Bronner's Peppermint Soap into a glass of water, soak the dentures for ten minutes, then scrub clean with cool water.

- **Heinz White Vinegar.** Soak dentures overnight in Heinz White Vinegar, then brush away tartar with a toothbrush. The vinegar kills bacteria and softens any plaque buildup for easy cleaning.

- **Jif Peanut Butter.** If a piece of chewing gum gets stuck to your dentures, cover the gum with a dollop of Jif Peanut Butter. The oils in the peanut butter dissolve the gum and it wipes clean. Then brush the dentures with toothpaste.

- **Krazy Glue.** If a tooth dislodges from a pair of dentures, Krazy Glue can be used to adhere it back in place.

- **L'eggs Sheer Energy Panty Hose.** Cut a small piece of nylon from a used, clean pair of L'eggs Sheer Energy Panty Hose and use it to polish dentures. The nylon is a mild abrasive.

- **Morton Salt.** While you're cleaning your dentures, dissolve one teaspoon of Morton Salt in a glass of warm water and rinse your mouth to clean and soothe your gums.

- **WD-40.** If a piece of chewing gum gets stuck in your dentures, spray WD-40 on the gum and it will slide right off. Be sure to brush the dentures thoroughly with toothpaste to remove the WD-40.

- **Ziploc Storage Bags.** When traveling, you can clean dentures inside a resealable Ziploc Storage Bag.

STRANGE FACTS

◆ Around 800 B.C.E., the Etruscans (the people living in the region known today as Tuscany, Italy) invented dentures, carving individual teeth from ivory, molding bridgework from gold, and extracting teeth from the dead to make dentures for the wealthy.

◆ During the Middle Ages, wealthy Europeans paid poor peasants for their healthy teeth, which were then extracted and set in bridgework made from ivory.

◆ In the 1600s, sturdy springs were used to keep dentures in place, requiring the wearer to clench his jaw to keep his mouth shut.

◆ Contrary to popular belief, George Washington did not wear false teeth made from wood. His dentures, made from ivory and gold, are on display in the Smithsonian Institution in Washington, D.C.

◆ During the Civil War and the Battle of Waterloo, unscrupulous traders collected teeth from the mouths of dead soldiers to be used in dentures.

◆ Around the time of the French Revolution, dentists in Paris developed dentures made from one piece of porcelain.

◆ After Charles Goodyear invented the vulcanization process for rubber in 1839, dentists were able to use rubber to fashion the first comfortable base to hold false teeth.

◆ In the *Austin Powers* movies, starring Mike Myers, secret agent Austin Powers has notoriously bad teeth. To achieve the effect, Meyers wore a specially crafted dental prosthesis.

Diaper Rash

- **Arm & Hammer Baking Soda.** Soothe diaper rash by adding a cup of baking soda to baby's bathwater.

- **Bag Balm.** Use Bag Balm, the salve created to relieve cracking in cow udders, on your baby's behind to moisturize and protect the dry skin.

- **ConAir Pro Style 1600 Hairdryer.** Drying your baby's bottom with a towel may irritate the diaper rash. Instead, dry your tot's buns with a blow-dryer set on low.

- **Crisco All-Vegetable Shortening.** You can prevent or cure diaper rash by buttering the baby's buns with Crisco All-Vegetable Shortening. The soybean oil and cottonseed oil in Crisco moisturize the dry, irritated skin.

- **Dickinson's Witch Hazel.** Applying witch hazel heals diaper rash.

- **Heinz White Vinegar.** If you use cloth diapers, launder them by adding a cup of Heinz White Vinegar during the rinse cycle. The vinegar will lower the pH level of the cloth diaper to the same level as the baby's skin, impeding diaper rash enzymes.

- **Kingsford's Corn Starch.** Sprinkle Kingsford's Corn Starch on the diaper rash and gently rub over the affected area. Cornstarch soothes the dry skin and promotes healing.

- **Ocean Spray Cranberry Juice Cocktail.** Feeding older infants two to three ounces of cranberry juice increases the acid in the child's urine, lowering the pH that irritates the skin.

- **Palmolive.** Add a few drops of Palmolive Dishwashing Liquid to the running warm water while filling a bathtub. Let the baby play in the bubbles for a few minutes (supervised by an adult, of course), then rinse well, towel dry, and diaper. Repeat daily until the rash clears up, which should take no longer than two days.

- **Pam Cooking Spray.** After giving the baby a bath, spray the diaper rash with Pam Cooking Spray. The oils in the cooking spray moisturize the skin and speed healing.

- **Phillips' Milk of Magnesia.** Using a cotton ball or sponge, dab milk of magnesia directly on the diaper rash. The antacid neutralizes the acids that cause the skin irritation.

SIDE EFFECTS
SMELLY DIAPERS

ARM & HAMMER BAKING SODA
Deodorize a diaper pail by sprinkling liberally with Arm & Hammer Baking Soda. If you use cloth diapers, mix one-half cup Arm & Hammer Baking Soda in two quarts water and soak diapers in the solution, then launder as usual.

BOUNCE
To deodorize a diaper pail, place a sheet of Bounce on the bottom of the pail.

PLAYTEX GENTLE GLIDE ODOR ABSORBING TAMPONS
Place a Playtex Gentle Glide Odor Absorbing Tampon in the bottom of the diaper pail to deodorize it.

TIDY CATS
Pour a few cups of Tidy Cats into the bottom of the plastic bag lining the diaper pail to absorb the odors of the diapers.

20 MULE TEAM BORAX
If you use cloth diapers, add one-half cup 20 Mule Team Borax to the hot water in your washer (along with your regular detergent) to eliminate stains and odors. The borax also helps make the diapers more absorbent.

ZIPLOC STORAGE BAGS
Keep extra Ziploc Storage Bags in your baby bag—especially when visiting friends' homes—so you can seal dirty diapers inside a plastic bag and carry the offending item in your baby bag until you can dispose of it properly.

• **Vaseline Petroleum Jelly.** Apply a thin coat of Vaseline Petroleum Jelly to a baby's clean, dry bottom before putting on a fresh diaper. The petroleum jelly moisturizes the skin, seals it from wetness, and speeds up healing.

STRANGE FACTS

◆ If you have a leak in your roof, placing a disposable diaper inside the bucket or pot positioned under the dripping water will absorb the droplets and the sound of the kerplunks.

◆ The ammonium hydroxide from urine built up in a wet diaper burns the skin, causing diaper rash.

◆ Digging a hole, placing an opened Pampers diaper—plastic side down—at the bottom, covering it with some dirt, and then planting a tomato plant over it produces healthy tomato plants with minimal watering. The disposable diaper retains water.

◆ In the disposable diaper trade, the baby's contribution is referred to as the "insult."

◆ Disposable diapers contain nontoxic superabsorbent granular flakes, roughly the size of salt grains, that swallow up urine, thickening into beads of gel.

◆ Disposable diapers, once fastened with small pieces of adhesive tape, now use Velcro-like hook-and-loop fasteners.

THE POOP ON PAMPERS

In 1957, Procter & Gamble bought the Charmin Paper Company and instructed its research scientists to devise new products for the paper business. Vic Mills, a grandfather who hated washing diapers, thought up the idea of a disposable diaper. Using a toy doll that wet its diapers, Procter & Gamble scientists began developing Mills' idea, creating Pampers. The original diaper, launched in Peoria, Illinois, in 1961, featured layers of creped tissue lined with rayon on the side that touched the baby's skin, pleated to fit better around the legs, padded with plastic on the outside, and attached together with pins.

In 1976, Procter & Gamble acquired Luvs, incorporating the idea of elastic around the leg opening into Pampers' design. To improve upon the absorbent paper core, scientists shifted to filling the diapers with finely shredded cellulose, which they called fluff, adding bulk to the diapers. Procter & Gamble also replaced the pin with adhesive tabs.

Meanwhile, two research scientists, Carlyle Harmon at Johnson & Johnson and Billy Gene Harper at Dow Chemical, had filed separate applications in 1966 for a patent on a polymer made of small flakes that absorbed up to three hundred times its weight in water. These flakes, sandwiched between layers of cloth, eliminated the need to stuff disposable diapers with fluff.

In the 1980s, Procter & Gamble began making Pampers with this superabsorbent polymer. Because the polymer requires more time than paper to absorb urine, scientists added an absorbent paper liner before the core to hold the liquid until the polymer fully absorbs it. The company also replaced the adhesive tabs with Velcro-like tabs that can be refastened easily.

INITIALLY, SUPERMARKETS AND DRUG-STORES did not know whether to stock Pampers in the convenience section, the food aisle, the paper product section, or the drug section.

THE AVERAGE BABY SECRETES seven milliliters of urine per second for a total of ten seconds.

THE SUPERABSORBENT POLYMER CORE in Pampers can easily hold all the urine secreted by a baby during the night.

NO ONE FULLY UNDERSTANDS how the superabsorbent polymers work.

SUPERABSORBENT POLYMERS are mixed in with the sealant on the walls of the Chunnel between England and France to absorb any water that might leak in, plugging the hole.

SUPERABSORBENT POLYMERS can absorb ten times more freshwater than salty water. Since urine contains salt, scientists are working to develop a purifying screen to remove the salt from urine before it hits the superabsorbent polymer, minimizing the amount of polymer needed and significantly reducing the thickness of disposable diapers.

Diarrhea

- **Campbell's Chicken Noodle Soup.** The salts and vitamins in a bowl of chicken soup actually help rehydrate and reenergize the body.

- **Coca-Cola.** When traveling through developing countries where the risk of getting diarrhea is high, drinking Coca-Cola helps minimize your chances of getting the trots. The acids in Coca-Cola help reduce the amount of *E. coli* bacteria in your intestines, inhibiting the production of toxins that would otherwise prevent your intestines from absorbing water.

- **Dannon Yogurt.** Taking antibiotics not only kills disease-bearing bacteria but also often kills the healthy bacteria necessary for proper digestion, resulting in diarrhea. To prevent diarrhea while taking antibiotics, eat Dannon yogurt with active cultures. The *Lactobacillus acidophilus* bacteria produce the bacteriocins necessary for proper digestion, restoring natural intestinal cultures.

- **Domino Sugar, Morton Salt,** and **ReaLemon.** Drinking plenty of fluids during a bout of diarrhea is essential to avoiding dehydration. To make your own rehydration solution, mix three teaspoons sugar, one teaspoon salt, and two teaspoons lemon juice in a tall glass of water. Drink the entire solution to replace the glucose, minerals, and vitamin C being flushed out of your body.

- **Gatorade.** Drinking Gatorade replenishes the electrolytes and glucose being drained from your body.

- **Jell-O.** When you're ready to eat again, start with clear, soft foods like Jell-O to give your bowels a rest until your symptoms improve.

- **Krispy Original Saltine Crackers.** When you feel able to eat, start with saltine crackers. They absorb the excess liquid in your stomach, and one ingredient—sodium bicarbonate—helps relieve indigestion.

- **Lipton Tea Bags.** Drink plenty of Lipton tea. The tannins in tea help stop the muscular contractions in the intestines, and the tea itself replaces fluids lost by the body.

- **Mott's Apple Sauce.** When you have the energy to eat, applesauce makes an excellent starter food that the body can easily digest.

- **SueBee Honey.** Eating honey helps relieve diarrhea, inhibiting the growth of such germs as *Salmonella*, *Shigella*, *E. coli*, and *V. cholerae* in the intestinal tract. (Honey should not be fed to infants under one year of age.)

- **Uncle Ben's Converted Brand Rice.** Eating plain Uncle Ben's Converted Brand Rice helps cure diarrhea.

- **Wonder Bread.** Once the diarrhea has subsided, eating unbuttered toast will help you get on your feet again.

If Montezuma's revenge has you on the run for more than a week, talk to your doctor.

STRANGE FACTS

- World travelers have given diarrhea such colorful nicknames as Montezuma's revenge, the Inca two-step, Delhi belly, the Hong Kong dog, the Casablanca crud, the Katmandu quickstep, the Zimbabwe shuffle, the Tiki trots, and the Tanzanian tango.

- Fossilized dinosaur droppings are called coprolites and are actually fairly common.

- The Ancient Greek physician Hippocrates (circa 460–377 B.C.E.), considered the father of modern medicine, incorrectly claimed that people with speech impediments are more likely to get protracted diarrhea.

- Though rudimentary toilets date back to 2000 B.C.E., the toilet did not become practical until 1861, when British plumber Thomas Crapper invented an advanced water-saving flush system.

- By the 1920s, the toilet had become a standard fixture in most newly built homes, though in developing nations, 2.9 billion people still don't have access to one.

- When Coors translated its "Turn It Loose" slogan into Spanish, it was mistranslated as "Suffer from Diarrhea."

- According to Charmin, the average American uses fifty-seven sheets of toilet paper a day. That's 1.5 miles of toilet paper per year.

- In 1978, Mr. Whipple, the fictional spokesperson for Charmin Toilet Tissue, was the third most recognized personality in America after Richard Nixon and Billy Graham.

- Toilet paper and facial tissues are made from wood pulp treated with plant resins to make it absorbent.

- An average toilet uses five to seven gallons of water every time it is flushed. A single leaky toilet can waste more than fifty gallons a day, amounting to 18,000 gallons a year.

- Gastroenterologists have confirmed that Michael Lotito of Grenoble, France, has the uncanny ability to eat and digest glass and metal. Since 1966, Lotito has eaten seven television sets, six chandeliers, a computer, ten bicycles, a supermarket cart, a Cessna aircraft, and a coffin. He has been nicknamed Monsieur Mangetout—French for "Mr. Eat-It-All."

- In 1996, Singapore launched the Clean Toilets Education Campaign, identifying clean public toilets and appreciation of music as markers for a more gracious society. Not flushing a public toilet is a criminal offense.

SIDE EFFECTS
CLEANING TOILETS

ALKA-SELTZER
Drop in two tablets (plop plop, fizz fizz), wait twenty minutes, then brush brush, flush flush. The citric acid and effervescent action clean vitreous china.

CASCADE
Pour one teaspoon Cascade into the toilet, brush well, let sit for ten minutes, brush again, and flush. The phosphates in Cascade will make the toilet sparkling clean.

CLEAN SHOWER
Spray Clean Shower inside the bowl and under the seat, then brush and flush.

CLOROX
Pour one cup Clorox Bleach into the toilet, let sit for ten minutes, brush, and flush.

COCA-COLA
Pour a can of Coca-Cola into your toilet, let it sit for one hour, brush, and flush. The citric acid, ascorbic acid, and phosphoric acid in Coke remove stains from vitreous china.

COUNTRY TIME LEMONADE
Pour two tablespoons Country Time Lemonade powdered mix in your toilet, brush well, then let sit for one hour. Then brush and flush. The citric acid removes stains from porcelain, and Country Time leaves your toilet smelling lemon fresh.

EFFERDENT
Drop two Efferdent tablets into the toilet bowl, let sit for five minutes, then scrub and flush. (Just be sure not to clean your dentures and the toilet at the same time.)

GATORADE
Pour two cups Gatorade into the toilet bowl, let sit for one hour, then brush and flush clean. The citric acid in Gatorade removes stains from vitreous china.

HEINZ WHITE VINEGAR
Pour in one cup Heinz White Vinegar, let stand for five minutes, and flush.

HUGGIES BABY WIPES
After cleaning the inside of the toilet bowl, wipe down the rim, the top and bottom of the toilet seat, and the outside of the bowl with a Huggies Baby Wipe.

KOOL-AID
Empty a packet of any flavor Kool-Aid into the toilet, scrub with a toilet brush, and flush clean. Soldiers in the military frequently use "bug juice" (generic Kool-Aid) to clean toilets and tank parts.

LISTERINE
Pour one-quarter cup Listerine into the toilet, let sit for thirty minutes, then brush and flush. The antiseptic mouthwash disinfects germs and the alcohol content cleans the toilet.

TANG
Put two tablespoons Tang powder in the toilet, wait fifteen minutes, then brush and flush. The citric acid in Tang cleans stains from porcelain.

Dry Hair

- **Alberto VO5 Conditioning Hairdressing.** To prevent the sun or a swim in a chlorinated pool from drying the oils in your hair, rub a dollop of Alberto VO5 Conditioning Hairdressing between your palms, and then run your fingers through your hair before going out in the sun or going for a swim.

- **Aunt Jemima Original Syrup.** To condition dry hair, massage Aunt Jemima Original Syrup into hair and directly into split ends, cover with a shower cap (or Saran Wrap) for thirty minutes, then shampoo and rinse thoroughly.

- **Budweiser.** After shampooing, rinse hair with Budweiser, let sit for five minutes, then rinse clean with water. Beer gives hair great body.

- **Carnation Condensed Milk, Heinz White Vinegar, and SueBee Honey.** Pour one fourteen-ounce can Carnation Condensed Milk into a bowl, and add one teaspoon Heinz White Vinegar and one teaspoon SueBee Honey. Mix well, then apply the mixture to dry hair. Wait five minutes, then rinse thoroughly.

- **Coca-Cola.** To give your hair a great shine, pour a can of Coca-Cola on your hair, working it in well, then rinse your hair with water.

- **Cool Whip.** Apply Cool Whip to dry hair, let sit for thirty minutes, then rinse well and shampoo. The coconut and palm kernel oils in Cool Whip condition hair for a luxurious shine.

- **Coppertone.** Apply a dollop of Coppertone sunscreen to your hair as a conditioner, then rinse clean. The emollients in Coppertone condition hair.

- **Downy.** If you're out of cream rinse, use a drop of Downy Liquid Fabric Softener in your final rinse. Your hair will be tangle-free and soft and smell April fresh.

- **Epsom Salt.** Combine three tablespoons of your regular conditioner with three tablespoons Epsom Salt. Heat the mixture in a microwave oven, then work the warm mixture through your hair and let it set for twenty minutes. Rinse with warm water. The Epsom Salt (magnesium sulfate) helps revitalize dry hair.

- **Heinz Apple Cider Vinegar.** Mix one-half cup Heinz Apple Cider Vinegar and one cup water in a sixteen-ounce trigger-spray bottle. After shampooing, spray your hair with the mixture. Vinegar adds highlights to brown hair, restores the acid mantle, and removes soap film and sebum oil.

- **Land O Lakes Butter.** Massage Land O Lakes Butter into dry hair, cover hair with a shower cap for thirty minutes, then shampoo and rinse thoroughly.

- **Miracle Whip.** Apply Miracle Whip to dry hair, let it set for thirty minutes, then rinse several times before shampooing thoroughly. The oils revitalize dry hair and give it a great shine.

- **Nestea.** Mix a quart of Nestea according to the directions (using warm water and without adding sugar), then use the tea as a final rinse after shampooing your hair. Nestea gives a natural shine to hair.

- **Reddi-wip.** If you're all out of cream rinse, use Reddi-wip whipped cream. Fill the cupped palm of your hand with Reddi-wip, apply to your hair (topping yourself with a maraschino cherry is optional), cover with a shower cap (or Saran Wrap), wait fifteen minutes, then rinse a few times before shampooing thoroughly.

- **Star Olive Oil.** Pour a few drops of Star Olive Oil in the cupped palm of your hand, rub your hands together, and then run your hands through your hair. The olive oil not only conditions your hair and scalp, it also gives your hair a nice shine.

- **SueBee Honey** and **Star Olive Oil.** Mix one tablespoon SueBee Honey and two teaspoons Star Olive Oil. Warm the mixture in a microwave oven, then use your fingers to rub the sticky concoction through your hair. Soak a towel in hot water, wring it out completely, wrap it around your head, and leave it on for twenty minutes. Then shampoo as usual, lathering well to remove the olive oil, leaving your hair with more body and fullness.

- **Wesson Corn Oil.** Warm three teaspoons Wesson Corn Oil in the microwave oven, massage the warm oil into dry hair, cover with a shower cap (or Saran Wrap) for thirty minutes, then shampoo and rinse thoroughly.

STRANGE FACTS

◆ English writer Samuel Johnson (1708–1784) incorrectly claimed, "The cause of baldness in men is dryness of the brain and its shrinking from the skull."

◆ When a cartoon character sticks a finger in an electrical outlet, we traditionally see flashes of the character's skeleton, and the smoldering character gains frizzy hair.

◆ In Mel Brooks's 1974 movie *Young Frankenstein*, Gene Wilder gets extraordinarily frizzy hair after giving the Frankenstein monster a jolt of electricity.

SIDE EFFECTS
FLYAWAYS

ALBERTO VO5 CONDITIONING HAIRDRESSING
Prevent flyaways in your hair created by static electricity by combing a dab of Alberto VO5 Conditioning Hairdressing through your hair.

BOUNCE
If you suffer from static electricity in your hair every time you brush it, wipe a sheet of Bounce over your hair and the static will magically disappear.

DOWNY
For flyaway hair, rub a few drops of Downy Liquid Fabric Softener in your palms, then run your hands through your hair. The fabric softener eliminates the static electricity, softens your hair, and makes it smell good, too.

STATIC GUARD
Spray Static Guard on the hairbrush before brushing your hair to tame the static electricity.

THE BUZZ ON BUDWEISER

In 1852, George Schneider founded the Bavarian Brewery in St. Louis, Missouri. When he went bankrupt eight years later in 1860, Eberhard Anheuser, a German immigrant and soap manufacturer who had loaned the Bavarian Brewery over $90,000, assumed control of the company. Anheuser was soon joined by his son-in-law, Adolphus Busch, who used refrigerated railroad cars to enlarge distribution and put teams of Clydesdale horses to work, transforming the brewery's carts into working advertisements. In 1876, Busch helped restaurateur Carl Conrad create a light beer like those brewed in the Bohemian town of Budweis, naming the beer Budweiser. Budweiser's popularity over darker beers helped the brewery grow rapidly.

When Adolphus Busch died in 1913, his son, August Busch, took over the Bavarian Brewery, renamed Anheuser-Busch, Inc., in 1919. During Prohibition, August Busch kept the company in business by selling yeast, refrigeration units, truck bodies, syrup, and soft drinks. When Prohibition was repealed, Busch resumed the brewing operation, delivering a case of Budweiser to President Franklin Roosevelt in a carriage drawn by Clydesdale horses, which have since become the company's symbol.

BUDWEISER WAS NOT the first "King of Beers." St. Louis A.B.C. Bohemian beer was billed as "King of All Bottle Beers," Michelob was called "King of Draught Beer," and both Regal Beer and Imperial Beer were touted as "King of Beers."

IN OCTOBER 1983, when Anheuser-Busch took a Cleveland florist to court for using the Budweiser slogan "This Bud's for You," Federal Judge Ann Aldrich ruled in favor of the florist, claiming it would be absurd for anyone to confuse flowers with beer.

ANHEUSER-BUSCH OPERATES twelve breweries in the United States, and the company's beer is sold in more than eighty countries.

ANHEUSER-BUSCH IS THE WORLD'S largest brewer and the self-proclaimed "King of Beers" in the United States (with the number one spot and 44 percent of the beer market).

◆ Hair is made from three layers of dead skin cells called keratin, the same hard protein that forms fingernails and toenails.

◆ Most hair follicles contain sebaceous glands that secrete oil into the follicle, keeping the hair lubricated and soft.

◆ The *arrector pili*, a muscle attached to most hair follicles, causes hair to stand on end, producing goose bumps.

Dry Shampoo

- **Arm & Hammer Baking Soda.** To give yourself a dry shampoo, sprinkle Arm & Hammer Baking Soda on your hair, work it in well, wait ten minutes, then brush the powder from your hair. The baking soda absorbs the oil from your hair.

- **Baby Magic Baby Powder.** Give your hair a dry shampoo by working Baby Magic Baby Powder into your hair, then brush out.

- **Gold Medal Flour.** When American pioneers crossed the country in covered wagons, the women used a handful of flour in their hair as a dry shampoo—a testimony to their ingenuity. To do the same, simply sprinkle Gold Medal Flour in your hair, work it in, and brush it out.

- **Kingsford's Corn Starch.** If you're sick in bed and can't take a shower, work Kingsford's Corn Starch into your oily hair, then brush it out for a dry shampoo.

- **Quaker Oats.** Apply dry Quaker Oats to your hair, work it through with your fingers, and brush it out. Oats absorb the sebum oil from your hair.

STRANGE FACTS

- ◆ In 1963, Beatle Ringo Starr told reporters, "I want to be a hairdresser or two." His first wife, Maureen, was a former Liverpool hairdresser. In 1985, his son Zak Starkey married the daughter of a hairdresser.

◆ An aerosol can of Klorane Oat Extract Dry Shampoo sells for $16.95.

◆ Since the Space Shuttle does not have a shower, the astronauts shampoo their hair with a rinseless shampoo originally developed for hospital patients who were unable to get out of bed to shower. To use the shampoo, astronauts simply wet their hair with a little water, squirt out some of the shampoo on their heads, lather, and towel dry.

◆ Russian cosmonaut Valery Polyakov, who lived aboard the Mir Space Station for 437 days, used wet towels to wash his skin and hair.

Dry Skin and Windburn

- **Alberto VO5 Conditioning Hairdressing.** Rub a dab of Alberto VO5 Conditioning Hairdressing on the lines around your eyes to moisturize the skin.

- **Arm & Hammer Baking Soda** and **ReaLemon.** Mix Arm & Hammer Baking Soda and ReaLemon lemon juice to make a paste, then rub the abrasive mixture into dry elbows.

- **Baby Magic Baby Powder.** Sprinkle Baby Magic Baby Powder on your hands and rub it into the skin to smooth rough hands.

- **Bag Balm.** Soothe chapped hands by rubbing on Bag Balm, the salve created in Vermont to relieve cracking in cow udders.

- **ChapStick.** Rubbing ChapStick on your face protects the skin from windburn while snow skiing.

- **Cheerios.** Using a blender, grind one cup Cheerios into a fine powder, then pour the powder into a large bowl. Rub the pulverized oat cereal over your hands to exfoliate the dry skin. Wash your hands with cool water, dry well, then apply a moisturizing cream.

- **Coppertone.** Rubbing sunscreen into your hands moisturizes the skin while simultaneously protecting it from sunburn. The emollients in Coppertone rejuvenate dry skin.

- **Cortaid.** Every time you finish washing your hands, rub a small dab of this hydrocortisone cream into your hands.

- **Crisco All-Vegetable Shortening.** Soak your hands in warm water for five minutes, then seal in the moisture by coating your hands with a small dab of Crisco All-Vegetable Shortening.

- **Dannon Yogurt.** Before taking a shower, cover your dry skin with Dannon Yogurt, wait ten minutes, then rinse clean. The yogurt moisturizes the skin.

- **Domino Sugar** and **Johnson's Baby Oil.** Place one teaspoon sugar in your palm, cover it with Johnson's Baby Oil, and rub your hands, elbows, and knees. Then wash with soap. The abrasive sugar exfoliates dry skin.

- **Fruit of the Earth Aloe Vera Gel.** Rub Fruit of the Earth Aloe Vera Gel into your hands to soothe and moisturize the skin.

- **Heinz White Vinegar.** To prevent the alkaline from wet concrete or plaster from cracking the skin or causing eczema, wash your hands with soap and water, then rub Heinz White Vinegar on your hands. The acetic acid in vinegar offsets the alkalinity.

- **Jif Peanut Butter.** To exfoliate and moisturize dry hands, elbows, and knees, rub the skin with Jif Extra Crunchy Peanut Butter. Let sit for two minutes, then wipe your hands clean with a sheet of paper towel. The oils in the peanut butter will moisturize your skin while the nuts exfoliate.

- **Johnson's Baby Oil.** Rub a few drops of Johnson's Baby Oil into your hands to moisturize the dry skin. (Just be sure to keep your hands out of the sun. Mineral oil makes your skin more susceptible to sunburn.)

- **Kingsford's Corn Starch.** Soften rough hands by applying Kingsford's Corn Starch as you would hand lotion.

- **Land O Lakes Butter.** To moisturize skin, massage Land O Lakes Butter into your skin, wait fifteen minutes, remove excess butter with a paper towel, then take a hot bath.

- **Lubriderm.** To prevent steam heat or air conditioning from drying out your skin, moisturize your skin with Lubriderm.

- **Miracle Whip.** Exfoliate dead skin by rubbing a dab of Miracle Whip into your feet, knees, elbows, or face. Let sit for a few minutes, then massage with your fingertips. Applying Miracle Whip as a skin cream also moisturizes the skin.

- **Morton Salt** and **Johnson's Baby Oil.** Mix Morton Salt and Johnson's Baby Oil to make an abrasive, moisturizing scrub to exfoliate dry skin.

- **Neosporin.** If you suffer from dry hands, rub Neosporin antibiotic ointment into the skin as a hand cream.

- **Pam Cooking Spray.** Spray your hands with a very light coat of Pam Cooking Spray and rub it into the skin. The oils moisturize dry skin.

- **Playtex Living Gloves.** Apply skin cream to your hands, then put on a pair of Playtex Living Gloves and do the dishes. The heat from the warm water will help the skin cream penetrate your skin.

- **Preparation H.** For dry, chapped hands, apply a dab of Preparation H and rub into the skin for soothing relief.

- **Quaker Oats.** Blend a cup of Quaker Oats into a fine powder, then pour the powder into a large bowl. Rub the powdered oats over your hands to exfoliate the dry skin. Wash your hands with cool water, dry well, then apply a moisturizing cream.

- **ReaLemon** and **Star Olive Oil.** Rejuvenate dry skin by applying ReaLemon lemon juice, rinsing, then rubbing in Star Olive Oil.

- **Skin-So-Soft.** Taking a moisturizing bath helps rejuvenate dry skin. Add two tablespoons of Skin-So-Soft to a warm bath as a bath oil. For more soothing bath ideas, see page 26.

- **Vaseline Petroleum Jelly.** Before going to bed, rub Vaseline into your hands, put on a pair of cotton gloves, and go to sleep. In the morning, your hands will feel remarkably soft. For dry feet, cover your feet with Vaseline, then put on a pair of socks. To moisturize your face, wash your face thoroughly and, while it's still wet, rub in a small dab of Vaseline.

- **Wesson Corn Oil.** Massage Wesson Corn Oil into your skin, wait fifteen minutes, remove the excess oil with a paper towel, then take a hot bath.

- **Ziploc Storage Bags** and **Vaseline Petroleum Jelly.** Coat your hands with Vaseline Petroleum Jelly, slip them inside two Ziploc bags, wait fifteen minutes, then wash hands with warm water.

Strange Facts

- ◆ Human skin is waterproof.

- ◆ Skin is the human body's largest organ.

- ◆ The outer layer of the epidermis is called the horny layer.

- ◆ Skin color is determined primarily by the amount of melanin, a brown pigment, produced in the skin. Melanocytes in the epidermis form melanin. All humans have the same number of melanocytes. Heredity determines how much melanin the melanoctyes produce.

- ◆ The 1971 movie *Skin Game* stars James Garner as a white con artist during slavery times who sells his black partner, played by Lou Gossett Jr., into slavery.

SIDE EFFECTS
SAVE YOUR SKIN

BABY MAGIC BABY POWDER
Wearing rubber gloves while washing the dishes can irritate skin. Sprinkle Baby Magic Baby Powder inside the gloves to reduce friction against the skin and to help the gloves slip on and off easily.

JOHNSON & JOHNSON COTTON BALLS
Stuff a Johnson & Johnson Cotton Ball into each fingertip of a pair of rubber gloves to prevent your fingernails from tearing through the gloves.

ZIPLOC STORAGE BAGS
When cutting up jalapeño peppers, put a Ziploc Storage Bag on each hand as an impromptu glove to keep the caustic heat from the peppers—which doesn't wash off easily—from getting on your skin.

- The 1989 Blake Edwards movie *Skin Deep* stars John Ritter as an alcoholic womanizer with no apparent redeeming traits.

- "Getting under someone's skin" means to irritate, "having a thick skin" means being impervious to criticism, "having a thin skin" means being sensitive to criticism, "no skin off your back" means having no consequence, "saving your skin" means avoiding death, and "skinning someone alive" means reprimanding someone or subduing an opponent.

Earache

- **Bounty** and **Dixie Cups.** Relieve an earache caused by the change in pressure in an airplane by dampening a sheet of Bounty Paper Towels with hot water, balling it up, and placing it in the bottom of a Dixie Cup. Then hold the Dixie Cup over your ear. The steam from the hot water will soften the wax in your ear, alleviating the pain.

- **ConAir Pro Style 1600 Hairdryer.** Switch your blow-dryer to a low, warm setting and, holding it more than a foot away, aim the nozzle at your ear. The warm air will gently relieve the pain in your ear.

- **Glad Flexible Straws.** If you don't have an eardropper, insert a Glad Flexible Straw into the liquid, cover the open end of the straw with your finger, hold the straw over your ear, and release your finger from the straw.

- **Johnson's Baby Oil.** If an insect gets stuck in your ear, gently pour a few drops of Johnson's Baby Oil into your ear, and the insect—being lighter than oil—will float to the surface. (If you have a perforated eardrum, do not put oil in your ear.)

- **Johnson's Baby Oil.** To relieve an earache, fill a pot with hot water from the tap, and place a bottle of baby oil in the pot of water until the temperature of the oil rises to the temperature of the water. With an eardropper, place a few drops of oil in your ear. The warm oil will gently relieve the pain. (If you have a perforated eardrum, do not put oil in your ear.)

- **Kodak 35mm Film Canisters.** Keep your earplugs for swimming or sleeping in a Kodak film canister.

- **Life Savers.** Relieve an earache caused by the change in pressure in an airplane by sucking on a Life Saver. The candy causes your mouth to salivate, and the resulting swallowing action opens the eustachian tubes in your ears.

- **Smirnoff Vodka.** If you don't have rubbing alcohol, fill an eardropper (or see "Glad Flexible Straws" above) with Smirnoff Vodka and squeeze it into the affected ear, then let it drain out. The alcohol in the vodka kills whatever bacteria are causing the pain in your ear.

- **Star Olive Oil.** Soothe an earache by warming two tablespoons Star Olive Oil in a microwave oven. Insert a few drops of the warmed oil into the affected ear, plug with cotton, and cover with a hot-water bottle.

- **Wesson Corn Oil.** Heat up two tablespoons Wesson Corn Oil, then put some drops of the warmed oil in the affected ear. Wait a few minutes for the oil to relieve the pain.

- **Wrigley's Spearmint Gum.** Alleviate an earache caused by a cold, sinus infection, allergy, or the change in pressure in an airplane by chewing a piece of Wrigley's Spearmint Gum. The muscular action of chewing will open the eustachian tubes (which run from the back of the throat to the middle ear).

- **Ziploc Storage Bags.** Fill a Ziploc Storage Bag with warm water, seal securely, and hold the bag against your ear as a warm compress. The warm bag conforms to the contours of your ear and provides relief.

Hear ye! Hear ye! If your earache lasts more than a day, is accompanied by a fever or hearing loss, or you have discharge, contact your doctor.

STRANGE FACTS

- ◆ The smallest bone in the human body is the stapes bone in the middle ear—the only bone that has yet to be broken in a ski accident.

- ◆ Around 350 B.C.E., the Greek philosopher Aristotle suggested that sound is carried to our ears by the movement of air. He was wrong. Sound travels in waves.

- The small bump of flesh just in front of your ear canal is called a tragus.

- On Christmas Eve in 1888, Post-Impressionist painter Vincent Van Gogh, suffering from a seizure, grabbed a knife and threatened to kill fellow artist Paul Gauguin, who was visiting him at the time. Van Gogh cut off part of his own left ear instead.

- In 1935, during an exhibition of Van Gogh's paintings at New York's Museum of Modern Art, prankster Hugh Troy hung on the wall a velvet-lined shadow box containing a piece of dried beef that he had carved into the shape of an ear with a sign that read, "This is the ear that Van Gogh cut off and sent to his mistress Dec. 24, 1888."

- In the 1966 movie *Fantastic Voyage*, starring Raquel Welch, the shrunken scientists traveling in a microscopic submarine inside a sedated human body pass through the inner ear. When a nurse in the outside surgery room accidentally drops a tool, the resulting sound, amplified by the eardrum, causes the ship to toss and turn uncontrollably.

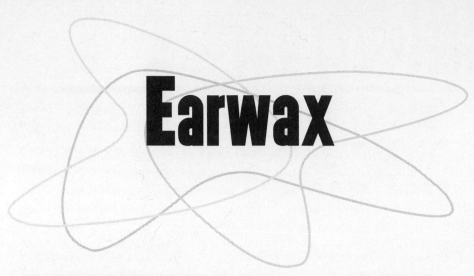

Earwax

- **Arm & Hammer Baking Soda.** Dissolve one teaspoon of baking soda in one cup warm water and flush into the ear using a small bulb syringe. Several flushes may be required to disoldge a hardened, impacted chunk of ear wax.

- **Colace Stool Softener.** To get rid of excessive ear wax, cut a hole in a Colace capsule and squeeze the liquid into the ear canal. Place a cotton ball in the ear to prevent the liquid from leaking out. You may need to repeat this procedure for several days to produce the desired result.

- **Hydrogen Peroxide.** A few drops of hydrogen peroxide in each ear will gently loosen excessive earwax. You may need to repeat for a few days, then rinse your ears using a rubber bulb syringe filled with water.

- **Johnson's Baby Oil.** A few drops of baby oil in each ear will gently loosen excessive ear wax. You may need to repeat for a few days, then rinse your ears using a rubber bulb syringe filled with water. (If you have a perforated eardrum, do not put oil in your ear.)

STRANGE FACTS

◆ The ear produces wax to prevent dust and dirt from entering the sensitive middle part of the ear.

HEARSAY ON Q-TIPS

In 1922, Leo Gerstenrang, an immigrant from Warsaw, Poland, who had served in the United States Army during World War I and worked with the fledgling Red Cross Organization, founded the Leo Gerstenrang Infant Novelty Co. with his wife, selling accessories used for baby care. After the birth of the couple's daughter, Gerstenrang noticed that his wife would wrap a wad of cotton around a toothpick for use during their baby's bath and decided to manufacture a ready-to-use cotton swab.

After several years, Gerstenrang developed a machine that would wrap cotton uniformly around each blunt end of a small stick of carefully selected and cured nonsplintering birch wood, package the swabs in a sliding tray-type box, sterilize the box, and seal it with an outer wrapping of glassine (later changed to cellophane). The phrase "untouched by human hands" became widely known in the production of cotton swabs. The *Q* in the name Q-Tips stands for *quality* and the word *tips* describes the cotton swab on the end of the stick.

In 1962, Chesebrough-Pond's Inc.—the company founded in 1955 when Chesebrough Manufacturing Company merged with Pond's Extract Company—bought Q-Tips. In 1987, Unilever—the company founded in 1885 in England as Lever Brothers by grocer William Hesketh Lever and his brother James—acquired Chesebrough-Pond's.

Q-TIPS COTTON SWABS were originally called "Baby Gays."

THE PRINCIPAL Q-TIPS manufacturing plant in Long Island City, New York, produces Q-Tips Cotton Swabs around the clock.

Q-TIPS COTTON SWABS are the best-selling baby product in the United States and the best-selling cotton applicator swab in the world.

◆ The medical term for earwax is *cerumen*, derived from the Latin word *cer* (meaning "wax"), the connective *-u*, and the suffix *-men* (meaning "substance").

◆ Ears enable humans to hear and maintain balance through equilibrium.

◆ The fleshy, curved part of the ear on the outside of the head is technically called the *auricle*, made entirely from cartilage covered with skin.

◆ The African elephant has the largest auricles of any mammal, measuring up to four feet wide.

- In humans, three small muscles attach the auricle to the head, and some people can use these muscles to wiggle their ears.

- In India, grasping your ear signifies repentance or sincerity.

- In Brazil, holding your earlobe between your thumb and forefinger is a gesture of appreciation.

- Crickets have ears on the inside of each front leg.

- Frogs have eardrums on the sides of their heads.

Eczema

- **Bag Balm.** Rubbing a dab of Bag Balm, the salve created to relieve cracking in cow udders, into the dry skin helps heal eczema.

- **Carnation Condensed Milk.** To treat oozing eczema, saturate a washcloth with Carnation Condensed Milk and place over the affected area for ten minutes, then rinse with cool water.

- **Crisco All-Vegetable Shortening.** To moisturize the dry skin and heal the eczema, rub Crisco All-Vegetable Shortening on the afflicted area.

- **Dickinson's Witch Hazel.** Apply Dickinson's Witch Hazel to the dry skin to cool it and speed healing.

- **Lubriderm.** After bathing, moisturize your skin by rubbing your body with a thin coat of Lubriderm. (In some cases, the lanolin in Lubriderm may irritate eczema.)

- **Noxzema.** Rub a dab of Noxzema Original Skin Cream into the dry skin to heal the eczema.

- **Quaker Oats** and **L'eggs Sheer Energy Panty Hose.** Cut off the foot from a clean, used pair of L'eggs Sheer Energy Panty Hose. In a blender, grind one cup Quaker Oats into a fine powder and pour into the panty hose foot. Tie a knot in the nylon, hang the sachet from the spigot in the bathtub, and fill the tub with warm water. Soak in the soothing oatmeal bath for thirty minutes, using the oatmeal sack as a washcloth.

- **Ziploc Freezer Bags.** Applying an ice pack helps relieve eczema. To make the ice pack, fill a Ziploc Freezer Bag with water and freeze it or fill it with ice cubes. Wrap the ice pack in a paper towel before applying. For other ways to make and apply an ice pack, see page 198.

STRANGE FACTS

- ◆ In 1914, pharmacist Dr. George Bunting combined medication and vanishing cream in the prescription room of his Baltimore drugstore at 6 West North Avenue to create "Dr. Bunting's Sunburn Remedy." He mixed and heated the skin cream in a huge coffeepot and then poured it into little blue jars. A customer told Dr. Bunting, "Your sunburn cream sure knocked my eczema," inspiring Bunting to change the name of "Dr. Bunting's Sunburn Remedy" to *Noxzema*—a clever combination of the misspelled word *knocks* and the last two syllables of the word *eczema*.

- ◆ Eczema is also known as "bricklayer's itch." The acids in brick mortar dry the skin, causing itching and burning.

- ◆ A strange folklore remedy holds that eczema can be cured by carrying a potato in your pocket.

- ◆ Albert Camus, author of *The Stranger*, wrote, "Style, like sheer silk, too often hides eczema."

- ◆ Approximately ten million Americans suffer from eczema.

- ◆ The United Kingdom celebrates National Eczema Week during the last week of September.

- ◆ In an episode of the television adventure series *Xena: Warrior Princess*, Gabrielle mockingly refers to Xena as Eczema.

Eyeglasses

CLEANING:

- **Bounce.** Wipe your glasses with a clean, used sheet of Bounce. The remaining antistatic elements in the Bounce sheet will prevent dust from sticking to your glasses for some time.

- **Coca-Cola.** Clean your eyeglasses with Coke. The phosphoric acid cleans the grunge from eyeglasses. Then rinse with water.

- **Colgate Toothpaste.** Polish the eyeglasses with a dollop of Colgate Regular Flavor Toothpaste.

- **Heinz White Vinegar.** A drop of Heinz White Vinegar cleans eyeglass lenses (but don't use vinegar on plastic lenses).

- **Huggies Baby Wipes.** In a real pinch, you can clean your glasses with a Huggies Baby Wipe. They remove all that grime and grunge and leave your glasses feeling pampered like a baby's bottom.

- **Lysol Tub and Tile Cleaner.** To clean the grime from glasses, spray the eyepieces with Lysol Tub and Tile Cleaner, let sit for five minutes, then rinse thoroughly with water.

- **Mr. Coffee Filters.** Mr. Coffee Filters are 100 percent virgin paper, so they do a great job cleaning glasses without leaving behind any lint.

- **Smirnoff Vodka.** Simply wipe the lenses with a soft, clean cloth dampened in Smirnoff Vodka. The alcohol in the vodka cleanses the glass and kills germs.

- **Tampax Tampons.** Rubbing the lenses of eyeglasses with a clean, unused Tampax tampon cleans them beautifully. The cotton absorbs grease and grime without leaving behind any lint.

DEFOGGING:
- **Barbasol Shaving Cream.** Rubbing a small dab of Barbasol Shaving Cream over both sides of the lenses prevents them from fogging up.

- **Bioré Facial Cleansing Cloths.** Cleaning your eyeglass lenses with Bioré Facial Cleansing Cloths prevents them from fogging up.

- **Colgate Toothpaste.** Rub a dab of Colgate Regular Flavor Toothpaste on the lenses, then wash clean with water, creating a thin film on the glasses that repels precipitation.

- **Dawn.** Rub a drop of Dawn Dishwashing Liquid on eyeglasses, then wipe them clean, leaving a thin film to prevent them from fogging up.

- **Pledge.** Keep eyeglasses from fogging up by spraying the lenses with Pledge, then wipe clean.

REPAIRING:
- **Band-Aid Bandages.** If your glasses break, put them back together temporarily with a Band-Aid Bandage.

- **Forster Toothpicks.** If you lose a screw from your eyeglasses, substitute a Forster Toothpick in its place until you can get them fixed properly.

- **Maybelline Crystal Clear Nail Polish.** To prevent the screws in eyeglasses from loosening, apply a small drop of Maybelline Crystal Clear Nail Polish to the threads of the screws before tightening them.

- **Oral-B Mint Waxed Floss.** Replace a missing screw from a pair of eyeglasses by tying a piece of Oral-B Mint Waxed Floss through the holes for a temporary repair.

- **Scotch Transparent Tape.** If the lens in your eyeglasses cracks, use a small piece of Scotch Transparent Tape to hold the lens in place temporarily.

- **Wrigley's Spearmint Gum.** In an emergency, put a small piece of chewed Wrigley's Spearmint Gum in the corner of the lens to hold it in place.

STRANGE FACTS

- Ten percent of *Star Trek* fans replace the lenses on their eyeglasses every five years whether they need to or not.

- Owls are the only birds that can see the color blue.

- The common goldfish is the only animal that can see both infrared and ultraviolet light.

- In the 1959 novel *Lord of the Flies* by William Golding, the boys of a private boarding school, stranded on an island, use a pair of eyeglasses to start fires. The glasses belong to a boy nicknamed Piggy.

- All United States presidents have worn glasses, though many chose not to be seen wearing them in public.

- In the 1992 movie *Wayne's World*, starring Mike Myers and Dana Carvey, Garth's glasses fog up whenever he gets too excited.

- In the 1999 movie *Notting Hill*, Hugh Grant stars as a London bookstore owner in love with an American movie star, played by Julia Roberts. Unable to find his eyeglasses, he wears his prescription swimming mask to the movies.

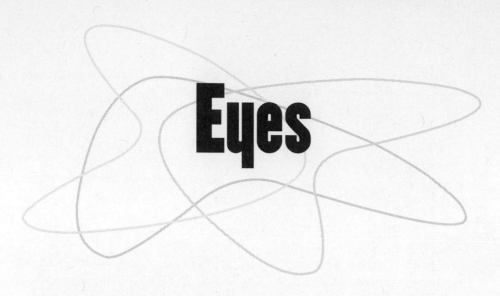

Eyes

- **Glad Flexible Straws.** Improvise an eyedropper by inserting a Glad Flexible Straw into the liquid, covering the open end of the straw with your finger, and lifting. The liquid will stay in the straw until you release your finger.

- **Lipton Tea Bags.** Soothe tired eyes or heal a sty on your eye by soaking two Lipton Tea Bags in warm water, then placing them over your closed eyes for twenty minutes. The tannins in the tea reduce the puffiness and revitalize tired eyes. Healing a sty may require several applications.

- **Post-it Notes.** Protect your eyes when using hair spray or coloring your hair by applying Post-it Notes over your eyebrows.

- **Preparation H.** To eliminate puffy bags under your eyes, carefully rub Preparation H into the skin around the eyes. The hemorrhoid ointment acts as a vasoconstrictor and relieves swelling. (Just be careful not to get it in your eyes.)

- **Uncle Ben's Converted Brand Rice.** Pour two cups Uncle Ben's Converted Brand Rice into a microwave-safe container and heat in the microwave for one minute. Carefully pour or spoon the hot rice into a sock (not too compactly), tie a knot in the end, and place the warm sock over your closed eyes for ten minutes to relieve any soreness. The sock conforms wherever applied.

STRANGE FACTS

◆ In Alfred Hitchcock's 1960 horror film, *Psycho*, the famous shower scene ends with an extreme close-up of Janet Leigh's eye, with her pupil tightly contracted. When people die, their pupils dilate.

◆ Our eyes remain the same size from birth, but our nose and ears never stop growing.

◆ In comic books, when Superman uses his x-ray vision to see through concrete walls, x-rays shoot from his eyes. Living creatures do not see by radiating light from their eyes. (X-rays are a more energetic form of light.) Instead, light enters the eye, is refracted by the cornea, passes through the pupil, is refracted by the lens, and forms an image on the retina, which is rich in nerve cells that are stimulated by light. To see through concrete walls, the nerve cells in Superman's retinas would have to be stimulated by x-rays.

◆ The flashes of color you see when you close and rub your eyes are called phosphenes.

◆ Camels have three eyelids to protect their eyes from blowing sand.

◆ The average eyebrow contains 450 hairs.

◆ The eyes' muscles are the most active muscles in the human body, moving an estimated 100,000 or more times a day.

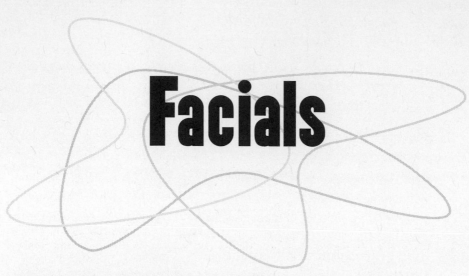

Facials

- **Arm & Hammer Baking Soda.** Mix one-half cup Arm & Hammer Baking Soda with water to form a paste. Apply the mixture to your face, let set until dry, then wash off with warm water, followed by cool water. Pat dry with a clean towel. The baking soda cleanses the pores and exfoliates dead skin.

- **Carnation NonFat Dry Milk.** Mix one-quarter cup Carnation NonFat Dry Milk with enough water to make a thick paste. Apply the milky paste to your face, let it dry, then wash it off.

- **Cheerios, SueBee Honey,** and **ReaLemon.** In a blender, grind one cup Cheerios into a fine powder on medium-high speed. In a bowl, mix the powdered Cheerios with enough SueBee Honey and ReaLemon lemon juice to make a thick paste. Apply the sticky substance to your face, let sit for ten minutes, then rinse off with warm water. The Cheerios are oats (absorbing the oils from the skin), the lemon juice contains citric acid (disinfecting the pores), and the honey is hygroscopic (moisturizing the skin).

- **Colgate Toothpaste.** Squeeze a dollop of Colgate Regular Flavor Toothpaste into the cupped palm of your hand, add a few drops of water, and rub your hands together to create a lather. Coat your face with the toothpaste lather, then rinse it thoroughly. Toothpaste is a mild abrasive that cleanses the skin.

- **Cool Whip.** Give yourself a moisturizing facial by covering your face with Cool Whip Whipped Topping. Let set twenty minutes, then wash your face clean with warm water, followed by cold water. The coconut and palm kernel oils in Cool Whip moisturize the skin.

- **Dannon Yogurt.** To tighten pores and cleanse skin, spread Dannon Yogurt (plain or any flavor you wish) over your face, wait twenty minutes, then wash off with lukewarm water.

- **Domino Sugar** and **Johnson's Baby Shampoo.** To make an exfoliating facial wash, mix one-quarter cup Domino Sugar, one teaspoon Johnson's Baby Shampoo, and one-quarter cup water to make a thick paste. Rub the grainy mixture over your face, then wash off with warm water, followed by cold water.

- **Dr. Bronner's Peppermint Soap.** Place a hand towel in a sink filled with hot water and add a dash of Dr. Bronner's Peppermint Soap. Wring out the towel, lay it over your face, and massage with your fingertips. The peppermint oil in the soap rejuvenates and invigorates the skin.

- **Elmer's Glue-All.** Coat your face with a thin layer of Elmer's Glue-All (avoiding your eyes). Let the glue dry (it takes approximately twenty minutes), then gently peel it off, exfoliating a thin layer of skin. Elmer's Glue-All is water soluble, so you can always wash it off with warm water should it stick your eyebrows. Your skin will feel baby-smooth.

- **Epsom Salt.** To cleanse and exfoliate your skin, wet your face, massage a handful of Epsom Salt over your skin, then wash it clean.

- **French's Mustard.** Apply French's Mustard as a face mask that both stimulates and soothes the skin.

- **Fruit of the Earth Aloe Vera Gel, SueBee Honey,** and **Kingsford's Corn Starch.** Mix equal parts Fruit of the Earth Aloe Vera Gel and SueBee Honey, blend thoroughly, then add enough Kingsford's Corn Starch to bring the consistency of the mixture to the thickness of a face cream. Spread the mixture on your face, let it dry thoroughly, then rub it off with a wet washcloth to gently exfoliate the skin.

- **Miracle Whip.** Give yourself a rejuvenating, moisturizing facial by applying Miracle Whip as a face mask. Miracle Whip cleanses the skin and tightens the pores. Leave on for twenty minutes, then wash off with warm water, followed by cold water. You may feel like a tuna fish sandwich, but the Miracle

Whip gives your face an amazingly wonderful tingling sensation—demonstrating the real miracle of Miracle Whip.

- **Mott's Apple Sauce.** Rub applesauce over your face, wait thirty minutes, and wash it off with lukewarm water. The applesauce cleans dry skin.

- **Pepto-Bismol.** Cover your face with Pepto-Bismol (avoiding your eyes), let dry, then rinse off with cool water to dry the oils from your skin. If you're suffering from a stomachache and taking Pepto-Bismol to soothe it, you might as well pamper yourself with a Pepto-Bismol facial at the same time.

- **Phillips' Milk of Magnesia.** Use a cotton ball to apply Phillips' Milk of Magnesia as a facial mask, let dry for thirty minutes, then rinse off with warm water, followed by cool water. The milk of magnesia absorbs the oils from your skin while cooling the skin at the same time, leaving your face minty fresh.

- **Quaker Oats** and **SueBee Honey.** Mix up a cup of warm Quaker Oats, add enough SueBee Honey to thicken, and apply the paste to your dry face, being sure the paste is warm but not hot enough to burn your skin. Let it sit for ten minutes, then rinse it off with warm water. Use a plastic or mesh drain cover to avoid clogging your pipes. Both the warmth and the honey draw the oil from your skin, and the oatmeal absorbs it.

- **ReaLemon.** Wash your face with ReaLemon lemon juice to lighten and exfoliate your skin. The lemon juice is a natural bleach.

- **Reddi-wip.** Using Reddi-wip as a facial mask moisturizes dry skin and gives it a healthy glow. Leave the Reddi-wip on for twenty minutes, then wash off this dessert topping with warm water, followed by cold water.

- **Smirnoff Vodka.** Using a cotton ball, apply Smirnoff Vodka to your face as an astringent to cleanse the skin and tighten the pores.

- **SueBee Honey, Carnation Evaporated Milk, Heinz Apple Cider Vinegar,** and **Gold Medal Flour.** Mix three tablespoons SueBee Honey, one-half cup Carnation Evaporated Milk, and four tablespoons Heinz Apple Cider Vinegar in a bowl. Add enough Gold Medal All-Purpose Flour to make a very thick paste. Apply as a face mask and let dry. Rinse off the mask with warm water, followed by cold water. The honey disinfects the skin and seals in moisture, the milk moisturizes, and the vinegar tightens the pores.

- **Tidy Cats.** Mix two handfuls of unused Tidy Cats with enough water to make a thick, muddy paste. Smear the mud over your face to create a deep-cleansing mud mask, let it set for twenty minutes, then rinse your face clean with water. The clay from the cat box filler detoxifies your skin by absorbing dirt and oil from the pores.

STRANGE FACTS

- ◆ The skeleton of the face consists of fourteen bones.

- ◆ In the 1995 movie *It Takes Two*, starring Mary-Kate and Ashley Olsen, one of the twins mistakes her father's girlfriend—wearing a white bathrobe, a white towel wrapped around her hair, and white facial cream—for a ghost.

- ◆ In the 1996 movie *Dunston Checks In*, starring Jason Alexander, a wealthy woman undergoing a facial treatment in the spa of a luxury hotel mistakes the orangutan jumping on her back for a masseuse.

- ◆ In the 2000 movie *Miss Congeniality*, Sandra Bullock, starring as an undercover cop who infiltrates a beauty pageant, spots her roommate lying in bed wearing a green facial mask and says, "My roommate is asleep, or she's, uh, starting to mold."

- ◆ Pat Davis, spa director at the Peninsula Hotel in Beverly Hills, told the *Los Angeles Times*, "A lot of fruit enzymes are great for exfoliating the skin." The spa offers a Pineapple Papaya Enzyme Scrub and Green Tea and Ginger Seaweed Mask.

- ◆ The Verabella salon in Beverly Hills offers a facial treatment called "Fall on Your Face," consisting of a cranberry-apple scrub and a pumpkin-pie peel. A second facial treatment, called "Champagne and Caviar," features a mask made from flat champagne mixed with powdered wheat germ and oatmeal, followed by a spongy sheet of collagen and caviar extract.

Fingernails and Toenails

- **Alberto VO5 Conditioning Hairdressing.** Soften dry cuticles by rubbing on a dab of Alberto VO5 Conditioning Hairdressing.

- **Arm & Hammer Baking Soda.** To whiten fingernails and toenails, add three tablespoons Arm & Hammer Baking Soda to one-half cup warm water. Soak your nails in the solution for fifteen minutes. Then softly brush across each nail with a nailbrush.

- **Bounce.** Rubbing your fingernails with a Bounce dryer sheet removes nail polish without nail polish remover.

- **ChapStick.** Condition dry, cracked cuticles by rubbing on ChapStick Lip Balm.

- **Colgate Toothpaste.** Remove ink or adhesive residue from your fingernails by rubbing on a dab of Colgate Toothpaste.

- **Coppertone.** To soften brittle fingernails, warm three teaspoons of Coppertone, and use it as a hot-oil treatment.

- **Efferdent.** To whiten fingernails that have yellowed, drop two Efferdent tablets in a bowl of water, let dissolve, then soak your fingernails in the denture cleanser for five minutes. Efferdent not only cleans stains from dentures, it cleans stains from fingernails.

- **Forster Toothpicks** and **Band-Aid Bandages.** After softening the nail and skin around an ingrown toenail and sterilizing the area with an antiseptic, use a

Forster Toothpick to lift the sharp edge of the nail away from the skin. Insert a small piece of gauze or cotton under the nail, then cover with a Band-Aid bandage to allow the nail to grow out. Change the dressing every day.

- **Heinz White Vinegar.** Soften cuticles by filling a bowl with Heinz White Vinegar and soaking your fingers in it for five minutes. Also, fingernail polish will adhere longer to nails that have been soaked in vinegar.

- **Jell-O** and **Q-Tips Cotton Swabs.** To strengthen fingernails, mix any flavor of Jell-O powder with enough water to make a paste. Using a Q-Tips Cotton Swab, paint the mixture on your fingernails. The gelatin in the Jell-O fortifies the nails, helping them grow longer and stronger. The darker-colored flavors of Jell-O will also color your nails and give them a pleasant fruit-flavored scent.

- **Jet-Puffed Marshmallows.** Polish your toenails by placing a Jet-Puffed Marshmallow between each toe before painting them.

- **Johnson's Baby Oil.** Soften brittle fingernails by warming a few tablespoons of Johnson's Baby Oil and soaking your nails in it for ten minutes.

- **Krazy Glue** and **Maybelline Crystal Clear Nail Polish.** Fix a broken fingernail by using a small drop of Krazy Glue to secure the nail in place, then coat it with Maybelline Crystal Clear Nail Polish.

- **Lipton Tea Bags** and **Maybelline Crystal Clear Nail Polish.** To fix a broken fingernail, cut a piece of gauze paper from a Lipton Tea Bag to fit the nail, coat the broken nail with Maybelline Crystal Clear Nail Polish, press the gauze paper over the wet nail polish, then paint with clear or colored nail polish.

- **Listerine.** Treat toenail fungus by soaking your toes in Listerine four times daily for a couple of weeks. Listerine is an antiseptic that kills germs.

- **Lubriderm.** Prevent hangnails by moisturizing your cuticles with Lubriderm every day to keep the flesh surrounding your nails soft.

- **Miracle Whip.** To strengthen your fingernails, soak them in Miracle Whip for five minutes, then wash them clean.

- **Mr. Coffee Filters** and **Krazy Glue.** Make nail wraps by cutting a piece of a Mr. Coffee Filter to the size of your fingernail and adhering it to the nail with a drop of Krazy Glue.

- **Orajel.** If you're suffering from an ingrown toenail, apply Orajel to numb the tissue around the nail so you can work on it.

- **Oral-B Toothbrush.** If you don't have a nailbrush, grab a clean, used Oral-B Toothbrush to give yourself a manicure or pedicure. Dip the toothbrush in soapy water to clean fingernails and toenails gently and effectively.

- **Pam Cooking Spray.** Moisturize cuticles by spraying them with Pam Cooking Spray.

- **ReaLemon and Heinz White Vinegar.** Soften brittle fingernails and whiten yellowing nails by soaking your fingernails in ReaLemon lemon juice for ten minutes, then brush nails with a mixture of equal parts Heinz White Vinegar and warm water. Rinse well.

- **ReaLemon and Q-Tips Cotton Swabs.** Prevent fingernail biting by using a Q-Tips Cotton Swab to paint your fingernails with a quick dab of ReaLemon lemon juice. Let dry for a tart reminder to stop biting your nails.

- **Saran Wrap and Scotch Transparent Tape.** To treat a hangnail, apply hand cream to the affected area before going to bed, wrap the fingertip with a piece of Saran Wrap, and secure it in place with Scotch Transparent Tape. The plastic wrap confines the moisture overnight, softening the cuticle.

- **Skin-So-Soft.** Mix two capfuls Skin-So-Soft in a cup of warm water, then soak your fingernails for fifteen minutes to soften cuticles.

- **Star Olive Oil.** Pour one-quarter cup Star Olive Oil in a bowl, warm it, then soak your fingertips in the oil for five minutes to condition the cuticles.

- **Tabasco Pepper Sauce and Q-Tips Cotton Swabs.** Prevent fingernail biting by using a Q-Tips Cotton Swab to paint your fingernails with a quick dab of Tabasco Pepper Sauce. Let dry. Should you absentmindedly put your fingernails in your mouth, the zesty tang will quickly get your attention, reminding you to stop biting your nails.

- **Vaseline Petroleum Jelly.** To moisturize cuticles, massage Vaseline Petroleum Jelly around your fingernails before going to bed, put on a pair of white cotton gloves, and go to sleep. By morning your cuticles will be soft and healthy.

- **Vicks VapoRub.** Treat toenail fungus by applying a thick coat of Vicks VapoRub to the affected nail several times a day.

- **Wesson Corn Oil.** Soaking your fingernails in warm Wesson Corn Oil moisturizes the nails and cuticles.

STRANGE FACTS

- ◆ Fingernails grow .02 inches per week—four times faster than toenails.

- ◆ As early as 3000 B.C.E., Egyptian women stained their fingernails with henna.

- ◆ The Chinese invented enamels and lacquers as early as 3000 B.C.E. and used the color of fingernail polish to indicate social status. In 600 B.C.E., the royal family of the Chou Dynasty had their nails painted gold and silver.

- ◆ In Ancient Egypt, Queen Nefertiti had her fingernails and toenails painted ruby red—a color forbidden to be painted on any other woman's nails.

- ◆ During World War II, the United States Fleet commander in the Pacific Theater (Admiral Chester Nimitz) and the Japanese Fleet commander (Admiral Isoroku Yamamoto) had each lost two fingers as the result of accidents while they were younger officers aboard ships.

- ◆ In 1952, Shridhar Chilla of Pune, Marharshtra, India, stopped cutting his fingernails. As of March 1997, he had the longest fingernails in the world on record. The fingernail on his left thumb measured four feet, seven inches.

- ◆ Actor James Doohan, best remembered as Mr. Scott on the television series *Star Trek*, is missing the entire middle finger on his right hand.

- ◆ Grateful Dead guitarist Jerry Garcia was missing the top two-thirds of the middle finger on his right hand.

- ◆ On the popular television comedy variety series *Rowan & Martin's Laugh-In*, the cast routinely bestowed the Flying Fickle Finger of Fate Award.

- ◆ The white, crescent-shaped part of your fingernail is called the lunule (from the word *luna*, meaning "moon").

THE RUB ON VICKS VAPORUB

In 1905, Lunsford Richardson, a pharmacist working in his brother-in-law's drug store in Selma, North Carolina, aspired to create an ointment to decongest sinuses and relieve chest congestion. In the backroom laboratory of the pharmacy, he blended menthol (a newly introduced extract from oil of peppermint), petroleum jelly, and other ingredients from the pharmacy shelf. He named his creation Richardson's Croup and Pneumonia Cure Salve. When rubbed on the forehead and chest, the salve—vaporized by body heat—stimulated blood circulation and decongested blocked sinuses.

Demand for the salve exceeded Richardson's wildest expectations, prompting the pharmacist to market his new remedy. Seeking a catchier name for the product, Richardson decided to name it in honor of his brother-in-law, Joshua Vick. He advertised Vicks VapoRub in local newspapers, with coupons redeemable for a free trial jar. He convinced the United States Postal Service to institute a new policy allowing him to send out advertisements for Vicks VapoRub addressed solely to "Boxholder," effectively creating the concept of junk mail. The 1918 Spanish Flu epidemic—killing twenty-five million people worldwide—sent sales of Vicks VapoRub skyrocketing, surpassing one million dollars.

- ◆ The Japanese have developed a low-cost, biodegradable plastic made from shrimp shells by combining *chitin*—an extract from the shells that is also found in human fingernails—with silicon. The resulting "chitisand" is stronger than petroleum-based plastics, decomposes in soil, and acts as a fertilizer.

- ◆ Fifty-eight percent of women in the United States paint their nails regularly.

- ◆ Working in pressurized space suits causes the fingerprints on the fingertips of space shuttle astronauts to be rubbed away.

- ◆ While the word *hangnail* seems to refer to the fact that the sliver of nail hangs from the cuticle, the word *hangnail* is actually derived from the Middle English prefix *ang-* (meaning "painful").

◆ Human fingernails are made of the same material as rhinoceros horns.

◆ The phrase "burn your fingers" means suffering injury by meddling, the phrase "have a finger in the pie" means to have a share in something, the phrase "keep your fingers crossed" means to hope for good luck, the phrase "put your finger on it" means to recall or locate something, the phrase "not lift a finger" means to refrain from taking action, the phrase "put the finger on someone" means to designate a victim or identify a criminal, and the phrase "slip through your fingers" means to let an opportunity pass you by.

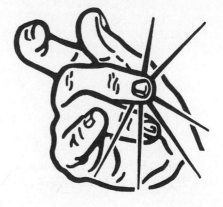

Flatulence

- **Altoids Peppermints.** Chewing two Altoids Peppermints relieves flatulence. The active ingredient is the peppermint, one of the oldest known remedies for gas.

- **Arm & Hammer Baking Soda.** When cooking beans, add one tablespoon Arm & Hammer Baking Soda to neutralize the gas.

- **Canada Dry Ginger Ale.** Drinking Canada Dry Ginger Ale helps release gas pockets in your stomach through burping, rather than through flatulence.

- **Coca-Cola.** To prevent flatulence, add a can of Coca-Cola to a pot of pinto beans when cooking to neutralize the gas.

- **Dannon Yogurt.** Eat a cup of Dannon Yogurt every day. The *Lactobacillus acidophilus* in the yogurt produces the bacteriocins necessary for proper digestion.

- **Heinz White Vinegar.** Before cooking beans, add three teaspoons Heinz White Vinegar to a pot of water and soak the beans in the solution overnight. The acetic acid in the vinegar dissolves some of the indigestible sugars in beans that would otherwise produce gas in your system.

- **Wrigley's Spearmint Gum.** Chewing a stick of Wrigley's Spearmint Gum helps settle the gases in the stomach—thanks to the oils in the spearmint.

- **York Peppermint Pattie.** Eating a York Peppermint Pattie relieves flatulence. Peppermint is an ancient cure for gas.

Strange Facts

◆ The average person passes gas eight to twenty times a day.

◆ Typical flatulent gas is composed of 59 percent nitrogen, 21 percent hydrogen, 9 percent carbon dioxide, 7 percent methane, and 4 percent oxygen.

◆ Ancient Greek physician Hippocrates (circa 460–377 B.C.E.), considered the father of modern medicine, incorrectly claimed that people suffering from jaundice are not susceptible to flatulence.

◆ The ancient Greek playwright Aristophanes laced his plays—including *The Clouds*, *The Acharnians*, *Peace*, and *Ecclesiazusae*—with jokes about farts.

◆ In "The Summoner's Tale" in *The Canterbury Tales* by Geoffrey Chaucer, the lord's squire solves the problem of how to divide a fart into thirteen equal portions.

◆ The phrase "to be hoist by one's own petard," apparently originated by William Shakespeare in his play *Hamlet*, means "to be undone by one's own devices." The word *petard* is French for "a loud discharge of intestinal gas," so Shakespeare's phrase more literally means to be flung by one's own flatulence.

◆ In his play *The Comedy of Errors*, William Shakespeare has Dromio of Ephesus tell Dromio of Syracuse:

> A man may break a word with you, sir, and words are but wind,
> Ay, and break it in your face, so he break it not behind.

◆ In 1776, Benjamin Franklin published a book of bawdy essays titled *Fart Proudly*.

◆ In his 1831 novel *The Hunchback of Notre Dame*, Victor Hugo wrote about farting prostitutes.

◆ In the 1890s, Joseph Pujol, a French music-hall entertainer who went by the stage name Le Petomane, was billed as "The Man with the Musical Derriere." Pujol used his uncanny ability to suck air into his rectum and expel it at will to imitate bird chirps and human voices, smoke cigarettes, and blow out candles—accompanied by an orchestra.

◆ German dictator Adolf Hitler once attempted to cure his chronic flatulence by drinking machine gun oil.

◆ In Mel Brooks' 1974 movie *Blazing Saddles*, cowboys sitting around a campfire at night eating beans fart excessively loudly, but when the movie airs on network television, the censors eliminate the thunderous sounds.

◆ In the 1984 movie *This Is Spinal Tap*, a "mockumentary" directed by Rob Reiner about a fictional heavy metal band, one of Spinal Tap's albums is titled *Break Like the Wind*.

◆ Screamin' Jay Hawkins said, "Do not eat beans; they talk behind your back."

◆ The CD *Pull My Finger*, released in 1999, contains ninety-nine recorded flatulent sounds. The best-selling CD has yet to win a Grammy Award.

◆ At the Academy Awards in 2000, ABC-TV refused to let Robin Williams sing the word *fart* when he performed the Oscar-nominated song "Blame Canada" from the film *South Park: Bigger, Longer and Uncut*.

◆ Paul Oldfield, a British performer who goes by the stage name Mr. Methane because of his ability use his flatulence to carry a tune, has made several appearances on *The Howard Stern Show*, where he farted the melodies of Rimsky-Korsakov's "Flight of the Bumblebee" and Deep Purple's "Smoke on the Water."

◆ Euphemisms for emitting flatulence include such colorful expressions as "blasting the chair," "breaking wind," "cutting the cheese," "floating an air biscuit," "making a one-gun salute," "shooting the cannon," "sounding the trumpet," and "stepping on a duck."

Fleas

- **Dawn.** To kill fleas in carpeting, pour one tablespoon Dawn Dishwashing Liquid into a sixteen-ounce trigger-spray bottle. Fill the rest of the bottle with water, shake well, and spray the carpet, upholstery, and floors. The soap dries up the insects, killing them almost instantly. After fifteen minutes, wipe the floors with a damp towel and vacuum the carpet.

- **Hartz 2-in-1 Flea & Tick Collar.** Kill fleas sucked into your vacuum cleaner bag by placing a Hartz 2-in-1 Flea & Tick Collar inside the bag.

- **Lysol.** Spray the carpet and upholstery with Lysol disinfectant spray. The antiseptic kills fleas. Repeat the following day to kill any newly hatched fleas.

- **Morton Salt.** Sprinkle Morton Salt on carpets, let sit for at least three hours, and vacuum thoroughly.

- **Pine-Sol.** Pour one-quarter cup Pine-Sol into a sixteen-ounce trigger-spray bottle, fill the rest of the bottle with water, shake well, and spray the soapy liquid on your carpets and upholstered furniture. Pine-Sol Liquid Cleaner kills fleas and simultaneously removes pet odors.

- **20 Mule Team Borax.** Sprinkle a light coating of 20 Mule Team Borax on the carpets and floors, let sit for twenty-four hours, and then vacuum. The borax kills all the fleas.

To rid your house of fleas, you must also rid your pet of fleas. To do so, see page 252.

STRANGE FACTS

♦ An adult female flea can lay one egg every hour during its 3-month life span.

♦ If an average human body were compacted to remove all the space between the nuclei of the atoms, the weight of that body would remain the same, but the size of that body would be smaller than a flea.

♦ The nursery rhyme "Ring around the rosy, a pocket full of posies, ashes, ashes, we all fall down" is about the deadly disease carried by rat fleas that caused the Great Plague of London from 1664 to 1665. The disease killed more than seventy thousand people—one out of every seven London citizens. The "ring around the rosy" describes the initial round rosy rash, the "pocket full of posies" refers to the alleged herbal remedies that infected people carried in their pockets, "ashes" is a mispronunciation of "achoo," describing the sneeze that came before "falling down" dead.

♦ In Walt Disney's 1992 animated movie *Aladdin*, one of Princess Jasmine's suitors accuses Aladdin of having fleas. Aladdin denies having fleas—as he scratches himself.

♦ By biting an infected rat or squirrel, fleas can spread typhus or bubonic plague.

♦ The common flea measures one-eighth inch in length and can jump up to thirteen inches. Proportionally, that's the equivalent of a human being jumping seven hundred feet.

♦ A flea circus features troupes of fleas leashed to objects such as tiny wagons that they pull across the small stage.

♦ In 1980, John Lennon told *Newsweek,* "Part of me is a monk. And part of me is a performing flea."

Flu

- **Alka-Seltzer.** Fill the bathtub with warm water and drop in six Alka-Seltzer tablets for a soothing bath to help soothe achy muscles (unless you are allergic to asprin, a key ingredient in Alka-Seltzer).

- **Altoids Peppermints.** Chewing two Altoids Peppermints helps clear up a stuffed-up nose. Peppermint relieves congestion.

- **Arm & Hammer Baking Soda** and **Epsom Salt.** Add one cup Arm & Hammer Baking Soda and one cup Epsom Salt to running bath water. Soak your body to relieve muscles made sore by the flu.

- **BenGay.** Rub a small dab of BenGay into your forehead, temples, and the back of your neck. The heat from the salve will gently soothe headache pain.

- **Campbell's Chicken Noodle Soup.** Sipping a bowl of hot Campbell's Chicken Noodle Soup actually helps decongest nasal passages while simultaneously rehydrating and reenergizing the body with essential salts.

- **ChapStick.** If your nose gets red and sore from blowing your nose too often, rub unflavored ChapStick on the tender spots to heal the irritation.

- **Dannon Yogurt.** Enhance your immune system by eating Dannon Yogurt. According to the *International Journal of Immunotherapy*, yogurt with active cultures enhances the body's immune system by increasing the production of gamma interferons, which play a key role in fighting certain viral infections.

- **Dial Soap.** Washing your hands frequently with Dial antibacterial soap may help you avoid contracting the flu from a sick family member—by killing any germs you may have inadvertently picked up.

- **French's Mustard.** Rub a generous amount of French's Mustard on your chest. Cover with a washcloth dampened with warm water and wrung, making an old-fashioned mustard plaster that relieves congestion.

- **Gatorade.** Drinking two quarts of liquids daily replaces vital bodily fluids lost through fever, flushes impurities from your system, relieves headaches caused by dehydration, and helps speed healing. Gatorade replaces electrolytes (the potassium and salt lost through fever and perspiration).

- **Gold's Horseradish.** Gold's Horseradish is a natural remedy for a congested nose. Simply eat some horseradish on a cracker.

- **Heinz Apple Cider Vinegar** and **SueBee Honey.** Mix one-quarter cup Heinz Apple Cider Vinegar with one-quarter cup SueBee Honey. Take one tablespoon six times daily. The vinegar kills bacteria and the honey soothes your throat.

- **Life Savers.** Sucking on Life Savers hard candy helps moisturize your throat, providing relief while simultaneously giving your body additional calories to reenergize and fight the virus.

- **Lipton Tea Bags.** Drinking hot tea replaces vital bodily fluids, flushes impurities from your system, relieves headache pain, and helps soothe your throat and decongest your sinuses.

- **Maxwell House Coffee** and **Glad Flexible Straws.** Sipping a cup of hot, black coffee through a plastic straw helps relieve chest congestion.

- **McCormick Garlic Powder.** Spice a bowl of chicken soup with McCormick Garlic Powder. Garlic is a natural antibiotic and antiseptic.

- **Morton Salt.** Dissolve one teaspoon salt in a glass of warm water and gargle with the solution three times a day to relieve your throat and loosen phlegm.

- **Morton Salt** and **Glad Flexible Straws.** To clear congested sinuses, dissolve one-half teaspoon Morton Salt in one cup warm water. Insert a Glad Flexible Straw into the liquid, cover the open end of the straw with your finger, insert the straw in your nostril, release your finger from the straw, and inhale the liquid. Repeat several times, and then blow your nose thoroughly.

- **Mott's Apple Sauce.** When you have the energy to eat, Mott's Apple Sauce makes a great starter food that the body can easily digest.

- **Pampers.** To give yourself a rejuvenating sponge bath and reduce your fever, saturate a Pampers disposable diaper with water (you'll be amazed at how much liquid it holds), wipe down your body, then place it over your forehead.

- **Popsicle.** Sucking on an ice-cold Popsicle brings instant relief to a sore throat. The sugars also help to coat the throat and give you energy.

- **Smirnoff Vodka.** To relieve a fever, use a washcloth to rub Smirnoff Vodka on your chest and back as a liniment.

- **Star Olive Oil** and **Gold's Horse Radish.** Mix one tablespoon Gold's Horse Radish in one-half cup Star Olive Oil. Let the mixture sit for thirty minutes. Apply as a massage oil to relieve achy muscles.

- **Stayfree Maxi Pads.** If you don't have a washcloth, saturate a Stayfree Maxi Pad with cold water and place it over your forehead to bring down a fever. A Stayfree Maxi Pad is the perfect size to fit on your forehead.

- **SueBee Honey.** To help yourself sleep at night, eat a teaspoon of SueBee Honey (or mix it into a cup of tea) before bedtime. Honey acts like a sedative. (Do not feed honey to infants under one year of age.)

- **Tabasco Pepper Sauce** and **Campbell's Tomato Juice.** Mix ten to twenty drops Tabasco Pepper Sauce in a glass of Campbell's Tomato Juice. Drink several of these decongestant tonics daily to help relieve congestion in the nose, sinuses, and lungs. Or gargle with ten to twenty drops Tabasco Pepper Sauce mixed in a glass of water to clear out the respiratory tract.

- **Vaseline Petroleum Jelly.** When your nose gets sore from too much blowing, apply a thin coat of Vaseline Petroleum Jelly around your nostrils.

- **Wilson Tennis Balls.** Put several Wilson Tennis Balls inside a sock and tie it at the end. Have a loved one roll this over your back to soothe achy muscles. This technique is frequently used by labor coaches to massage the backs of women in labor.

- **York Peppermint Pattie.** Eating a York Peppermint Pattie helps clear sinuses. Peppermint relieves congestion.

- **Ziploc Freezer Bags.** Applying an ice pack to your head relieves headache pain and fever. To make an ice pack, fill a Ziploc Freezer Bag with water and freeze it or fill it with ice cubes. Wrap the ice pack in a paper towel before applying. For other ways to make and apply an ice pack, see page 198.

- **Ziploc Storage Bags.** Keep a gallon-size Ziploc Storage Bag on hand so you can dispose of used tissues. Seal the bag to avoid spreading germs.

STRANGE FACTS

- ◆ Fever, headache, hacking cough, muscle ache, and extreme fatigue usually accompany the flu, but rarely accompany colds. A runny nose, sore throat, and sneezing are common symptoms of a cold. The flu is never associated with sneezing.

- ◆ The common cold generally lasts longer than the flu.

- ◆ The flu is caused by three main types of viruses: Influenza A, B, and C, which have an uncanny ability to mutate into a multitude of other forms. Surviving one flu virus makes you immune only to that one particular strain or mutation.

- ◆ Antibiotics cannot cure the flu. Antibiotics kill bacteria, not viruses.

- ◆ In 1918, the Spanish Flu killed more than twenty million people worldwide.

- ◆ Most flu vaccines are made from dead influenza viruses.

- ◆ In March 1976, at the request of President Gerald Ford, Congress appropriated 135 million dollars for a federal campaign to inoculate the entire United States population against a virus with swine flu characteristics that had first appeared a month earlier among soldiers at Fort Dix in New Jersey. Vaccinations began in the fall, resulting in twenty-three deaths and hundreds of lawsuits against the government for adverse reactions, including heart attacks and paralysis. The government ended the program in December 1976.

- ◆ Most deaths associated with the flu are actually caused by secondary infections—such as bacterial pneumonia.

A SHOT OF SMIRNOFF VODKA

In 1818, Pierre Smirnoff began distilling and bottling vodka in Moscow, Russia. In 1886, Czar Alexander II awarded the House of Smirnoff the honor of purveyor to the court, an honor the company held through the reign of Nicholas II, who was killed in the Bolshevik Revolution in 1917.

When the Bolsheviks confiscated all private industry, they seized all neutral grain spirit, demineralized water, and filtered water. Among the many people they arrested, the Bolsheviks jailed Vladimir Smirnoff, then head of the House of Smirnoff, and sentenced him to death.

In 1918, Smirnoff escaped to France and opened new plants in Constantinople, Poland, and Paris. In 1933, Smirnoff gave fellow Russian refugee Rudolf Kunett (whose family had provided Smirnoff with an alcohol by-product of the beet sugar manufacturing process) the exclusive right to sell Smirnoff Vodka in North America—anticipating the repeal of Prohibition later that year. Kunett began building the first vodka plant in the United States in Bethel, Connecticut. But unable to raise $1,500 for a mandatory sales license, he sold the American arm of Smirnoff to G. F. Heublein and Brothers, remaining as company president.

SMIRNOFF VODKA has been James Bond's choice of vodka for his "shaken, not stirred" vodka martini for eighteen movies, starting with *Dr. No* in 1962.

LEGEND HOLDS that the screwdriver—a mixture of vodka and orange juice—was invented by an American engineer in the Middle East, who stirred the concoction with a screwdriver.

IN THE 1920S, Fernand Petiot, an American working at Harry's Bar in Paris, created the Bloody Mary (originally called "The Bucket of Blood") by mixing vodka with tomato juice and adding a stalk of celery. Tabasco Pepper Sauce was added to the recipe in the 1930s at the King Cole Bar in New York's St. Regis Hotel.

VODKA—MADE FROM BARLEY, corn, rye, or potatoes—varies from 80 to 100 proof and is not aged. The alcoholic beverage is colorless, odorless, and tasteless.

ADVERTISEMENTS FOR SMIRNOFF VODKA have featured Benny Goodman, Tony Randall, Robert Goulet, Groucho and Harpo Marx, Sid Caesar, Zsa Zsa Gabor, and Johnny Carson.

IN THE COLDEST REGIONS OF RUSSIA, construction workers add vodka to the transmission fluid of gas-powered machines and vehicles to prevent the transmission fluid from freezing when the temperature drops below zero degrees Fahrenheit.

SMIRNOFF IS the most popular spirit in the United States.

Food Poisoning

- **Coca-Cola.** Open a can of Coca-Cola, let it sit until it goes flat (roughly thirty minutes), then drink the defizzed real thing. Letting the bubbles out of the soda prevents the carbonation from further upsetting your stomach.

- **Domino Sugar, Morton Salt,** and **ReaLemon.** Drinking plenty of fluids during a bout of diarrhea is essential to avoiding dehydration. To make your own rehydration solution, mix three teaspoons sugar, one teaspoon salt, and two teaspoons lemon juice in a tall glass of water. Drink the entire solution to replace the glucose, minerals, and vitamin C being flushed out of your body.

- **Gatorade.** Relieve the pangs of food poisoning by rehydrating your body with Gatorade. Drinking Gatorade replaces the electrolytes (particularly potassium, sodium, and glucose) flushed out of your system by vomiting and diarrhea.

- **Krispy Original Saltine Crackers.** When you're feeling ready for food again, start with bland foods like saltine crackers, which you can easily digest.

- **Uncle Ben's Converted Brand Rice.** Eating plain Uncle Ben's Converted Brand Rice will help cure diarrhea.

Let a doctor figure out what's eating you if your nausea, vomiting, diarrhea, or stomach pain continues for more than twelve hours.

STRANGE FACTS

◆ Staphylococcal bacteria, the cause of most food poisoning, is produced when food is left too long without refrigeration. The bacteria release poisons into the contaminated food.

◆ Salmonella bacteria cause the second most common form of food poisoning. The bacteria, usually found in raw meat, can cause diarrhea, vomiting, and fever. Instead of releasing poisons into the food, salmonella bacteria reproduce in the digestive tract.

◆ Botulism, another form of food poisoning, is caused when *Clostridium botulinum* spores get into improperly canned food. Without oxygen, the spores become active bacteria and secrete *botulinus* toxin into the food. While rare, botulism can cause paralysis and death.

◆ During turbulent times in European monarchies, kings would often have a royal food taster who would eat small portions of food prepared for the king to test if it was poisoned.

◆ In Alfred Hitchcock's 1941 movie *Suspicion*, Joan Fontaine stars as a wealthy woman who suspects that her charming husband is trying to murder her, possibly with a glass of poison milk.

◆ In the 1942 movie *Arsenic and Old Lace*, starring Cary Grant, two old ladies invite lonely old men into their home and poison them with elderberry wine.

◆ In Alfred Hitchcock's 1946 movie *Notorious*, starring Cary Grant, a postwar Nazi spy slowly attempts to murder a counterspy, played by Ingrid Bergman, by poisoning her coffee.

◆ The twigs and foliage of cherry trees, if eaten, cause death.

Foot Ache

- **Adolph's Meat Tenderizer.** Add enough water to Adolph's Meat Tenderizer to make a paste, and rub it into your feet to tenderize them.

- **Alberto VO5 Conditioning Hairdressing.** To soothe tired feet, coat your feet with Alberto VO5 Conditioning Hairdressing before going to bed, covering them with a pair of socks. In the morning, your feet will feel rejuvenated.

- **Alka-Seltzer.** Plop four Alka-Seltzer tablets in a pan of warm water, plop your feet into the alkaline solution, and let them fizz fizz for fifteen minutes (unless you are allergic to aspirin, an ingredient in Alka-Seltzer).

- **Arm & Hammer Baking Soda.** Dissolve three tablespoons Arm & Hammer Baking Soda in a basin of warm water and soak your feet in the solution to relieve the achiness.

- **Bounce.** Put one sheet of Bounce in a basin of warm water and soak your feet in it for ten minutes to moisturize tired soles.

- **Bubble Wrap.** Cut foot pads from Bubble Wrap and slip them into your shoes. They'll cushion your feet for up to six hours.

- **Cool Whip.** Coat your feet with Cool Whip, let sit for fifteen minutes, then wash your feet clean. The nondairy dessert topping cools achy feet and the oils soften the skin.

- **Crisco All-Vegetable Shortening.** Massage your feet with a dab of Crisco All-Vegetable Shortening, using your thumb to work the sole of your foot. The shortening also works wonders between the toes.

- **Epsom Salt** and **Lubriderm.** Soak your feet in a pan of warm water mixed with two tablespoons Epsom Salt, then rinse your feet with cool water, pat them dry, and rub in Lubriderm.

- **French's Mustard.** Fill a pan with warm water, mix in three tablespoons French's Mustard, and soak your feet in the mustard bath.

- **Heinz White Vinegar.** Swabbing your feet with Heinz White Vinegar helps to cool and dry them.

- **Land O Lakes Butter.** To soothe tired feet, rub Land O Lakes Butter into your feet, wrap in a damp, hot towel, and sit for ten minutes.

- **Miracle Whip.** Warm up one-half cup Miracle Whip in a microwave oven, apply a thick coating of the dressing to your feet, let sit fifteen minutes, and then wash clean. Your feet will feel miraculously healed.

- **Nestea.** Mix Nestea according to the directions in two quarts warm water, soak your feet in the mixture, then rinse clean. The tannin in the tea soothes tired feet.

- **Pam Cooking Spray.** Spray your foot with Pam Cooking Spray and use your thumb to massage the sole, then concentrate on the area between the toes.

- **Quaker Oats, Carnation Condensed Milk,** and **SueBee Honey.** Mix one cup Quaker Oats, one-half cup Carnation Condensed Milk, and one-third cup SueBee Honey in a dishpan. Place your feet in the pan, coat them with the mixture by rubbing your feet back and forth, and let soak for twenty minutes. Your feet will feel like a million bucks.

- **Scotch-Brite Heavy Duty Scrub Sponge.** Use a Scotch-Brite Heavy Duty Scrub Sponge for a cushion support in your shoe. One sponge, cut in half, will provide comfort for your feet when you walk.

- **Smirnoff Vodka.** To cool down your feet, swab them with Smirnoff Vodka. The alcohol in the vodka works like a liniment to cool and dry your feet.

- **Tabasco Pepper Sauce.** Rub the hot sauce onto your feet. Tabasco Pepper Sauce, made from a type of pepper called *Capsicum frutescens*, contains the alkaloid capsaicin, which has been proven to numb pain when applied topically. If you feel a burning sensation on the skin, apply a thin coat of Colgate Toothpaste over the dried Tabasco Pepper Sauce to relieve the irritation and possibly elevate the analgesia from the capsaicin. Do not apply Tabasco Pepper Sauce to an open wound.

- **Vicks VapoRub.** To soothe aching feet, apply a thick coat of Vicks VapoRub and cover with a pair of socks before going to bed. By morning, your feet will be moisturized and rejuvenated.

- **Wesson Corn Oil.** Warm one-half cup Wesson Corn Oil in a microwave oven. Rub the warmed oil into your feet, wrap in a damp, hot towel, and let set for ten minutes. Wash your feet clean.

- **Wilson Tennis Balls.** For an excellent foot massage, roll your bare foot over a Wilson Tennis Ball for several minutes.

- **Ziploc Freezer Bags.** Using an ice pack relieves swollen feet and ankles. Fill a Ziploc Freezer Bag with water and freeze it or fill it with ice cubes. Wrap the ice pack in a paper towel before applying. For other ways to make and apply an ice pack, see page 198.

Strange Facts

- ◆ If you lace your shoes from the inside to the outside, the fit will be snugger around your big toe.

- ◆ Feet are ticklish because of the high concentration of nerve endings.

- ◆ In Greek mythology, when the Greek hero Achilles was born, his mother held him by his heel and dipped him in the river Styx to make him invincible. During a battle, Paris shot a poison arrow, hitting Achilles in the heel, his only vulnerable spot, killing the hero.

- ◆ In the children's fairy tale "Cinderella," as told by Charles Perrault in his 1697 book, Cinderella's evil stepsisters mangle their feet in an attempt to squeeze them into Cinderella's little glass slipper.

- ◆ Neil Armstrong first stepped on the moon with his left foot.

- ◆ On January 26, 1977, George Meegan of Great Britain started walking the 19,019 miles from Ushuaia, on the southern tip of South America, to Prudhoe Bay in Northern Alaska, arriving 2,426 days later on September 18, 1983.

- ◆ The world record for balancing on one foot is held by Amresh Kumar Jah, who stood on just one foot for seventy-one hours, forty minutes in Bhiar, India, from September 13 to September 16, 1995.

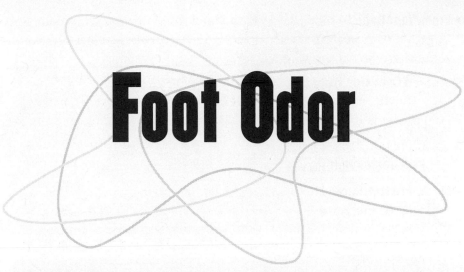

Foot Odor

- **Alka-Seltzer.** Dissolve two Alka-Seltzer tablets in a quart of warm water and soak your feet in the solution for fifteen minutes twice a week (unless you are allergic to aspirin, a key ingredient in Alka-Seltzer). The baking soda in the Alka-Seltzer increases the acid level on your feet, inhibiting odor-producing bacteria.

- **Arm & Hammer Baking Soda.** Dissolve two tablespoons Arm & Hammer Baking Soda in one gallon warm water. Twice a week, soak your feet in the solution for fifteen minutes. The baking soda solution raises the acid level on your feet, inhibiting odors.

- **Dial Soap.** Washing your feet with Dial Soap gets rid of the bacteria that thrive on perspiration and produce vile-smelling odors.

- **Heinz White Vinegar.** Add one cup Heinz White Vinegar to a gallon of water and soak your smelly feet in the solution for fifteen minutes. The acid in the vinegar lowers the pH level of your skin, neutralizing odors.

- **Jell-O.** Soaking your feet in ready-made Jell-O for twenty minutes deodorizes smelly feet. Jell-O comes in twenty-five flavors, giving you a nice selection of fruit scents. Now they'll come running to kiss your feet.

- **Kingsford's Corn Starch.** After a shower, powder your feet with Kingsford's Corn Starch and frequently sprinkle the inside of your shoes with corn-starch to keep them dry as well.

- **Lipton Tea Bags** and **Kingsford's Corn Starch.** Boil three or four Lipton Tea Bags in one quart water for ten minutes. Add enough cold water to make a comfortable soak. Soak your feet for twenty to thirty minutes, then dry them and apply Kingsford's Corn Starch. Do this twice a day until foot odor is under control. Then continue twice a week to keep odor under control. The tannin in the tea is a drying agent, giving you a measure of control over foot perspiration.

- **Listerine.** Soaking your feet in Listerine kills any odor-causing bacteria.

- **Morton Salt.** Dissolve one cup Morton Salt in a gallon of warm water and soak your feet in the solution. The salt water solution dries the skin.

- **Right Guard.** Spray your smelly feet with Right Guard to deodorize them. (Do not use deodorant on athlete's foot fungus. The deodorant will sting the lesions.)

- **Smirnoff Vodka.** After washing your feet, swab them with Smirnoff Vodka. The alcohol in the vodka dries your feet.

- **Stayfree Ultra Thin Maxi Pads.** Stayfree Ultra Thin Maxi Pads make excellent shoe insert pads. Not only are they the perfect size, but they are also available with deodorant—killing two birds with one stone.

- **Ziploc Storage Bags.** To avoid powdering the floor, fill a gallon-size Ziploc Storage Bag with foot powder and dip your feet in the bag.

STRANGE FACTS

- Sprinkling garlic powder in someone's shoes will eventually cause the victim's breath to smell like garlic.

- In the 1900s, Sicilian-born Frank Betenia toured as a sideshow attraction with the Ringling Brothers circus because he had three legs.

- In his 1922 epic poem *The Waste Land*, T. S. Eliot wrote:
  O the moon shone bright on Mrs. Porter
  And on her daughter
  They wash their feet in soda water.

◆ In the 1960s Hanna-Barbera animated television series *The Flint-stones*, Fred Flintstone stands on his toes when he bowls, earning him the nickname "Twinkle Toes."

◆ Dan Aykroyd has webbed toes, which can be seen in the 1979 cult movie *Mr. Mike's Mondo Video*, starring former *Saturday Night Live* writer Michael O'Donoghue.

◆ In the 2000 movie *Best in Show*, directed by Christopher Guest, Eugene Levy plays a dog owner with two left feet.

Freckles and Sunspots

- **Coppertone.** Freckles can sometimes be prevented by using sunscreen lotions such as Coppertone that contain para-aminobenzoic acid (PABA). Freckles are caused by an accumulation of the skin pigment melanin, which responds unevenly to sunlight.

- **Gold's Horseradish, Heinz Apple Cider Vinegar,** and **Mr. Coffee Filters.** Place one tablespoon Gold's Horseradish in a bowl and use the spoon to spread out the horseradish evenly. Pour just enough Heinz Apple Cider Vinegar into the bowl to cover the horseradish. Let sit for ten days, then strain through a Mr. Coffee Filter. Dilute the liquid with an equal amount of water, and use a cotton ball to apply to freckles and sunspots twice a day to minimize them (and in some cases, make them disappear completely). Be sure to avoid using around the eyes and on irritated skin. Store the remaining liquid in an airtight container.

- **ReaLemon.** Apply ReaLemon lemon juice to the freckles or sunspots, and let sit for fifteen minutes, then rinse your skin clean. Lemon juice is a safe skin bleach.

STRANGE FACTS

- ◆ Skin damaged by the sun produces more melanin, the pigment that gives the skin its color and creates the appearance of suntanned skin, resulting in sunspots.

- Freckles are caused by small buildups of melanin.

- In her poem "Inventory," published in her 1927 book *Enough Rope*, Dorothy Parker wrote:

  Four be things I'd been better without:
  Love, curiosity, freckles, and doubt.

- In the *Pippi Longstocking* books, author Astrid Lindgren depicts Swedish Pippi with long red pigtails and a face full of freckles.

- In the 1970s television show *The Partridge Family*, middle child Danny Partridge, played by Danny Bonaduce, is a precocious freckle-faced redhead.

- In the 1982 movie *Annie*, little orphan Annie has red curly hair and a face full of freckles.

- As a child, pop artist Andy Warhol contracted Saint Vitus' dance, a disease that left brownish blotches all over his body, prompting his classmates in grade school to nickname him "Spot."

Green Hair

- **Arm & Hammer Baking Soda.** Prevent chlorine from dyeing blond hair green by filling the cupped palm of your hand with Arm & Hammer Baking Soda and using it to wash your hair. Baking soda raises the alkalinity of chlorine.

- **Bayer Aspirin.** Dissolve six Bayer Aspirin tablets in a tall glass of warm water. Rub the solution into your hair to make the green disappear (unless you are allergic to aspirin).

- **Campbell's Tomato Juice.** Saturate your hair with tomato juice, cover your hair with a plastic shower cap, wait fifteen minutes, then rinse well and shampoo thoroughly. The acid in the tomatoes neutralizes the chlorine.

- **Canada Dry Club Soda.** Rinse your green hair with Canada Dry Club Soda to change blond hair dyed green by chlorine back to blond.

- **Heinz Apple Cider Vinegar.** To prevent chlorine from turning blond hair green, apply Heinz Apple Cider Vinegar to your hair, let set for fifteen minutes, then rinse clean. The vinegar deep cleans the hair down to the roots.

- **Heinz Ketchup.** Massage Heinz Ketchup through your hair, let it dry, then shampoo. The ketchup eliminates the chlorine, cleanses the hair, and leaves hair feeling soft and silky.

- **Kool-Aid.** Empty a packet of banana-flavored Kool-Aid into the cupped palm of your hand, add enough water to make a thick paste, and massage the drink mix into your hair to return your green hair to its blond color.

WHAT'S SHAKING WITH HEINZ?

In the seventeenth century, English sailors whose ships were docked in Singapore discovered that local natives ate *kechap*—a tangy sauce made from fish brine, herbs, and spices—with their fish and fowl dishes. Upon returning home to Britain, the sailors, yearning for the sauce, tried to re-create it, substituting mushrooms, walnuts, cucumbers, and later tomatoes, for the ingredients they were missing. *Ketchup*, as the British called the surrogate sauce, became a national favorite.

Meanwhile, Maine sea captains acquired a taste for Singaporean *kechap* and for the exotic tomato, relished in Mexico and the Spanish West Indies. Maine families were soon growing tomatoes in their gardens and making *kechap*—which they called *catsup*—to use on codfish cakes, baked beans, and meat.

Making ketchup at home required that the tomatoes be parboiled and peeled. The puree had to be continually stirred on the stove to prevent the pulp from sticking to the cauldron and burning.

Fortunately for housewives, Henry J. Heinz introduced the first mass-produced, bottled ketchup in 1876. Heinz had started his condiment business in Pittsburgh, Pennsylvania, in 1869, marketing horseradish in clear glass bottles to show customers that his product—unlike that of his competitors—was not mixed with cheap fillers. Heinz quickly earned the public trust, expanding his product line to include pickles, sauerkraut, and vinegar, delivered by horse-drawn wagons to grocers in the Pittsburgh area.

IN 1896, while riding an elevated train in New York City, company founder Henry J. Heinz spotted an advertisement for a shoe store announcing "21 Styles" of shoes. Inspired by the concept, Heinz immediately decided to use it to advertise his pickles and condiments. Although Heinz made more than sixty different products at the time, he settled on the slogan "57 Varieties" because he liked the way it looked in print.

TODAY, HEINZ HAS OVER three thousand varieties, but still uses the "57 Varieties" slogan.

HEINZ INTRODUCED HIS BOTTLED KETCHUP during a depression. The banking industry had collapsed just one year earlier in 1875.

IN 1981, to save money on government-subsidized school lunches, the United States Department of Agriculture announced its plan to classify ketchup as a vegetable and sunflower seeds as meat. Public ridicule prompted the Reagan administration to withdraw the plan.

WHEN HEINZ KETCHUP leaves the bottle, it travels at a speed of twenty-five miles per year.

IN 2001, HEINZ INTRODUCED Blastin' Green and Funky Purple Ketchup.

KETCHUP IS THE BEST-KNOWN CONDIMENT in the world, and Heinz Ketchup is America's favorite.

- **Ocean Spray Cranberry Juice Cocktail** and **ReaLemon.** Mix two parts Ocean Spray Cranberry Juice Cocktail with one part ReaLemon lemon juice. Massage the juicy mixture into your hair. The solution instantly removes the green buildup.

- **ReaLemon.** Rinse green hair with full-strength ReaLemon lemon juice until the green vanishes.

STRANGE FACTS

◆ In the 1948 movie *The Boy with Green Hair*, starring Dean Stockwell and Pat O'Brien, a young war orphan's hair turns green, making him a target of bigotry and prejudice.

◆ In an episode of *Gilligan's Island*, Gilligan wakes up one morning to discover that his hair has turned completely white without any explanation. The Professor eventually deduces the cause: the crude bleach Gilligan used to clean the castaways' laundry. We never learn how the castaways make bleach.

◆ In the final episode of *The Brady Bunch*, Greg buys a bottle of Neat & Natural Hair Tonic from his brother Bobby, which turns his hair orange.

◆ Hip-hop singer Pink gets her name from the fact that she dyed her hair bright pink—although she claims that her name will remain Pink regardless of the color of her hair.

◆ In the animated television series *Doug*, Doug's best friend Skeeter has green skin, his friend Phoebe has purple hair and aqua skin, his nemesis Roger Klotz has orange hair, Roger's friends have green and purple hair, assistant principal Mr. Bone has pink hair, and Roger's teacher, Mrs. Wings, has turquoise skin.

◆ In the 2002 movie *Big Fat Liar*, starring Amanda Bynes and Frankie Muniz, a Hollywood bigwig dives into a swimming pool and emerges with bright blue skin—because the pool water was tainted with blue dye.

Gum in Hair

- **Jif Peanut Butter.** Rub a dollop of Jif Peanut Butter into the wad of chewing gum stuck in a head of hair, working it in well, then comb the gum out. The oils in the peanut butter dissolve the chewing gum.

- **Johnson's Baby Oil.** Pour a few drops of Johnson's Baby Oil into the gum and massage it with your fingers. The mineral oil—a clear, colorless, oily liquid with little odor or taste—dissolves the gum, making it easy to comb out of hair.

- **Noxzema.** To remove chewing gum from hair, rub a dollop of Noxzema—the skin cream originally poured into little blue jars from a huge coffeepot—into the gum, then comb through the hair gently.

- **Pam Cooking Spray.** A quick spritz of Pam Cooking Spray on the wad of chewing gum helps to free it from hair.

- **Skin-So-Soft.** Rub a dollop of Skin-So-Soft into the chewing gum, then comb out the dissolved goo painlessly.

- **Spray 'N Wash.** Spray the chewing gum liberally with Spray 'N Wash, rub the liquid into the gum, then comb from hair.

- **WD-40.** Spraying a wad of chewing gum stuck in hair with this water displacement solution, originally formulated for the space program to prevent moisture from corroding wires in Mercury and Gemini rockets, dissolves the gum, making it easy to comb from hair. Then shampoo hair well.

- **Wesson Vegetable Oil.** Pour a capful of Wesson Vegetable Oil over the wad of gum, rub it in a circular motion with your fingers, then comb it out. Shampoo, and follow it by a vinegar rinse to remove the excess oil from hair.

STRANGE FACTS

- ◆ In 1848, John Curtis produced the first commercially available chewing gum, which he called State of Maine Pure Spruce Gum.

- ◆ In the 1860s, American businessman Thomas Adams began selling chicle, a gum from the sapodilla tree, indigenous to the Yucatán desert in Mexico.

- ◆ Posters advertising the 1972 movie *The Candidate* depicted a cavalier Robert Redford blowing a bubble-gum bubble.

SIDE EFFECTS
DIRTY BRUSHES, COMBS, AND CURLING IRONS

ARM & HAMMER BAKING SODA
Mix four tablespoons of Arm & Hammer Baking Soda in a glass of warm water, and soak hairbrushes and combs in the alkaline solution for thirty minutes. Then rinse clean.

CUTEX NAIL POLISH REMOVER
Wipe a cool, unplugged curling iron with a cotton ball saturated with Cutex Nail Polish Remover to remove grime and sticky residue. Wipe clean again with a water-dampened paper towel.

LYSOL and ORAL-B TOOTHBRUSH
Soak hairbrushes in Lysol Tub & Tile Cleaner for five minutes, scrub with a used, clean Oral-B Toothbrush, and then rinse and dry well.

PARSONS' AMMONIA
Add three tablespoons Parsons' Ammonia to one quart warm water, soak dirty hairbrushes and combs in the solution, and rinse them well.

S.O.S STEEL WOOL SOAP PADS
Scrubbing a cool, unplugged curling iron with an S.O.S Steel Wool Soap Pad removes hair-spray buildup easily and effortlessly.

STICKING WITH BAZOOKA

In 1938, four brothers—Abraham, Ira, Philip, and Joseph Shorin—founded the Topps Company in Brooklyn, New York, to market single pieces of chewing gum for one cent each. These became popular "change makers" on store counters throughout the country. After World War II, the company's defense-minded slogan, "Don't Talk Chum, Chew Topps Gum," became a catchphrase among American soldiers and civilians working in defense plants.

In 1947, Topps developed pink Bazooka Bubble Gum, named after the crude wind instrument played by vaudeville entertainer Bob Burns, who fashioned his "Bazooka" from two gas pipes and a funnel in the 1930s. Bazooka Bubble Gum—with its distinctive name, taste, smell, and red, white, and blue wrapper—soon became an American icon. In 1953, the company added Bazooka Joe comics to each piece of gum to charm kids. The comics also include premium offers. In 1994, the company moved into new headquarters at the Topps building in lower Manhattan.

BOB BURNS, also known as "The Arkansas Philosopher," appeared in several motion pictures in the 1930s, including *The Singing Vagabond*, *The Big Broadcast of 1937*, *Wells Fargo*, and *The Arkansas Traveler*.

THE BAZOOKA, the portable rocket launcher developed during World War II, got its name because it resembled a musical contraption, the Bazooka, played and invented by Bob Burns.

THE NAME *BAZOOKA JOE* is a play on the slang expression "Joe Palooka," meaning "a foolish, clumsy person."

BAZOOKA JOE WEARS a distinctive black eye patch over his right eye, sports a backward baseball cap on his head, and pals around with his friends A.J., Mort, and Kara.

TOPPS HAS DEVELOPED more than five hundred different Bazooka Joe comics. The company tries not to repeat a joke for at least five years so that the comics are fresh for each new generation of kids.

IN 1951, Topps began producing baseball trading cards, expanding its array of cards over the decades for other sports, pop stars, movies, and Pokémon characters.

A PSYCHOLOGICAL STUDY identified Bazooka Bubble Gum as one of the most frequently recognized tastes and smells that trigger memories.

- The first product to have a UPC bar code on its packaging was Wrigley's gum.

- On July 19, 1994, Susan Montgomery Williams of Fresno, California, blew the world's largest recorded bubble from bubble gum. It measured twenty-three inches in diameter.

- In the February 1997 issue of *British Archaeology*, Elizabeth Aveling described the oldest piece of chewing gum in the world: a 6,500-year-old piece of birch tar, embedded with human tooth marks, that had been found in a bog in Sweden.

Hair Coloring

- **Country Time Lemonade.** To get the rust color out of your hair, pour a dollop of your regular conditioner in the cupped palm your hand, add enough Country Time Lemonade powdered mix to make a thick paste, then using a little hot water to dilute the paste, apply it to your hair. Let set for five minutes, then rinse clean.

- **Hunt's Tomato Paste** and **Q-Tips Cotton Swabs.** If you want to be a red-head, wash your hair thoroughly with shampoo, rub Hunt's Tomato Paste into your hair, then rinse lightly. For red streaks, use a Q-Tips Cotton Swab to apply paste to strands of hair.

- **Jell-O.** Dye your hair temporarily by making a thick paste with any flavor Jell-O powder and water. Apply the paste to your hair, let it dry, then rinse. If you have darker hair, the coloring will last through a few shampoos. If you're blond, the color may last a while longer.

- **Kool-Aid.** If you'd like to find out how you look with purple hair or rainbow streaks, mix the contents from a packet of any flavor Kool-Aid with a little water to make a thick paste and apply it to your hair. The coloring is non-toxic and will last through a few shampoos if you have medium or dark hair. Blonds may find that the coloring lasts longer.

- **Lipton Tea Bags.** Use several Lipton Tea Bags to brew a strong pot of tea by letting the tea bags steep for ten minutes. Let the tea cool, pour it into a trigger-spray bottle, and spray your hair. Wearing sunscreen, sit in the sun for an hour. The tea will give your brown or red hair highlights.

- **Maxwell House Coffee.** Highlight brown or red hair by rinsing it with Maxwell House Coffee for a rich and shiny color.

- **Mrs. Stewart's Liquid Bluing.** Adding a couple of drops of Mrs. Stewart's Liquid Bluing to the rinse water when washing gray or white hair eliminates yellowing and gives hair a lush whiteness that products made especially for this purpose cannot achieve. Mrs. Stewart's Liquid Bluing is perfectly safe, and a few drops cost less than a penny.

- **ReaLemon.** To create blond highlights, rinse your hair with one-quarter cup ReaLemon lemon juice in three-quarters cup water and, wearing sunscreen, sit in the sun until your hair dries. Lemon juice is a natural bleach.

- **7-Up.** Prevent the burning, itchy feeling from hair-coloring products by adding two tablespoons 7-Up to the formula before dyeing your hair.

STRANGE FACTS

- ◆ The Assyrians began dyeing their hair around 1500 B.C.E.

- ◆ The ancient Greeks revered light-colored hair, and most of their great heroes had golden-blond hair. Many dark-haired Greeks used soaps and alkaline bleaches imported from Phoenicia to lighten or redden their hair. Others dusted their hair with yellow flour, talc made from yellow pollen, and gold dust.

- ◆ Ancient Romans of the upper classes preferred dark hair, and elderly senators and consuls dyed their graying hair with a concoction made by boiling walnut shells and leeks. To prevent graying, men went to bed wearing a paste made from herbs and earthworms.

- ◆ Drawings depict early Saxon men with hair and beards dyed blue, red, green, and orange.

- ◆ In the 1600s, many Europeans erroneously believed that frequently combing gray hair with a lead comb could restore the hair to its original color.

- ◆ When England's Queen Elizabeth I dyed her hair bright reddish orange, thousands of her faithful subjects followed suit.

- During the sixteenth century, French aristocrats powdered their hair with perfumed wheat flour. By 1790, the French were powdering their hair with a wide assortment of colors, including blue, pink, and violet.

- In 1909, French chemist Eugène Schueller created the first safe, permanent, commercial hair dye, founding the French Harmless Hair Dye Company. A year later, he changed the company name to L'Orèal.

- In the 1937 classic movie *The Wizard of Oz*, when Dorothy, the Scarecrow, the Tin Man, and the Cowardly Lion enter the gates of the Emerald City, they discover the Horse of a Different Color, which

SIDE EFFECTS
WHOOPS!

AJAX
If you dye your hair too dark, wash your hair with a handful of Ajax cleansing powder to lighten the color, being careful not to get any in your eyes.

ALBERTO VO5 CONDITIONING HAIRDRESSING
To prevent hair coloring from dyeing your skin, rub a dab of Alberto VO5 Conditioning Hairdressing along your hairline on your forehead and around your ears.

CHAPSTICK
Rubbing ChapStick along your hairline before coloring your hair prevents hair coloring from dyeing the skin.

FANTASTIK
If you dye your hair too dark, wash your hair with Fantastik. Just spray Fantastik in

your hair, work it in well, then rinse. Be careful not to get any in your eyes. Repeat for up to four days and the hair coloring will lighten.

REYNOLDS WRAP
When dyeing your hair, wrap the ear pieces of your eyeglasses in Reynolds Wrap to avoid dyeing them.

SPIC AND SPAN
If you color your hair too dark, use Spic and Span diluted with water to remove the excess color. Be careful not to get any in your eyes.

VASELINE PETROLEUM JELLY
Prevent hair coloring from dyeing your skin by rubbing Vaseline Petroleum Jelly along your hairline before coloring your hair.

changes color from scene to scene. To achieve this special effect, stage-hands dyed white horses different colors by sponging them with Jell-O powder. The horses licked off most of the Jell-O between shots, making the scene difficult to shoot.

◆ In 1950, only 7 percent of women in the United States colored their hair.

◆ The advertising catchphrases "Does She or Doesn't She?" and "Only Her Hairdresser Knows for Sure," used to advertise Clairol hair dyes, popularized the idea of hair coloring.

◆ Executives at *Life* magazine, finding lewd connotations in the line "Does She or Doesn't She?" initially refused to run the advertisements for Clairol.

◆ Today, three out of four women in the United States color their hair.

Hair Gel

- **Barbasol Shaving Cream.** A small dab of Barbasol Shaving Cream combed through your hair will keep it in place. If you use a blow-dryer once you've applied shaving cream to your hair, you can make your hair stand up on end.

- **Budweiser.** Pour a can of Budweiser into a trigger-spray bottle and spray your hair lightly. The beer works just like hair spray to hold your hair in place. Of course, if you use too much beer in your hair and get pulled over by the police, you might have difficulty explaining why you smell like a brewery.

- **Close-Up Red Gel Toothpaste.** Squeeze a dollop of Close-Up gel and use it as hair gel to spike your hair. The red gel holds any hairstyle in place, making your head kissably fresh.

- **Coca-Cola.** Mix equal parts Coca-Cola and water in a trigger-spray bottle and shake well. After getting out of the shower or bath, spray a light coat of the diluted Coke over your hair to give your locks a tousled look.

- **Coppertone.** In a pinch, Coppertone sunscreen makes an excellent hair gel.

- **Domino Sugar.** Make an excellent hair-setting lotion by mixing one part Domino Sugar with two parts warm water in a trigger-spray bottle. Use it just like hair spray.

- **Elmer's Glue-All.** Pour a dollop of Elmer's Glue-All in the cupped palm of your hands, rub your hands together, and comb your fingers through your hair to apply the glue evenly to your hair. Comb your hair with the fine teeth of the comb to remove the excess glue. Style your hair to your liking and let the glue dry. This technique works particularly well for spiking hair. (Elmer's Glue-All is water soluble and washes out of hair with regular shampoo.)

- **Fruit of the Earth Aloe Vera Gel.** Mousse your hair with Fruit of the Earth Aloe Vera Gel. It doubles as an effective hairstyling gel.

- **Jell-O.** If you've got a hot date or big job interview and you're all out of mousse, hair spray, and styling gel, go to your refrigerator and grab a bowl of Jell-O. A little dab'll do ya. Just rub some Jell-O through your hair and comb. It works just like mousse. Or use a teaspoon of Jell-O powder dissolved in a cup of warm water. Jell-O comes in twenty-five flavors, giving you a nice variety to work with. (Topping the Jell-O in your hair with whipped cream is optional.)

- **Phillips' Milk of Magnesia.** Mix two tablespoons Phillips' Milk of Magnesia in one cup water in a trigger-spray bottle. Spray the setting liquid in your hair, comb well to spread the solution equally, then set your hair, and let it dry.

- **Vaseline Petroleum Jelly.** After brushing your hair, rub a dab of Vaseline Petroleum Jelly between your palms and then run your hands through your hair for an amazing shine.

STRANGE FACTS

- ◆ The average person has 150,000 hairs on his or her head.

- ◆ The British did not comb their hair until the Danish invaded in 789 C.E. and began teaching the English living on the coast to comb their hair regularly.

- ◆ Clairol introduced its Mist Stick curling iron in Germany only to discover that in German the word *mist* is slang for "manure."

- ◆ In the 1998 comedy movie *There's Something about Mary*, starring Ben Stiller, co-star Cameron Diaz mistakes a bodily fluid for hair gel.

Hand Cleanser

FOOD-COLORING STAINS:
- **Colgate Toothpaste.** A dab of Colgate Toothpaste removes food coloring from hands and Kool-Aid mustaches from kids' faces.

GARLIC AND ONION ODORS:
- **Arm & Hammer Baking Soda.** Fill the cupped palm of your hand with Arm & Hammer Baking Soda, rub the powder all over your hands, then rinse clean to remove the smell of garlic or onions.

- **Heinz White Vinegar.** To get rid of the smell of garlic or onions on your hands, pour Heinz Vinegar (white or apple cider) over your hands, rubbing them together well, and then rinse them with water.

- **Huggies Baby Wipes.** After chopping garlic or onions, clean your hands with Huggies Baby Wipes to remove the smell from your skin.

- **Morton Salt.** To remove the stench of garlic or onion odor from hands, wet your hands and rub one teaspoon Morton Salt between them, concentrating on fingertips and nails.

- **ReaLemon.** Lemon juice removes garlic, onion, and fish odors from your hands. Simply rub the citrus juice on your skin, then rinse it with water.

PAINT AND GREASE:
- **Crisco All-Vegetable Shortening.** Instead of using caustic chemicals to clean paint and grease from hands, keep a tub of Crisco All-Vegetable Shortening in the garage or workshop. A dab rubbed between your hands

dissolves paint and grease, and—unlike turpentine, acetone, or mineral spirits—Crisco moisturizes your skin.

- **Johnson's Baby Oil.** Massage a few drops of Johnson's Baby Oil into your grease- or paint-covered hands, and then wash them with soap and water. The grease and paint will wash right off.

- **Land O Lakes Butter.** Need an emergency hand cleanser that is both effective and nontoxic? Open the refrigerator, grab a stick of Land O Lakes Butter, and rub a small chunk between your hands, then wash them with soap and water. The butter not only cleans your hands, but leaves them smelling like popcorn.

- **Miracle Whip.** Rubbing a dollop of Miracle Whip on your skin will remove grease, grime, and paint—and moisturize your skin at the same time.

- **Morton Salt.** To clean grease from hands, lather up your hands with soap, then sprinkle a generous amount of Morton Salt into your cupped palm, and continue scrubbing. Salt breaks down greases, and the grit makes for an abrasive scrub.

- **Pam Cooking Spray.** Rather than using caustic solvents like turpentine, acetone, and mineral spirits to clean paint and grease from hands, simply spray your hands with Pam Cooking Spray. Rub the vegetable oil into your skin, and then wash with ordinary soap and water. The cooking oil also moisturizes your skin.

- **Star Olive Oil** and **Domino Sugar.** Pour a dollop of Star Olive Oil into the cupped palm of your hand followed by an equal amount of Domino Sugar. Gently rub your hands together for several minutes, then rinse them thoroughly and dry. The olive oil removes paint and grease with help from the abrasive grit of the sugar—leaving your hands clean, soft, and moisturized.

- **WD-40.** If you get your hands covered with grease or paint, simply spray WD-40 on your hands, wipe your hands clean with a paper towel, and wash them thoroughly with soap and water.

- **Wesson Corn Oil** and **Dawn.** Pour equal amounts Wesson Corn Oil and Dawn Dishwashing Liquid into your cupped palm, scrub yourself with the mixture, and then rinse with water. The unusual combination of vegetable oil and dishwashing detergent cleanses the pores and leaves hands soft and moist.

Strange Facts

◆ Around 2000 B.C.E., the Hittites washed their hands with the ash of the soapwort plant and water.

◆ Around 600 B.C.E., the Phoenicians blended goat fat with wood ash to make the world's first soap, introducing the cleansing product to the Greeks and Romans.

◆ During World War I, when an Allied blockade prevented Germany from importing the natural fats used to make soaps, German chemists H. Gunther and M. Hetzer developed a wartime substitute—the first commercial detergent. Detergent had been invented in 1890 by German chemist A. Krafft.

◆ Unlike soaps, detergents do not leave behind soap scum or bathtub rings or cause yellowing in fabrics.

◆ Murphy's Oil Soap is the product most commonly used to clean elephants.

◆ The process for making soap is called saponification.

Hangover

- **Alka-Seltzer.** Dissolve two Alka-Seltzer tablets in a glass of water and drink the resulting fizzy liquid before going to bed to help lessen the effects of a hangover in the morning. Alcohol dehydrates your body cells, but the water rehydrates the body and the aspirin in Alka-Seltzer prevents the onslaught of a headache.

- **Campbell's Chicken Noodle Soup.** A bowl of Campbell's Chicken Noodle Soup helps replace the salt and potassium lost as a result of alcohol consumption.

- **Campbell's Tomato Juice.** Drink a glass of tomato juice. The fructose accelerates the body's ability to burn alcohol, flushing it from the body faster.

- **Gatorade.** Alcohol dehydrates the body, resulting in a hangover with a wicked headache. Drinking Gatorade throughout the day of the hangover replaces electrolytes (the potassium and salt lost through perspiration) and relieves headache pain almost immediately.

- **Hershey's Milk Chocolate.** Eating a Hershey's bar replenishes the amino acids that have been depleted from your body by the alcohol. Chocolate also contains caffeine, an ingredient also found in some pain relievers, which helps pep you up a bit.

- **Maxwell House Coffee.** Drink a couple of cups of Maxwell House Coffee. Coffee acts as a vasoconstrictor, reducing the swelling of blood vessels that causes headache.

- **SueBee Honey** and **Krispy Original Saltine Crackers**. Honey is a concentrated source of fructose. Eating SueBee Honey on Krispy Original Saltine Crackers helps your body flush out whatever alcohol remains in the body.

- **Tang.** Drinking a tall glass of Tang helps relieve a hangover—thanks to the vitamin C.

STRANGE FACTS

- ◆ As early as the sixth century B.C.E., the Greeks originated the custom of drinking to the health of a relative or friend so the host could publicly sip the wine first to reassure guests that it had not been poisoned.

- ◆ Ancient Romans originated the custom of dropping a piece of burnt toast into a cup of wine so the charcoal would reduce the acidity of inferior wine, mellowing the flavor. The combination of adding toast to wine and drinking to the health of a friend or relative gave birth to the phrase "making a toast."

- ◆ In the fifteenth century, amethyst was believed to cure drunkenness.

- ◆ In the eighteenth century, the British began making toasts to people who were not present, frequently beautiful women, making them the "toast of the town."

- ◆ "There is an old-time toast which is golden for its beauty," wrote Mark Twain in *Pudd'nhead Wilson's New Calendar*. "'When you ascend the hill of prosperity may you not meet a friend.'"

- ◆ W. C. Fields said, "A woman drove me to drink and I never even had the courtesy to thank her."

- ◆ Drama critic George Jean Nathan said, "I drink to make other people interesting."

- ◆ According to *Guinness World Records*, White Horse Scotch Whiskey makes the smallest bottles of liquor now sold in the world. The bottles are two inches high and contain 1.184 milliliters (less than one-eighth teaspoon).

- ◆ Typical toasts include "Bottoms up," "Here's mud in your eye," "Cheers," "Down the hatch," "*Skoal*," "*Prosit*," "*À votre santé*," "*Salud*," "*L'chiam*," "*Nazdorov'e*," and "Here's looking at you."

Headache

- **BenGay.** Rub a small dab of BenGay into your forehead, temples, and the back of your neck. The heat from the salve will gently soothe your pain.

- **Gatorade.** Headaches are frequently a symptom of dehydration. Drinking two glasses of Gatorade replaces electrolytes (the potassium and salt lost through perspiration) and relieves headache pain almost immediately.

- **Lipton Tea Bags.** Use two Lipton Tea Bags in one cup hot water for twenty minutes. Drinking this very strong cup of tea will relieve a migraine headache.

- **Maxwell House Coffee.** Drink a couple of cups of Maxwell House Coffee. Coffee acts as a vasoconstrictor, reducing the swelling of blood vessels that causes headache.

- **McCormick Basil Leaves, Aunt Jemima Original Syrup**, and **Mr. Coffee Filters.** Bring three cups water to a boil, pour into a ceramic teapot, and add one teaspoon ground basil. Cover and let steep for thirty minutes. Strain through a Mr. Coffee Filter, if necessary. Drink as tea. Sweeten to taste with Aunt Jemima Original Syrup.

- **Ziploc Freezer Bags.** Applying an ice pack to your head relieves headache pain. Fill a Ziploc Freezer Bag with water and freeze it or fill it with ice cubes. Wrap the ice pack in a paper towel before applying. For other ways to make and apply an ice pack, see page 198.

Don't be hard-headed! If your headache doesn't go away after a day or two, head for your doctor.

STRANGE FACTS

◆ The average man's brain weighs forty-nine ounces. The average woman's brain weighs forty-four ounces.

◆ Shortly after the Bayer Company started marketing heroin, its new morphine-derived painkiller, in 1898, doctors began prescribing heroin to treat headaches. In 1924, the United States banned the manufacture of heroin, but by then there were plenty of addicts to create a demand for heroin on the black market.

◆ In 1949, Portuguese neurosurgeon Antonio de Egas Moniz received the Nobel Prize in medicine for originating the prefrontal lobotomy, a barbaric surgical procedure in which parts of the front of the brain are removed to correct severe personality disorders. American neurologist Walter Freeman and American neurosurgeon James Watts popularized the lobotomy (frequently performed with a rudimentary ice pick) and claimed that the operation—despite its dubious results—separated the prefrontal lobes ("the rational brain") from the thalamic brain ("the emotional brain"). By 1955, after more than fifty thousand people in the United States had received lobotomies, leaving them sluggish and lethargic, critics correctly labeled the irreversible operation "mutilation" and the lobotomy was finally seen for what it really is—a sadistic form of restraint, not a cure. Surprisingly, the Soviet Union, teeming with psychiatric abuse, had stopped giving patients lobotomies four years earlier.

◆ While playing golf in 1970, Vice President Spiro Agnew hit professional golfer Doug Sanders in the head with a golf ball. A year later, Agnew hit a husband and wife with one shot.

◆ The lot numbers for the cyanide-tainted Tylenol capsules scare in 1982 were MC2880 and 1910MD.

◆ "Not tonight, I have a headache" is possibly the most well-known and well-used excuse of all time.

THE HEADS-UP ON BAYER ASPIRIN

The ancient Romans used the bark of the willow tree to fight fevers. The leaves and bark of the willow tree contain a substance called salicin, a naturally occurring compound similar to acetylsalicylic acid, the chemical name for aspirin.

In 1897, Felix Hoffmann, a German chemist working for the Farbenfabriken Bayer drug company, began seeking a way to treat his father's severe arthritic pain. Hoffmann researched acetylsalicylic acid, a drug first synthesized by French chemist Charles Frédéric von Gerhardt in 1853. Von Gerhardt had abandoned his discovery, convinced that salicin extract was more effective. Hoffmann, however, tested the acetylsalicylic acid on his father, alleviating his pain and reducing the swelling. The Bayer company decided to market the new drug, producing it from the meadowsweet plant, known by the scientific name *Spiraea ulmaria*, and calling the product Aspirin, a brand name derived from the letter *a* from *acetyl*, *spir* from *spiraea*, and the common medical suffix *-in*. By 1899, the Bayer Company was providing aspirin to physicians.

After Germany's defeat in World War I, the Allies forced Bayer to give up both trademarks as part of Germany's war reparations. At the Treaty of Versailles in 1919, Germany gave Bayer's trademark on aspirin to France, England, Russia, and the United States—enabling other manufacturers to make and distribute the drug.

IN 400 B.C.E., Greek physician Hippocrates prescribed the bark and leaves of the willow tree to relieve pain and fever.

BAYER ASPIRIN was originally marketed in 1899 as a powder to be mixed in a beverage. Bayer did not introduce aspirin tablets until 1900.

BAYER, FOUNDED BY FRIEDRICH BAYER in 1863 to develop synthetic dyes, became a pioneer in the modern German chemical industry—developing the first synthetic pesticide in 1892, synthetic rubber in 1915, a treatment for African sleeping sickness in 1921, and the first sulfa drug in 1935.

ASPIRIN IS the best-selling drug worldwide.

IN 1948, Dr. Lawrence Craven, a general practitioner in California, noticed that the four hundred men to whom he prescribed aspirin had not suffered any heart attacks. He regularly recommended to all patients that "an aspirin a day" could dramatically reduce the risk of heart attack.

THE MEDICINE KITS taken to the moon by the Apollo astronauts included Bayer Aspirin tablets.

IN 1988, the Food and Drug Administration approved aspirin for reducing the risk of heart second attack, preventing first myocardial infarction in patients with unstable angina, and preventing ministrokes in men.

IN A 1996 NATIONAL SURVEY on inventions, conducted by MIT, twice as many people chose aspirin over the personal computer as an invention they could not live without.

Heartburn

- **Canada Dry Ginger Ale.** Drinking Canada Dry Ginger Ale helps relieve an upset stomach. The ginger seems to absorb the gastric acid.

- **French's Mustard.** Aid digestion by using French's Mustard as a condiment and cooking ingredient. Mustard's properties for aiding digestion have never been disputed.

- **Heinz Apple Cider Vinegar.** Mix two teaspoons Heinz Apple Cider Vinegar in one cup water, and sip it during your meal. In many cases, heartburn is caused by low stomach acid, and the acetic acid in the vinegar corrects this inadequacy.

- **Phillips' Milk of Magnesia.** A tablespoon of Phillips' Milk of Magnesia helps relieve heartburn by quelling the acids in your stomach.

- **Uncle Ben's Converted Brand Rice.** Eating Uncle Ben's Converted Brand Rice, a food high in complex carbohydrates, absorbs acid in the stomach, relieving heartburn.

 Take heart! Most problems with heartburn are mild and occasional. However, if you have severe or daily discomfort or difficulty swallowing, see your doctor.

- **Wrigley's Spearmint Gum.** To relieve heartburn, chew a stick of Wrigley's Spearmint Gum. The act of chewing gum stimulates the production of saliva, which neutralizes stomach acid and corrects the flow of digestive juices. Spearmint also helps aid digestion.

STRANGE FACTS

- The medical term for heartburn is *pyrosis*, from the Greek root *pyr*, meaning "fire" or "heat."

- Heartburn has absolutely nothing to do with the heart. Heartburn is a burning sensation behind your breastbone caused when a muscle—the lower esophageal sphincter—malfunctions and lets gastric acid flow up from the stomach into the esophagus.

- Gastric acid in the stomach is almost as strong as battery acid.

- Approximately 25 million Americans get heartburn every day. That's roughly one out of every ten people.

- The 1986 movie *Heartburn*, written by Nora Ephron and directed by Mike Nichols (and based on Ephron's novel of the same name), starred Jack Nicholson and Meryl Streep as a mismatched married couple.

- In Italian, heartburn is *bruciore di stòmaco*, meaning "stomach burn."

Hemorrhoids

- **Baby Magic Baby Powder.** After toweling yourself dry from a shower or after finishing a bowel movement, gently powder your bum with Baby Magic Baby Powder. This will help reduce friction during the day, preventing further irritation.

- **Dannon Yogurt.** Use a cotton ball to apply Dannon Yogurt to the rectal zone. The yogurt soothes the burning pain of hemorrhoids and the live cultures in yogurt kill the bacteria in yeast infections, which cause rectal itching.

- **Desitin.** Applying a dab of Desitin, used to relieve diaper rash, also soothes the burning pain of hemorrhoids—thanks to the zinc oxide in the ointment.

- **Dickinson's Witch Hazel** and **Stayfree Maxi Pads.** Use Dickinson's Witch Hazel to saturate a Stayfree Maxi Pad, then press the pad against the rectum, leaving it in place for ten minutes to cool the hemorrhoid.

- **Huggies Baby Wipes.** Use unscented Huggies Baby Wipes as gentle, frictionless toilet paper to avoid aggravating sensitive hemorrhoids. Don't flush the baby wipe—it could clog the toilet.

- **Jif Peanut Butter.** In a pinch, a dab of Jif Peanut Butter will soothe hemorrhoids when used as an ointment. The oils in the peanut butter provide the relief. (To avoid further irritation, avoid the chunky.)

- **Kellogg's Raisin Bran.** Eating one cup Kellogg's Raisin Bran every morning adds seven grams of all-important fiber to your diet, preventing hemorrhoids in the first place by helping your body produce soft bowel movements.

- **Noxzema.** Originally developed as a sunburn ointment, Noxzema relieves burning pain—especially when applied to a hemorrhoid.

- **Orajel.** This topical pain reliever for toothache pain doubles as highly effective anti-itch and pain relief ointment for hemorrhoid discomfort by numbing the area. Simply apply directly.

- **Orville Redenbacher's Gourmet Popping Corn.** Eating thirty grams of fiber daily, found in foods such as popcorn, softens bowel movements, preventing the straining that incites hemorrhoids.

- **Vaseline Petroleum Jelly.** Lubricating an inch inside your rectum with Vaseline Petroleum Jelly before each bowel movement will help the stool pass through without damaging your anus.

STRANGE FACTS

- ◆ Eighty percent of all Americans have hemorrhoids during their lifetime.

- ◆ Hemorrhoids are simply varicose veins in the anus.

- ◆ Napoleon reportedly suffered from hemorrhoids. Some historians claim that the pain contributed to his defeat at the Battle of Waterloo.

- ◆ In 1879, British manufacturer Walter Alcock invented the world's first roll of perforated toilet paper and spent the next ten years trying to mass-produce and market it in prudish Victorian England.

- ◆ In the 1880s, American paper manufacturers Edward and Clarence Scott marketed the first roll of toilet paper in the United States, sold in plain brown wrappers. Eventually the product was named Scott Tissue Toilet Paper.

- ◆ Before the advent of toilet paper, Americans used old mail-order catalogs, newspapers, and fliers as reading material and toilet paper.

- ◆ During the 1990 primary campaign for Florida governor, Democratic candidate Bill Nelson, in an attempt to force his opponent, Lawton Chiles, to reveal all his health records, disclosed that he had once had hemorrhoids. Chiles won the election.

THE SCOOP ON KELLOGG'S

In the 1890s, Dr. John Harvey Kellogg directed the Adventist Battle Creek Sanitarium in Battle Creek, Michigan. As a Seventh-Day Adventist, Kellogg invented various health foods based on Adventist beliefs in health care, with help from his brother, William Keith Kellogg. While trying to invent a more digestible form of bread, the brothers ran dried wheat dough through rollers, accidentally inventing Granola, a cereal they served to patients at the sanitarium.

THE KELLOGG BROTHERS were the sons of a broom maker.

THE KELLOGG BROTHERS invented peanut butter, but failed to patent it.

C. W. POST, a former patient of the Kellogg brothers at the Battle Creek Sanitarium, launched Grape-Nuts, a cereal similar to Granola.

ALTHOUGH HE INVENTED Granola, Dr. John Harvey Kellogg breakfasted daily on seven graham crackers.

IN 1928, the Kellogg Company introduced Kellogg's Rice Krispies as "The Talking Cereal." In 1933, a year after the phrase "Snap! Crackle! Pop!" was printed on the box, a tiny, nameless gnome wearing a baker's hat appeared on the side of the box. He eventually became known as Snap, and in the mid-1930s he was joined by Crackle (wearing a red-striped stocking cap) and Pop (in a military hat). Snap, Crackle, and Pop are the Kellogg Company's oldest cartoon characters.

THE AVERAGE AMERICAN CUPBOARD contains four different brands of cereal.

THE KELLOGG COMPANY makes twelve of the top fifteen cereals in the world, including All-Bran, Froot Loops, Corn Flakes, Raisin Bran, Rice Krispies, and Special K.

IN FRONT OF THE KELLOGG FACTORY in Battle Creek, Michigan, stands a giant statue of Tony the Tiger.

IN 1964, Kellogg and the Post Cereal Company, eager to cash in on the concept of freeze-dried foods popularized by the space program, added freeze-dried fruits to their corn flake cereals. However, consumers quickly discovered that the pieces of freeze-dried fruit in the corn flakes had to soak in milk for nearly ten minutes before they reconstituted, by which time the corn flakes were soggy and unappetizing.

IN 1986, the Kellogg Company stopped giving tours of its Battle Creek factory to prevent industrial spies from unearthing its secret recipes.

WILLIAM KELLOGG WAS OBSESSED with the number seven. Born the seventh son to a seventh son on the seventh day of the week on the seventh day of the month with a last name seven letters long, Kellogg always booked hotel rooms on the seventh floor and insisted that his Michigan license plates end in a seven—which fails to explain the introduction of Kellogg's Product 19. It is not known whether Kellogg drank 7-Up.

Herpes

- **Castor Oil.** Fold a wool flannel cloth in half, saturate with one cup castor oil, place on your belly, cover with a piece of plastic, and then apply a heating pad set on the highest setting you can handle, and let sit for an hour. Repeat daily for the first month, then three times a week. Increase the number of treatments during a herpes attack. According to some doctors, castor oil packs strengthen your immune system, which then keeps the herpes virus from acting up.

- **Conair Pro Style 1600 Hairdryer.** If toweling dry after a bath or shower causes pain to the sores on your private parts, hold a blow dryer set on low warm about a foot away from your body and gently dry your genitals. The warm air from the blow dryer may also help dry out the lesions.

- **Fruit of the Earth Aloe Vera Gel.** Apply a dab of Fruit of the Earth Aloe Vera Gel to the affected area and cover with a small dressing like gauze to hold the aloe gel in place.

STRANGE FACTS

- ◆ There is no cure for genital herpes.

- ◆ Genital herpes is a sexually transmitted disease caused by a virus known as herpes simplex 2—not to be confused with the virus herpes simplex 1, which causes cold sores.

- Every year an estimated 500,000 Americans contract genital herpes.

- Forty percent of people infected with herpes never have any recurrences of the disease after the initial outbreak. The remaining sixty percent may have five or more outbreaks a year.

- Doctors have discovered that people infected with herpes who have diets high in lysine and low in arginine tend to have fewer outbreaks.

- German composer Ludwig Beethoven, Italian explorer Christopher Columbus, English explorer Captain James Cook, American general George Armstrong Custer, French Emperor Napoleon Bonaparte, French impressionist Paul Gaugin, Russian Tsar Peter the Great, German philosopher Friedrich Nietzsche, and American gangster Al Capone all had syphilis.

- According to the Bible, King Solomon had seven hundred wives and somewhere between sixty and three hundred mistresses.

- In his memoirs, Italian adventurer Giovanni Giacomo Casanova claimed that he seduced thousands of women.

- Russian Tsarina Catherine the Great had more than eighty lovers and advocated having sex six times a day.

- Russian mystic Rasputin seduced hundreds of women from all walks of life.

- When asked how she wrote her memoirs, Mae West replied, "I do my best work in bed."

Hiccups

- **Domino Sugar.** One effective folklore remedy for getting rid of the hiccups is to swallow a heaping teaspoon of Domino Sugar—dry, without water. The texture of the sugar seems to reprogram the nerve receptors that control the diaphragm.

- **Heinz Apple Cider Vinegar.** Many people cure hiccups by drinking one teaspoon Heinz Apple Cider Vinegar stirred into one cup warm water.

- **Jif Peanut Butter.** For many people, eating one heaping spoonful Jif Peanut Butter is a definite cure for the hiccups.

- **ReaLemon.** A little-known cure for the hiccups is to quickly swallow a jigger of ReaLemon lemon juice. The sour taste of lemon may shock the diaphragm's nerves out of spasm.

STRANGE FACTS

- ◆ There is no surefire cure for the hiccups, nor do doctors know what causes hiccups.

- ◆ The Ancient Greek philosopher Plato insisted that the cure for hiccups was to gargle while holding your breath.

- ◆ Hiccups are involuntary contractions of the diaphragm.

◆ Men get hiccups more often than women.

◆ Twenty-eight-year-old Charles Osborne of Anthon, Iowa, started hiccuping in 1922 and continued hiccuping every 1.5 seconds until February 1990. He died the following year.

◆ Most doctors agree that the worst time to get the hiccups is while a patient is undergoing surgery.

Hives

- **Dickinson's Witch Hazel.** Chill a bottle of Dickinson's Witch Hazel in the freezer for fifteen minutes, then use a cotton ball to apply this astringent to the hives.

- **Listerine.** Use a cotton ball to apply the antiseptic astringent Listerine to your hives to stop the itching.

- **McCormick Cream of Tartar.** Make a paste of water and McCormick Cream of Tartar and apply to the hives. When the paste crumbles off, reapply.

- **Pepto-Bismol.** Apply Pepto-Bismol, a pink alkaline liquid, to your hives to temporarily relieve the itch.

- **Phillips' Milk of Magnesia.** Dab Phillips' Milk of Magnesia on your hives. The alkalinity helps relieve the itch.

- **Ziploc Freezer Bags.** Holding an ice pack against the hives soothes the itching. Fill a Ziploc Freezer Bag with water and freeze it or fill it with ice cubes. Wrap the ice pack in a paper towel before applying. For other ways to make and apply an ice pack, see page 198.

STRANGE FACTS

♦ In the Marx Brothers' 1930 movie *Animal Crackers*, Mrs. Rittenhouse's butler is named Hives.

- The scientific name for hives is *urticaria*.

- Hives is the skin version of an allergic attack, caused when the irritated cells release histamine. Histamine causes blood vessels to leak fluid in deep layers of the skin.

- In A. A. Milne's children's book *Winnie the Pooh*, Pooh Bear uses a blue balloon to ascend to a beehive in a tall tree, convinced that the bees will mistake him for a cloud. The bees swarm after him.

- In German, hives are called *Nesselsucht*.

- In the 1962 movie *That Touch of Mink*, Cary Grant stars as millionaire businessman Philip Shayne, whose attempts to woo inexperienced Cathy Timberlake (played by Doris Day) cause the young lady to break out in hives. In the end, the couple marries and goes off on a honeymoon, where Philip breaks out in hives.

- The Hives are a Swedish rock band from Fagersta, Sweden.

Ice Packs

MAKING:

- **Green Giant Sweet Peas.** Use a plastic bag of frozen Green Giant Sweet Peas as an ice pack. If the bag of peas feels too cold, put a paper towel between your skin and the bag. The sack of peas conforms to the contours of your body, and you can refreeze the peas for future ice-pack use—just label the bag for ice-pack use only. If you want to eat the peas, cook them after they thaw the first time, never after refreezing.

- **Jell-O and Ziploc Freezer Bags.** Prepare Jell-O according to the directions on the box and let cool enough to pour into a Ziploc Freezer Bag until three-quarters full. Seal the bag securely and freeze, and you have a homemade, flexible ice pack. When the Jell-O melts, simply refreeze.

- **Orville Redenbacher's Gourmet Popping Corn and Ziploc Freezer Bags.** Pour one cup unpopped kernels of corn into a small Ziploc Freezer Bag, and place it in the freezer to make an ice pack that easily conforms to your body.

- **Playtex Living Gloves.** Fill a Playtex Living Glove with ice, tie the cuff securely to prevent leaks, and freeze. Use the frozen glove as an ice pack.

- **Scotch-Brite Heavy Duty Scrub Sponge and Ziploc Freezer Bags.** Saturate a sponge with water, slip it inside a Ziploc Freezer Bag, and keep it in the freezer as a ready-made ice pack.

- **Smirnoff Vodka, Ziploc Freezer Bags, and McCormick Food Coloring.** Pour one-half cup Smirnoff Vodka and one-half cup water into a Ziploc Freezer

Bag (add five drops of blue food coloring for easy identification), and freeze. The alcohol doesn't freeze, but the water does—giving you a slushy, refreezable ice pack.

- **Stayfree Maxi Pads** and **Ziploc Freezer Bags.** Saturate a Stayfree Maxi Pad with water, slip it inside a Ziploc Freezer Bag, and keep it in the freezer as a ready-made ice pack.

- **Trojan Condoms.** In a pinch, you can fill a Trojan Condom with water (making a relatively large water balloon), tie a knot in the end, and freeze.

USING:
- **Bounty Paper Towels.** To protect the skin when using an ice pack, wrap the ice pack in a Bounty Paper Towel.

- **L'eggs Sheer Energy Panty Hose.** To protect the skin when using an ice pack, cut off one leg from a pair of L'eggs Sheer Energy Panty Hose and slip the ice pack inside.

STRANGE FACTS

- ◆ Approximately one-tenth of the earth's surface is permanently covered with ice. If all the ice melted, the sea would rise by about two hundred feet and many of the world's largest cities—including New York, Los Angeles, London, and Tokyo—would be underwater.

- ◆ Ice floats because expansion makes it lighter than water.

- ◆ Ice skating was invented as a form of winter transportation, most likely by the Scandinavians, who fashioned skates from the bones of elk, ox, and reindeer some two thousand years ago.

- ◆ In 1876, the Glaciarium, the world's first mechanically refrigerated ice skating rink, opened in London, on King's Road, Chelsea.

- ◆ The slang word for diamonds is "ice."

- ◆ In 1946, playwright Eugene O'Neill wrote *The Iceman Cometh.*

- ◆ On the 1960s television series *Batman*, the role of cold-blooded villain Mr. Freeze was played by George Sanders, Otto Preminger, and

Eli Wallach. In the 1997 movie *Batman and Robin*, Arnold Schwarzenegger starred as Mr. Freeze. The character was based on Mr. Zero, a villain who first appeared in a February 1959 *Batman* comic book.

◆ "Breaking the ice" means to initiate conversation, "cutting no ice" means failing to impress, "putting something on ice" means to suspend a course of action for the time being, and "walking on thin ice" means being in a precarious situation.

Indigestion

- **Alka-Seltzer, Domino Sugar,** and **McCormick Vanilla Extract.** Drop two Alka-Seltzer tablets in a glass of water, then add one teaspoon Domino Sugar and a few drops of McCormick Vanilla Extract to improve the taste. The combination should settle your indigestion.

- **Arm & Hammer Baking Soda.** According to the instructions on the side of the box of Arm & Hammer Baking Soda, drinking one-half teaspoon baking soda dissolved in one-half glass water relieves indigestion. (Sodium bicarbonate does neutralize an acid stomach, but read the instructions on the side of the box carefully before using it.)

- **Canada Dry Ginger Ale.** Drink Canada Dry Ginger Ale to soothe indigestion and cause you to burp out the troubling gas. Ginger helps promote digestion.

- **Coca-Cola.** Open a can of Coca-Cola, let it sit until it goes flat (roughly thirty minutes), then drink the defizzed real thing. Coca-Cola was originally invented as an elixir to cure upset stomachs, and it still works. Letting the bubbles out of the soda prevents the carbonation from further upsetting your stomach.

- **Heinz Apple Cider Vinegar.** Drink one teaspoon Heinz Apple Cider Vinegar in one-half cup water for quick relief from an upset stomach. The vinegar adds acid to your stomach, which may soothe the pain by acidifying a stomach that is not producing enough gastric acid.

- **McCormick Cream of Tartar.** Dissolve one teaspoon McCormick Cream of Tartar in a glass of water and drink the solution. Cream of Tartar, the powdery residue found in wine casks, relieves gas in the stomach by producing burps.

- **Orville Redenbacher's Gourmet Popping Corn.** Eating fiber at the first sign of a stomachache can head off the problem. Orville Redenbacher Gourmet Popping Corn contains one gram of fiber in every one-cup serving.

- **SueBee Honey.** Taking two teaspoons SueBee Honey tends to relieve indigestion, perhaps because this sweet antibacterial inhibits the growth of such germs as *Salmonella*, *Shigella*, *E. coli*, and *V. cholerae* in the intestinal tract. (Honey should not be fed to infants under one year of age.)

STRANGE FACTS

- The word *gourmand* means "a person who enjoys good food but tends to overeat."

- Abraham Lincoln's mother, Nancy, died when the family dairy cow ate poisonous mushrooms and she drank the milk.

- The average American consumes 1,500 pounds of food each year.

- The lining of your digestive system is shed every three days.

- *Hara kiri* is an impolite way of saying the Japanese word *seppuku*, which literally means "belly splitting."

- The expression "give the cold shoulder," meaning to snub someone with indifference, originated during the Middle Ages when Europeans fed unwanted houseguests leftover beef shoulder to get them to leave.

- The phrase "If I'm wrong, I'll eat my hat" originally referred to an unpopular and revolting dish called hatte—made from a strange array of ingredients, usually eggs, veal, tongue, and kidney.

- Cows have four stomachs.

- Unless your stomach produces a new layer of mucus every two weeks, it will digest itself.

◆ In November 1974, plastic surgeon Howard Bellin performed a tummy tuck on Virginia O'Hare of Poughkeepsie, New York, and accidentally moved her belly button two inches off center. O'Hare sued for malpractice and settled for $200,000.

HAVE A COKE AND A SMILE

WHEN THE COCA-COLA COMPANY introduced Coke in China, the name was transliterated as Kekoukela, without any regard for the actual meaning of the sounds in Chinese. In different dialects, the phrase Kekoukela translates as "bite the wax tadpole" or "female horse stuffed with wax." The Coca-Cola Company then researched forty thousand characters to find the phonetic equivalent kokou kole, which translates to "happiness in the mouth."

THE PEOPLE OF NORTHERN IRELAND consume more Diet Coke per capita than the people of any other nation.

IN MARCH 1982, a Coca-Cola bottler in Cookeville, Tennessee, launched a contest in which players would win $100,000 if they collected bottle caps embossed with individual letters of the alphabet to spell out HOME RUN. The bottler ordered just a few bottle caps printed with the letter R so the chances of winning the contest would be a million to one. When huge numbers of winners began turning up, the bottler discovered that the printer had made 18,000 caps embossed with the letter R—costing the bottler more than $100,000 in prize awards before the bottler backed out of the contest.

Insect Bites

- **A.1. Steak Sauce.** Relieve itching from insect bites by applying A.1. Steak Sauce over the affected area.

- **Adolph's Meat Tenderizer.** Make a paste of Adolph's Meat Tenderizer and water, and immediately apply to the sting. The enzymes in meat tenderizer break down the proteins in insect venom.

- **Alka-Seltzer.** Dissolve two Alka-Seltzer tablets in a glass of water, saturate a cotton ball with the mixture, and place it on the bite for twenty minutes (unless you are allergic to aspirin, an ingredient in Alka-Seltzer).

- **Arm & Hammer Baking Soda.** Make a paste of Arm & Hammer Baking Soda and water, apply it to the affected area, and let it dry. The sodium bicarbonate neutralizes the alkalinity, eliminating the itch.

- **Ban Antiperspirant.** Applying Ban Antiperspirant to mosquito bites helps stop the itching. Aluminum chloride, the drying compound in the anti-perspirant, seems to dry up the insect secretions in the skin.

- **Bayer Aspirin.** Wet the skin and rub a Bayer Aspirin tablet over the bite to help control inflammation (unless you are allergic to aspirin).

- **BenGay.** Applying BenGay to a mosquito or flea bite provides instant relief. The heat and menthol seem to scratch the itch for you.

- **Betty Crocker Potato Buds.** Mix Betty Crocker Potato Buds with enough water to make a thick paste and apply to the bite.

- **Carnation NonFat Dry Milk.** Mix five ounces Carnation NonFat Dry Milk and twelve ounces water in a mixing bowl, fill the rest of the bowl with ice cubes, and sprinkle two tablespoons salt over the ice. Saturate a washcloth with the milk, and apply to the infected area as a compress for twenty minutes, three or four times daily.

- **Colgate Toothpaste.** Applying a dab of Colgate Regular Flavor Toothpaste to insect bites (especially from fire ants) relieves the itch instantly.

- **Coppertone.** Applying Coppertone sunscreen to insect bites alleviates the itching.

- **Epsom Salt.** Dissolve one tablespoon Epsom Salt in one quart hot water. Chill, and then dip a clean, soft cloth into the solution and place it on the bite for twenty minutes.

- **Fruit of the Earth Aloe Vera Gel.** Apply Fruit of the Earth Aloe Vera Gel to the affected area to relieve the stinging pain and soothe the skin.

- **Heinz White Vinegar.** Use a cotton ball to dab mosquito and other bug bites with Heinz White Vinegar straight from the bottle.

- **Ivory Soap.** Wet a bar of Ivory Soap and gently rub it over the insect bite to relieve the itching.

- **Lay's Potato Chips.** Grind up Lay's Potato Chips into a powder with a mortar and pestle, add enough water to make a paste, and apply to insect bites to relieve the itching.

- **Lipton Tea Bags.** Dampen a Lipton Tea Bag with warm water and press it on the bite. The tannic acid in the tea will soothe the pain and relieve swelling.

- **Listerine.** Saturate a cotton ball with Listerine and dab mosquito and other bug bites to help stop the itching.

- **McCormick Curry Powder.** Make a smooth paste of curry powder and water, immediately apply it to the insect bite, and let it dry to relieve the pain. This insect bite remedy is used by Ayurvedic healers in India.

- **Miracle Whip.** Rub a dab of Miracle Whip on mosquito bites to relieve the itching.

- **Morton Salt.** Mix water with salt to make a thick paste, and apply the mixture to the bite.

- **Mrs. Stewart's Liquid Bluing.** In a booklet on treating snake and insect bites, the University of Arizona recommends using Mrs. Stewart's Liquid Bluing to treat the bite of a red harvester ant. The company has also received countless letters over the years reporting that a dab of Mrs. Stewart's Liquid Bluing immediately relieves the discomfort of a bee sting.

- **Orajel.** To relieve the itch from insect bites almost instantly, dab Orajel on the bite, numbing the area from pain.

- **Parsons' Ammonia.** Use a cotton ball to dab Parsons' Ammonia onto a mosquito bite, and the pain ceases almost immediately.

- **Phillips' Milk of Magnesia.** The antacid in Phillips' Milk of Magnesia helps this cool, white liquid—when dabbed on an insect bite—eliminate the itching.

- **Preparation H.** A dab of Preparation H soothes stings and reduces the swelling of welts from insect bites.

- **Rolaids.** Crush a Rolaids tablet, mix it with a little water to make a paste, and apply it to the bite. Within moments, the antacid should relieve the itching.

- **Skin-So-Soft.** Applying Skin-So-Soft over insect bites alleviates itching.

- **Tidy Cats.** Mix a handful of Tidy Cats with water to make a paste and apply to the sting and let dry. The clay in the cat box filler anesthetizes the sting.

- **Vicks VapoRub.** Coating insect bites with Vicks VapoRub instantly stops the itching—due to the ecalyptus and menthol in the salve.

- **Wish-Bone Thousand Island Dressing.** Applying a drop of Wish-Bone Thousand Island Dressing over the insect bite and rubbing it into the skin area alleviates itching.

- **Ziploc Freezer Bags.** Applying an ice pack to an insect bite anesthetizes the sting and prevents swelling. Fill a Ziploc Freezer Bag with water and freeze it or fill it with ice cubes. Wrap the ice pack in a paper towel before applying. For other ways to make and apply an ice pack, see page 198.

CHIGGERS:

- **Maybelline Crystal Clear Nail Polish.** Paint Maybelline Crystal Clear Nail Polish over chigger bites. The nail polish seals off the air, and the chiggers, burrowed into the skin, suffocate, putting a swift end to the itching.

- **Selsun Blue Dandruff Shampoo.** A few dabs of this blue dandruff shampoo on chigger bites stops the itching.

LEECHES:

- **Colgate Toothpaste.** Applying Colgate Toothpaste to a leech on your skin dries the creature, causing it to release its grip and fall off.

- **Morton Salt.** Sprinkling Morton Salt on the leech will kill it by reverse osmosis, causing the creature to fall off, shrivel up, and die.

STRANGE FACTS

- ◆ Mosquitoes of the genus *Anopheles* carry malarial parasites of the genus *Plasmodium*, and are believed to have caused an estimated 50 percent of all human deaths (excluding wars and accidents).

- ◆ In 1804, French chemist Armand Seguin erroneously concluded that the ingredient in the bark of the cinchona tree that cured malaria was gelatin. Seguin published his wrong findings, prompting physicians to treat their malaria patients with clarified glue. The ingredient in the cinchona bark that cures malaria is quinine.

- ◆ Ants do not chew their food. Instead, they move their jaws sideways, like scissors, to extract the juices from the food.

- ◆ Research indicates that mosquitoes are attracted to people who have recently eaten bananas.

- ◆ Mosquitoes do not live on the continent of Antarctica.

- ◆ In 1658, Puritan leader Oliver Cromwell, suffering from malaria, refused to take the cure—the bark of the cinchona tree—because he wrongly believed the bark remedy to be part of a Catholic plot to poison non-Catholics. Cromwell died of malaria.

Insect Repellent

- **Bounce.** Wearing a sheet of Bounce through a belt loop or the flap on the backside of a baseball cap repels mosquitoes and other insects. The fragrance in Bounce is oleander, a natural insect repellent. If one sheet of Bounce doesn't keep the insects away from you, insert more sheets in your other belt loops—turning yourself into an interesting fashion statement.

- **Clorox.** Before going outside, fill a bathtub with warm water, add two capfuls of Clorox Bleach, and soak in the solution for fifteen minutes (without getting the chlorinated water in your eyes).

- **Coppertone.** Slathering Coppertone on skin not only prevents sunburn, but the sunscreen also repels insects.

- **Johnson's Baby Oil.** Rubbing a thin coat of Johnson's Baby Oil on exposed skin creates a protective barrier against gnat bites.

- **L'eggs Sheer Energy Panty Hose.** To avoid leeches when walking through swampy areas, wear a pair of L'eggs Sheer Energy Panty Hose.

- **Listerine.** Rubbing Listerine over your body repels horseflies and other winged insects.

- **McCormick Garlic Powder.** Dousing your meals with garlic powder causes your body to give off a faint odor that insects find unpleasant.

- **Parsons' Ammonia.** To repel mosquitoes, kibbutzniks in Israel mix together one teaspoon ammonia and one-quarter cup rubbing alcohol and apply the solution to the skin.

- **Skin-So-Soft.** This skin cream also happens to double as the best mosquito repellent available, according to *Outdoor Life*, *Field and Stream*, and advice columnist Dear Abby.

- **Vicks VapoRub.** Apply Vicks VapoRub to your skin to repel insects, including mosquitoes. Insects hate the smell of Vicks VapoRub. (People also tend to dislike the smell of Vicks VapoRub, so you can also repel pesky neighbors, in-laws, and door-to-door salesmen.)

STRANGE FACTS

- The "Hazards to Humans—Warning" on the back of many commercial insect repellents reveals they often contain at least four ingredients that cause brain damage: butane, DEET, isobutane, and propane.

- The average housefly lives for one month.

- In his book *The Insects*, naturalist Url N. Lanham reports that female aphids are born pregnant.

- The praying mantis is the only insect that can turn its head.

- The world's termites outweigh the world's humans ten to one.

- In the 1954 sci-fi movie *Them*, starring Edmund Gwenn (best remembered for his role as Kris Kringle in *Miracle on 34th Street*), radiation from atomic bomb tests in the New Mexico desert causes a plague of colossal mutant ants.

- Scientists have discovered more than 900,000 different types of insects.

- Some insects taste with their feet, some have ears on their legs, and most smell with their antennae and breathe through holes in their sides.

- An ant can lift up to fifty times its weight.

- An insect's skeleton is on the outside of its body. The insect's muscles are attached to the inside of the skeletal wall.

Insomnia

- **Arm & Hammer Baking Soda.** Taking a warm, soothing bath an hour before going to bed relaxes the body and increases the deep stage of sleep. Dissolve one-half cup Arm & Hammer Baking Soda in a bathtub filled with warm water for a tranquilizing bath. For other ways to enhance a calming bath, see page 26.

- **McCormick Basil Leaves** and **Aunt Jemima Original Syrup.** Bring three cups water to a boil, pour it into a ceramic teapot, and add one level teaspoon basil. Cover the teapot and let the tea steep for thirty minutes. Sweeten to taste with Aunt Jemima Original Syrup. Drink an hour before bedtime.

- **SueBee Honey.** A teaspoon of honey at bedtime acts as a sedative to the nervous system—usually within an hour. (Honey should not be fed to infants under one year of age.)

- **Twinkies.** Having a small snack before bed, like a Twinkie, subdues hunger pangs that might otherwise keep you tossing and turning.

STRANGE FACTS

- ◆ The phrase "sleep tight" originated when mattresses rested on top of ropes woven through the bed frame. A bed key was used to tighten sagging ropes.

- The first written version of "Sleeping Beauty," published in *Pentamerone* by Italian Giambattista Basile in 1636, differs significantly from the version turned into an animated movie by Walt Disney. In the original story, a married nobleman discovers the sleeping princess, rapes her, and leaves. Nine months later, the sleeping beauty gives birth to twins—one of whom sucks the poison splinter from his unconscious mother's finger, waking her from slumber. When the nobleman's wife discovers her husband's indiscretion, she has the twins captured and orders her cook to kill them and bake them into a hash, which she feeds to her husband. When the vengeful wife learns that her cook actually freed the twins and cooked the hash from goat meat, she orders her henchmen to burn the twins' mother at the stake—prompting the nobleman to rescue her.

- In the children's fairy tale "The Princess and the Pea," by Hans Christian Andersen (1805–1875), a princess, sleeping on a tower made from twenty straw mattresses and twenty featherbeds with a single pea under the bottom mattress, tosses and turns all night, unable to get any sleep—proving that she really is royalty.

- On the night of June 5, 1944, German dictator Adolf Hitler took sleeping pills and gave orders that he not be woken. At dawn on June 6, 1944, the Allied Forces launched their D-day invasion of Normandy Beach with parachute landings. German General von Rundstedt immediately ordered two Panzer divisions to defend the region. However, German headquarters in Berlin ordered that Von Rundstedt halt the two Panzer divisions—until he received direct authorization from Adolf Hitler. When Hitler finally woke up, the Allies had won the invasion.

- Humans spend a third of their lives sleeping.

- Roosters do not crow only at dawn. They crow all the time to mark their territory and attract a mate. The crowing is more noticeable in the morning to people who do not wish to be roused from sleep.

- Fish sleep with their eyes open because they do not have eyelids.

- Armadillos sleep an average of 18.5 hours every day.

- When asked by reporters what she wore to bed, Marilyn Monroe smiled coyly and replied, "Chanel No. 5."

INSIDE TWINKIES

In 1930, during the Depression, Jimmy Dewar, manager of the Schiller Park Bakery near Chicago, saw a need for a new, low-priced product. Since pans used only during the six-week strawberry season to make "Little Short Cake Fingers" sat idle for most of the year, Dewar decided to inject the same cakes with a banana-cream filling and make them a year-round item that he would sell two for a nickel. On a business trip to St. Louis, Dewar saw a billboard advertising "Twinkle Toe" shoes, inspiring him to name his new cakes "Twinkies." In the 1940s, World War II created a banana shortage, prompting the company to replace the banana-cream filling in Twinkies with vanilla-cream filling.

BEGINNING IN 1930, Twinkie inventor Jimmy Dewar ate three Twinkies a day—until the day he died in 1981.

INTERSTATE BAKERIES CORPORATION, maker of Hostess Twinkies, also makes Wonder Bread.

HOSTESS BAKERIES can produce up to one thousand Twinkies per minute.

AMERICANS EAT more than five hundred million Twinkies every year.

IN THE 1950S, Howdy Doody, Buffalo Bob, and a cowhand named Twinkie the Kid praised Twinkies on the children's television show *The Howdy Doody Show*.

ON THE LANDMARK TELEVISION SERIES *All in the Family*, Archie Bunker insisted on having a Twinkie in his lunch box.

IN 1976, authorities in Kings Mill, Ohio, used Twinkies and bananas as bait to capture escaped baboons.

WHEN SAN FRANCISCO city supervisor Dan White stood trial for the 1978 murder of Mayor George Moscone and supervisor Harvey Milk, his lawyer insisted that White suffered from a "diminished mental capacity" because his diet consisted of candy bars and Twinkies.

IN 1980, Continental Baking celebrated the Twinkie's 50th birthday with a ten-foot-long Twinkie that weighed over a ton and was the equivalent of 32,300 regular Twinkies.

IN 1988, DC Comics celebrated Superman's fiftieth birthday with an eight-foot-tall cake made from Twinkies.

TWINKIES HAVE APPEARED in several movies, including *Ghostbusters*, *Grease*, *Die Hard*, and *Sleepless in Seattle*.

THE *NEW YORK TIMES* named Chicago the "Twinkie Capital of the World," because the average person in Chicago eats more Twinkies than citizens of any other American city.

BY 1997, Lewis Browning, having eaten one Twinkie every day since 1941, had consumed 20,440 Twinkies. He boasted: "Nobody likes Twinkies like I do!"

IN 1999, President Bill Clinton's administration selected the Twinkie as "an object of enduring American symbolism" to be included in the White House millennium time capsule.

Jellyfish Stings

- **Adolph's Meat Tenderizer.** Make sure whenever you go to the beach to take along Adolph's Meat Tenderizer. To relieve a jellyfish sting, dissolve the meat tenderizer in salt water and pat it on the affected area. The papain enzyme in meat tenderizer deactivates venom protein.

- **Arm & Hammer Baking Soda.** Applying a paste made from a tablespoon of Arm & Hammer Baking Soda and water to the jellyfish sting instantly kills the pain.

- **Barbasol Shaving Cream.** If you have difficulty removing jellyfish tentacles from your skin, apply a dab of Barbasol Shaving Cream, then scrape out the tentacles.

- **Clorox.** Pouring some Clorox Bleach onto a jellyfish sting eliminates the pain, disinfecting the venom. Once the pain dissipates, rinse thoroughly to remove the bleach from skin.

- **Coca-Cola.** Pouring the real thing over a jellyfish sting relieves the stinging pain. The acids in the Coke seem to neutralize the venom.

- **Heinz White Vinegar.** Pouring Heinz White Vinegar over the sting relieves the pain.

- **L'eggs Sheer Energy Panty Hose.** To avoid jellyfish stings in the first place, wear a pair of L'eggs Sheer Energy Panty Hose when swimming in the ocean.

- **MasterCard.** Remove jellyfish tentacles embedded in the skin by scraping with the edge of a credit card. Do not touch the tentacles with your bare hands. Otherwise, they'll sting your hands as well.

- **Parsons' Ammonia.** Neutralize a jellyfish sting by dabbing on Parsons' Ammonia.

- **Smirnoff Vodka.** If you don't have rubbing alcohol, splash Smirnoff Vodka over the affected area to disinfect and alleviate the sting.

- **Star Olive Oil.** Applying Star Olive Oil to jellyfish stings provides welcome relief.

STRANGE FACTS

- ◆ A jellyfish is 95 percent water.

- ◆ A type of jellyfish found off the coast of England is the longest animal in the world.

- ◆ In 1870, an Arctic jellyfish washed up in Massachusetts Bay with a bell diameter of seven feet, six inches, and tentacles stretching 120 feet.

- ◆ Australian box jellyfish (also known as sea wasps) have killed more than seventy people off the coast of Australia in the past one hundred years. Their poison is more deadly than any snake venom.

- ◆ Biologists refer to the jellyfish as a medusa. In Greek mythology, Medusa was a gorgon—a winged woman with snakes as hair. Anyone who looked at a gorgon was turned to stone.

- ◆ Some kinds of jellyfish are no larger than a pea.

- ◆ The *Polyorchis* jellyfish, found along the Pacific coast of the United States, glows like an electric lightbulb.

Kidney Stones

- **Country Time Lemonade.** Drinking a tall glass of Country Time Lemonade several times a day prevents kidney stones from forming. The citric acid in Country Time Lemonade prevents the calcium in bodily fluids from fusing together.

- **Mr. Coffee Filters** and **Kodak 35mm Film Canisters.** Carry several Mr. Coffee Filters in a Kodak 35mm Film Canister in your pocket. Urinate through the filter. If no stone passes, flush the filter. If you do pass a stone, put the filter and stone in the canister and take it to the doctor to determine the best course of treatment.

- **Ocean Spray Cranberry Juice Cocktail.** Cranberries help slow the formation of kidney stones and can help dissolve some calcium-type kidney stones. Drinking two glasses of Ocean Spray Cranberry Juice Cocktail every day acidifies the urine—perhaps dissolving the calcium oxalate that accumulates in the kidneys to form stones or possibly preventing bacteria from joining together to promote stones.

Leave no stone unturned! Once you pass a kidney stone, have your doctor evaluate it to determine what type of stone you have and which treatments are appropriate to prevent future attacks.

STRANGE FACTS

◆ Kidney stones are crystals of uric acid, calcium, phosphates, and other minerals that form in the urine.

◆ Men are four times more likely than women to get kidney stones.

◆ Eighty percent of all kidney stones are less than five millimeters in diameter and are fully capable of being squeezed through the ureter (the tube connecting the kidney with the bladder).

◆ In 1685, when English King Charles II fell ill from kidney disease, doctors detrimentally let blood, unnecessarily cut off his hair, pointlessly applied blistering agents on his scalp, and foolishly put plasters of pitch and pigeon dung on the bottom of his feet. They inflicted further harm by blowing the herb hellebore up his nose to make him sneeze nonexistent humors from his brain, and then had him drink antimony and sulfate of zinc to senselessly induce vomiting. The doctors then further weakened the king by giving him purgatives to cleanse his bowels and spirit of human skull to supposedly stop the convulsions. During this time they also administered a plethora of tonics, herbs, and drugs, and finally let another twelve ounces of his blood. After five days of this "treatment," King Charles II curiously died.

◆ In colonial America, barber-surgeons called stonecutters commonly performed lithotomies, cutting open patients—without the use of anesthesia (which had yet to be invented)—to remove kidney stones.

◆ Benjamin Franklin attempted to cure his kidney stones by eating blackberry jelly every night before going to bed.

◆ In September 1992, Lieutenant Colonel Don Snelgrove crashed the eighteen-million-dollar F-16 Air Force jet he was piloting. The United States Air Force determined, after a one-year investigation, that Snelgrove crashed because he was distracted while trying to urinate in his plastic "piddle pack."

Knee Pain

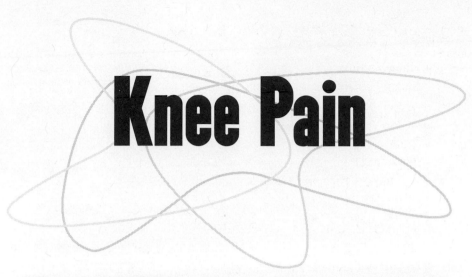

- **BenGay** and **Saran Wrap.** Apply BenGay to the sore spot, then wrap your knee with Saran Wrap. The plastic wrap increases the heat of the liniment. Be careful not to burn the skin.

- **Bubble Wrap** and **Scotch Packaging Tape.** When working in the workshop, crawling under the house or in the attic, roller skating, or playing contact sports, improvise knee pads by folding two sheets of Bubble Wrap to form cushions and taping them to each knee with Scotch Packaging Tape.

- **French's Mustard.** Rub French's Mustard over your knees, massaging it into the skin. When the mustard dries, rinse and repeat.

- **L'eggs Sheer Energy Panty Hose.** Cut off the calf section of a pair of panty hose and wear it over your knee as an impromptu knee brace.

- **Scotch-Brite Heavy Duty Scrub Sponge.** When you're scrubbing the floor or cleaning the bathtub, place a Scotch-Brite Heavy Duty Scrub Sponge under each knee. Or sew pockets onto the knees of an old pair of pants and slip the sponges inside.

- **Stayfree Maxi Pads.** Peel off the adhesive strip and stick a Stayfree Maxi Pad to each knee for a comfortable, disposable set of knee pads.

- **Uncle Ben's Converted Brand Rice.** Pour two cups Uncle Ben's Converted Brand Rice into a microwave-safe container and heat in the microwave for one minute. Carefully pour or spoon the hot rice into a sock (not too compactly), tie a knot in the end, and place the warm sock over your knee for ten minutes to relieve the pain. The sock conforms wherever applied.

- **Ziploc Freezer Bags.** Applying an ice pack to an injured knee will soothe the pain and ease the swelling. Fill a Ziploc Freezer Bag with water and freeze it or fill it with ice cubes. Wrap the ice pack in a paper towel before applying. For other ways to make and apply an ice pack, see page 198.

STRANGE FACTS

- ◆ Babies are born without kneecaps. They form sometime between the ages of two and six.

- ◆ Before leaving Portland, Oregon, to become a White House intern for President Bill Clinton in 1995, Monica Lewinsky reportedly told her friend Kathlyn Bleiler, "I'm going to the White House to get my presidential knee pads."

- ◆ The knee is more likely to be injured than any other joint, because the knee cannot twist.

- ◆ The kneecap is not attached to any other bone. It is held in place by muscles.

- ◆ Classical ballet dancer Mikhail Baryshnikov suffers from recurrent knee problems.

- ◆ Tennis professional Martina Navratilova, the most successful woman in the history of professional sports, had double knee reconstruction.

- ◆ A hilarious joke is called a knee-slapper.

- ◆ Former United States President Gerald Ford has two artificial knees.

Lactose Intolerance

- **Dannon Yogurt.** Being lactose intolerant means your small intestine does not produce enough lactase, the enzyme that digests lactose. Scientific research has shown that live, active cultures boost the body's immune system and help the body digest proteins and lactose. Yogurt helps the estimated fifty million Americans who are milk intolerant and incapable of digesting lactose, the principal sugar found in milk. Because of its high levels of live active cultures, Dannon Yogurt can be eaten by lactose-intolerant people, providing them with all the nutritional benefits of milk. Yogurt provides nearly 1.5 times more calcium than milk does. A single serving of Dannon yogurt provides 25 to 40 percent of daily calcium requirements.

- **L'eggs Sheer Energy Panty Hose** and **Dannon Yogurt.** Yogurt cheese has the same consistency as cream cheese but is much lower in fat. It can be used as a spread for bagels, toast, and crackers, or as a low-calorie, low-fat, low-cholesterol substitute for cream cheese in traditional cheesecake recipes. To make yogurt cheese, cut one leg from a clean pair of L'eggs Sheer Energy Panty Hose at the knee, pour two cups Dannon Plain Yogurt into the panty hose, tie the end around the kitchen faucet, and place a bowl underneath. The whey drains from the yogurt and the curds remain inside the panty hose. Empty the curds into a Rubbermaid container, seal the cover, and refrigerate for twenty-four hours. Makes approximately one cup yogurt cheese.

- **Tums.** If you're not drinking milk or eating yogurt, you need to get your calcium from another source. Eating a couple of Tums tablets a day may do the trick.

STRANGE FACTS

◆ To digest the sugar (lactose) in milk and other dairy products such as butter and ice cream, your body produces the enzyme lactase. The older you get, the less lactase your body produces. Without lactase, undigested lactose accumulates in the intestine, frequently causing cramps, diarrhea, and gas.

◆ In the Monty Python Flying Circus 1972 movie *And Now for Something Completely Different*, a seductive housewife entices a milkman to follow her inside her house and upstairs, where she directs him through a bedroom door. The milkman finds himself locked in a room with other delivery men.

◆ Lactose-intolerant actress Whoopi Goldberg appeared in a "Got Milk?" magazine ad with a lactose-free milk moustache.

◆ Cow milk contains between 3.7 and 5.1 percent lactose. Rhinoceros milk contains 7.2 percent lactose. Whale milk contains 1.8 percent lactose. Sea lion milk does not contain any lactose.

◆ Human milk contains between 6.2 and 7.5 percent lactose.

◆ Milk has been proclaimed the official state beverage in Arkansas, Delaware, Louisiana, Minnesota, Mississippi, New York, North Carolina, North Dakota, Pennsylvania, South Carolina, South Dakota, Vermont, Virginia, and Wisconsin.

Lice

- **Aqua Net Hairspray.** To prevent head lice from being attracted to a head of hair, spray a light coat of Aqua Net Hairspray on the hair before leaving the house. The lice will be repulsed by the smell of the hair spray.

- **Clorox.** When treating hair for lice, add two teaspoons Clorox to a sink full of water and soak all combs, brushes, barrettes, and hair clips in the solution, then rinse them thoroughly with water.

- **Crisco All-Vegetable Shortening** and **Heinz White Vinegar.** Rub a thick coat of Crisco All-Vegetable Shortening into the hair and roots well, saturating the hair. Put on a shower cap, or wrap the head with Saran Wrap (above the eyes, nose, and mouth), and let sit two hours. Shampoo hair thoroughly. The oils in vegetable shortening suffocate head lice and also condition hair. Rinse hair with Heinz White Vinegar (see below), then rinse again with water. Comb hair with a nit comb. Repeat one week later.

- **Glad Trash Bags.** Place all comforters, quilts, and stuffed animals in Glad Trash Bags, tie shut, and store in the garage for two weeks. Lice cannot survive without a human host. The eggs take one week to hatch, so after two weeks all the lice will be dead.

- **Heinz White Vinegar.** Adult lice lay eggs, called nits, which stick like glue to the hair shafts. After treating hair with Crisco All-Vegetable Shortening (see above), or any of the brand-name products listed below, rinse hair with Heinz White Vinegar. The vinegar dissolves the "glue," allowing you to comb the nits from hair easily with a nit comb.

- **Johnson's Baby Oil** and **Dawn.** Saturate hair with Johnson's Baby Oil, cover with a shower cap (or wrap the head with Saran Wrap—avoiding the eyes, nose, and mouth), and let sit for two hours. The lice drown in the baby oil. Wash the baby oil from hair with Dawn Dishwashing Liquid. Repeat one week later.

- **Kraft Real Mayonnaise** and **Heinz White Vinegar.** Saturate hair completely with a thick coat of Kraft Real Mayonnaise, working the mayonnaise in the hair and roots well. Wrap hair with Saran Wrap (above the eyes, nose, and mouth) or put on a shower cap. Let set for two hours. Shampoo hair thoroughly. The olive oil in the mayonnaise kills head lice and nits. The mayonnaise is also an excellent hair conditioner. Rinse hair with Heinz White Vinegar (see page 221), then rinse clean with water and comb hair with a nit comb. Repeat one week later.

- **Listerine.** Wet the hair and scalp with Listerine, cover with a shower cap, and wait two hours. The thymol in the Listerine kills lice and prevents reinfestation.

- **Lysol.** To clean brushes and combs (particularly a nit comb), soak the items in Lysol, then rinse them with water.

- **Paul Mitchell Tea Tree Shampoo.** To avoid getting lice, shampoo regularly with Paul Mitchell Tea Tree Shampoo. Tea tree oil, from the melaleuca tree, is a natural lice repellent. (Once your hair is infested with lice, however, washing your hair with tea tree oil shampoo will not get rid of them.)

- **Star Olive Oil** and **Heinz White Vinegar.** Saturate hair with olive oil, cover with a shower cap (or wrap the hair in Saran Wrap—avoiding the eyes, nose, and mouth) and let set for two hours to kill head lice and make removing nits easier. Follow by rinsing with Heinz White Vinegar (see page 221), and comb out the nits with a nit comb.

STRANGE FACTS

- ◆ Medicated lice shampoos may cause serious side effects in children and should never be used without a doctor's supervision.

- ◆ Most people resort to a lice shampoo containing the pesticide pyrethrin (derived from chrysanthemums) or permethrin (a synthetic form of pyrethrin). Recent studies indicate that lice are becoming pyrethrin resistant.

♦ The medical term for a lice infestation is *pediculosis*.

♦ The word *louse*, the singular form of the word *lice*, is slang for "a bad person."

♦ The word *nitwit* originated from the false idea that head lice infest only poor, uneducated children.

♦ The term *nit-picking* originated from the tedious act of having to pick every nit from the head of a person infested with lice.

♦ The expression "going over it with a fine-tooth comb" stems from combing the hair of a lice-infested person with a fine-tooth comb to get rid of all the nits.

♦ Lice burrow into the scalp to feed on human blood. A chemical in their saliva stops blood from clotting. This chemical causes the incessant itching.

♦ Female lice lay up to ten eggs a day.

Makeup

- **Alberto VO5 Conditioning Hairdressing.** A dab of Alberto VO5 Conditioning Hairdressing on a tissue or cotton ball gently removes makeup.

- **Carnation NonFat Dry Milk.** Mix one teaspoon Carnation NonFat Dry Milk with warm water, apply with a cotton ball, wipe clean, and rinse.

- **Cool Whip.** Wet face with lukewarm water, spread a handful of Cool Whip on face, rinse clean with lukewarm water, and blot dry. The oils in Cool Whip also moisturize the skin.

- **Crisco All-Vegetable Shortening.** A dab of Crisco All-Vegetable Shortening removes makeup and moisturizes the skin.

- **Huggies Baby Wipes.** Wiping your face with a Huggies Baby Wipe removes lipstick, blush, rouge, eyeliner, eye shadow, and oil-based clown makeup.

- **Johnson's Baby Oil.** Dab on baby oil, wait ten minutes, and remove with cotton balls. Baby oil gently removes mascara, leaving a thin, protective film that moisturizes lids and lashes.

- **Johnson's Baby Shampoo.** Remove waterproof eye makeup without any tears by dabbing a few drops of Johnson's Baby Shampoo on a cotton ball and applying to the lids and wiping clean.

- **Q-Tips Cotton Swabs.** In a pinch, use a Q-Tips Cotton Swab as a substitute for an eye-shadow brush.

- **Reddi-wip.** To remove makeup, spread a handful of Reddi-wip on your face, rinse clean with lukewarm water, and blot dry. The whipped cream also moisturizes the skin.

- **Skin-So-Soft.** Rubbing a dab of Skin-So-Soft over your face removes makeup while simultaneously making your skin oh-so-soft. After cleaning off the makeup, wash your face with water.

- **Star Olive Oil.** Remove makeup by lathering your skin with Star Olive Oil, and then wipe it off. Olive oil acts as a moisturizer and does not dry your face like soap can.

- **Vaseline Petroleum Jelly.** A dab of Vaseline Petroleum Jelly cleans mascara, eyeliner, lipstick, and rouge from skin.

STRANGE FACTS

- Cleopatra used pomegranate seeds for lipstick.

- Ancient Egyptian women used green eye shadow (made from powdered malachite), blue-black lipstick, and red rouge. They also outlined their eyes and darkened their lashes with a black paste called kohl, and glittered their eyes with crushed sparkling beetle shells.

- Ancient Egyptians and Greeks used kohl pencils to connect their eyebrows above the nose.

- In the Bible, the evil Queen Jezebel "painted her face" (2 Kings 9:30).

- In eighteenth-century Europe, women ate Arsenic Complexion Wafers to attain a white complexion. The arsenic poisoned the blood.

- For centuries, European women used rouge and lipstick made from cinnabar, a poisonous red sulfide of mercury.

- In the 1920s, jars of lip color and skin cream were found in King Tut's tomb, dating back to around 1350 B.C.E.

- Fifty-three percent of women will not leave the house without adorning themselves with makeup.

Marital Relations

- **Chloroseptic.** Prevent premature ejaculation by spraying Chloroseptic on an erection to numb the sensitivity. Wipe off the excess to avoid anesthetizing your partner's private parts.

- **Colgate Toothpaste.** Rubbing a small dab of Colgate Toothpaste over a hickey conceals the redness and speeds healing.

- **Cool Whip.** Give new meaning to the phrase "dessert topping" by adding Cool Whip to an evening of passion.

- **Dannon Yogurt.** Use Dannon Yogurt as an all-natural vaginal lubricant that also combats yeast infections.

- **Halls Mentho-Lyptus.** Enhance romance by placing a mentholated lozenge in your mouth to give your partner an interesting tingle.

- **Hershey's Shell Topping.** Squirt Hershey's Shell Topping on an ice cream cone and within two minutes the chocolate dries into a hard shell that's fun to eat. The same effect can be achieved by dipping parts of your body in this chocolate topping, making them hard to resist.

- **Hershey's Syrup.** A dollop of seductive chocolate syrup poured on the right spot can put the romance back in your love life.

- **Jell-O.** Empty seven to ten boxes of Jell-O powder in a bathtub, add just enough hot water to dissolve it, then add cold water until the Jell-O starts to get slimy, then get in with your loved one. (To clean the Jell-O out of the bathtub, simply run the hot water. Some Jell-O flavors may stain the bathtub.)

- **McCormick Vanilla Extract.** A dab of vanilla extract behind each ear makes an alluring fragrance. Some people consider vanilla to be an aphrodisiac. In 1995, the Smell and Taste Research Institute revealed that the smell of vanilla had a sexually arousing effect on men (older men responded more positively than younger men).

- **Orajel.** Prevent premature ejaculation by applying Orajel to an erection. Wipe off the excess gel to avoid numbing the sensations of the partner.

- **Reddi-wip.** In the best-selling book *Everything You Always Wanted to Know About Sex (But Were Afraid to Ask),* author Dr. David Reuben first suggested using whipped cream to enhance activities in the bedroom.

- **SueBee Honey.** Sweeten your love life behind closed doors with a few drops of honey.

STRANGE FACTS

◆ The wedding cake was originally thrown at the bride as a symbol of fertility—just as rice is today.

◆ In *Macbeth*, Shakespeare wrote that alcohol "provokes the desire, but it takes away the performance."

◆ The 1716 book *Onania, of the Heinous Sin of Self-Pollution* incorrectly claimed that masturbation leads to insanity. By 1764, eighty editions of the book had been published. In the first American textbook of psychiatry, published in 1812, Dr. Benjamin Rush furthered this myth by incorrectly claiming that masturbation causes "seminal weakness, impotence, dysury, tabes orsalis, pulmonary consumption, dyspepsia, dimness of sight, vertigo, epilepsy, hypochondriasis, loss of memory, manalgia, fatuity and death."

◆ James Buchanan was the only president of the United States who never married. During his term in office, his niece Harriet Lane played the role of the First Lady.

◆ The hula was originally a religious dance performed by Hawaiians to promote fertility.

◆ Green M&M's are considered to be an aphrodisiac. At bridal showers, guests often present the future bride with a bag of M&M's with all the green candies carefully removed and placed in a second bag specifically reserved for the wedding night. An M&M/Mars brochure states: "Although many consumers ask us about the special qualities of green M&M's Chocolate Candies, we cannot explain any extraordinary 'powers' attributed to this color, either scientifically or medically."

◆ In an episode of *Gilligan's Island*, Mary Ann reveals that back home in Kansas she used a drop of honey behind each ear as perfume.
   "Did you attract many boys that way?" asks Ginger.
   "Not very many boys," admits Mary Ann. "But lots of flies."

◆ In the 1960s, the United States Agency for International Development shipped a 139-year supply of condoms to Thailand. The condoms had a shelf life of five to ten years.

◆ A Trojan Condom can be used to make a chocolate bowl. Simply inflate the Trojan condom to the size of a grapefruit. Melt four ounces of Hershey's Baking Chocolate, and one ounce Land O Lakes Butter together and put in a bowl, dip the balloon in about half way, swaying the balloon side to side and back and forth. Sit the balloon on a piece of Cut-Rite Wax Paper, let dry, then use a pair of scissors to snip a hole in the condom to slowly deflate. Peel off the condom and you have a chocolate bowl to fill with sweets.

◆ In 1970, Procter & Gamble hired model Marilyn Briggs to pose in a white terry-cloth robe with her baby on the front of the Ivory Snow box. Three years later, Procter & Gamble discovered that Marilyn Briggs was porn actress Marilyn Chambers, star of the 1972 hardcore X-rated film *Behind the Green Door*.

◆ To advertise its new leather first-class seats in Mexico, American Airlines literally translated its "Fly in Leather" slogan to "Vuela en Cuero," which means "Fly Naked" in Spanish.

◆ In his 1972 movie *Everything You Always Wanted to Know About Sex*, Woody Allen said, "Is sex dirty? Only if it's done right."

◆ The Ramses brand condom is named after the great Egyptian pharaoh Ramses II, who fathered more than 160 children.

THE JOY OF HERSHEY'S SYRUP

In 1887, Milton Hershey, a thirty-year-old Pennsylvania Dutchman who had worked as an apprentice to a candy maker, founded Lancaster Caramel Company and began manufacturing caramels. In 1900, inspired by a new chocolate-making machine he had seen at the 1893 Chicago Exposition, he sold his caramel company for one million dollars to start a chocolate factory in Derry Church, Pennsylvania, to manufacture America's first mass-marketed five-cent chocolate bar. In 1905, the factory was completed and Hershey began producing individually wrapped Hershey's Milk Chocolate Bars, followed by Hershey's Milk Chocolate Kisses in 1907, the Mr. Goodbar candy bar in 1925, and Hershey's Syrup in 1926. In 1988, Hershey's bought Cadbury's candy business in the United States, acquiring Peter Paul, Cadbury, and Caramello. In 1993, Hershey introduced Hugs, a white-and-dark chocolate product shaped like Hershey's Kisses.

DERRY CHURCH, PENNSYLVANIA, the home of Hershey Foods, was renamed Hershey in 1906.

IN 1909, Hershey and his wife founded the Milton Hershey School, a school for orphaned children near the chocolate plant. In 1918 Hershey donated the entire Hershey's Chocolate Corporation to the Milton Hershey School, and for years the company existed solely to fund the school. Although Hershey Foods is now publicly traded, the Milton Hershey School still controls 77 percent of the voting shares. Former Hershey Foods chairman William Dearden (1976–1984) was a Hershey School graduate, as are many Hershey employees.

DURING THE DEPRESSION, Milton Hershey put people to work by building a hotel, golf courses, a library, theaters, a museum, a stadium, and other facilities in Hershey, Pennsylvania.

THE UNIVERSALLY POPULAR HERSHEY BAR was used overseas during World War II as currency.

MILTON HERSHEY REFUSED to advertise his product, convinced that quality would speak for itself. Even after Hershey's death in 1945, the company refused to advertise—until 1970, when Hershey began losing sales to Mars.

IN 1990, during Operation Desert Storm, Hershey Foods sent 144,000 "heat-resistant" milk chocolate Desert Bars—capable of withstanding up to 100 degrees Fahrenheit—to American troops in Saudi Arabia.

IN 1995, MCI teamed up with Hershey to offer free long-distance calling to consumers who bought an eight-ounce or larger bag of Hershey's Kisses, Hershey's Hugs, or other chocolate products.

HERSHEY'S SYRUP IS the best-selling chocolate syrup in the world.

- Only humans and horses have hymens.

- During mating season, lions mate every twenty-five minutes for three days straight.

- Colonel Harland Sanders, who at the age of seventy founded Kentucky Fried Chicken, talked his wife into hiring his mistress as their live-in housekeeper, according to the Colonel's daughter, Margaret Sanders, in her book, *The Colonel's Secret: Eleven Secret Herbs and a Spicy Daughter*. Sanders later divorced his wife, married his mistress, and took both women with him to Washington, D.C., to attend a presidential inauguration.

- The most common method of shooting a marble is known as *fulking*.

- Roseanne Barr once said, "Men read maps better than women because only men can understand the concept of an inch equaling a hundred miles."

- Frank Perdue's chicken slogan, "It takes a strong man to make a tender chicken" was translated into Spanish as "It takes an aroused man to make a chicken affectionate."

- In the United States, the word *shag* is far less offensive than in other English-speaking countries, where the word is slang for "fornicate." In Singapore, authorities forced a movie distributor to change the title of the film *Austin Powers: The Spy Who Shagged Me* to *Austin Powers: The Spy Who Shioked Me*. The word *shioked* in Singapore means "treated nicely."

Memory Loss

- **CoverGirl Nailslicks.** Color code your keys by painting the tops with different bright colors of CoverGirl Nailslicks polishes. For instance, paint the top of your house key bright red, your car key bright blue, your spouse's car key bright green. If you do the same thing to the keys for every member of your family, even the youngest child will know which key is "Mommy's house key." You can also use glow-in-the-dark nail polishes.

- **Forster Clothes Pins.** Clip reminder notes to the sun visor in your car with a Forster Clothes Pin.

- **Post-it Notes.** To remember necessary chores, appointments, or things to do, write a reminder to yourself on Post-it Notes and stick them to the middle of your bathroom mirror, over the light switch in your office at work (so you see it before turning off the light), and on the inside of your front door before leaving on a vacation (so you don't forget to turn off all the lights, lock the doors, shut off the gas, check the windows, and take your airline tickets).

STRANGE FACTS

- "The advantage of a bad memory," wrote German philosopher Friedrich Nietzsche, "is that one enjoys several times the same good things for the first time."

- In the 1939 movie *The Wizard of Oz*, the Wizard claims, "I'm an old Kansas man myself," yet he takes off from the Emerald City in a hot-air balloon painted with the words "Omaha State Fair," which could only take place in Nebraska.

- In 1955, Elvis Presley recorded the song "I Forgot to Remember to Forget." In 1964, the Beatles recorded a version of "I Forgot to Remember to Forget" for exclusive broadcast on BBC radio.

- In May 1974, Bhandaanta Vicittabi Vumsa recited sixteen thousand memorized pages of Buddhist canonical texts in Yangon, Myanmar.

- According to China's Xinhua News Agency, Gon Yangling, a twenty-six-year old from Harbin, China, memorized more than fifteen thousand telephone numbers.

- In June 1996, at the London Zoo in England, Dominic O'Brien memorized the order of a deck of cards that had been shuffled once in 38.29 seconds.

Menopause

- **Dannon Yogurt.** When estrogen levels drop, a woman's bones start losing calcium, weakening the bones and possibly leading to osteoporosis. Yogurt provides nearly 1.5 times more calcium than milk. A single serving of Dannon Yogurt provides 25 to 40 percent of daily calcium requirements.

- **Huggies Baby Wipes** and **Ziploc Storage Bags.** To deal with hot flashes, carry a handful of Huggies Baby Wipes in a gallon-size Ziploc Storage Bag. Wipe your forehead to ease the intensity of the hot flash.

- **Tums.** To get extra calcium in your diet to compensate for the fact that bones start losing calcium when estrogen production decreases, eat three regular Tums or two extra-strength Tums daily.

STRANGE FACTS

◆ Left-handed women go through menopause an average of five years before right-handed women. The average menopausal age for left-handed women is 42.3 years, while the average age for right-handed women is 47.3 years.

◆ In the biblical Book of Genesis, Sarah becomes pregnant with her first child, Isaac, long after she has gone through menopause.

◆ Human females are the only mammal on earth known to stop menstruating.

◆ The menstrual cycle ends suddenly for some women, while in other women, the menstrual cycle occurs less regularly over a period of months or years before ceasing completely.

◆ In a 1972 episode of the television comedy series *All in the Family*, Edith Bunker goes through menopause, marking the first time this previously taboo topic was discussed on a prime-time network television show.

Menstruation

- **Altoids Peppermints.** Chewing two Altoids Peppermints relieves menstrual cramping. The active ingredient is the peppermint.

- **Arm & Hammer Baking Soda.** To get rid of menstrual odors, lightly powder yourself and a panty liner with Arm & Hammer Baking Soda.

- **Arm & Hammer Baking Soda** and **Epsom Salt.** Add one cup Arm & Hammer Baking Soda and one cup Epsom Salt into running bath water. Soak your body to relax your muscles and relieve cramps.

- **Bounce.** To remove menstrual smells, line your bathroom garbage pail with Bounce dryer sheets, filling the room with the delightful scent of oleander.

- **Canada Dry Ginger Ale.** Drinking Canada Dry Ginger Ale may relieve cramps and nausea. Herbalists classify ginger as a carminative (an herbal remedy that settles the intestines and releases gas).

- **Carnation NonFat Dry Milk.** Calcium lessens the severity of cramps. Add one teaspoon Carnation NonFat Dry Milk to the dishes you cook, such as casseroles, soups, and drinks. Each teaspoon contains roughly sixty-two milligrams of calcium.

- **Gatorade.** Relieve cramps by drinking Gatorade. The thirst quencher increases the potassium in your body.

- **Hershey's Milk Chocolate Bar.** If you feel a craving for chocolate before your period, eat a Hershey's Milk Chocolate Bar to appease those raging hormones.

- **Kellogg's Raisin Bran.** Relieve the symptoms of premenstrual syndrome by loading up on fiber, which helps flush out excess estrogen from your body. Eating one cup of Kellogg's Raisin Bran every morning adds seven grams of all-important fiber to your diet.

- **Kleenex Tissues.** In a pinch, several folded Kleenex Tissues can be used as an impromptu panty liner.

- **Lay's Potato Chips.** Relieve premenstrual syndrome by eating Lay's Potato Chips before you are about to have your period. Before menstruating, women lose a lot of fluid. Potato chips are high in carbohydrates, which cause your body to retain fluid and also give your body more energy.

- **Tums.** Calcium lessens the severity of cramps. Take three regular Tums or two extra-strength Tums daily. Tums are also available in peppermint, which soothes cramping as well.

- **York Peppermint Pattie.** Eating a York Peppermint Pattie relieves menstrual cramping (thanks to the peppermint), and the chocolate soothes those cravings.

- **Ziploc Storage Bags.** Carrying a supply of tampons inside a Ziploc Storage Bag prevents them from getting dirty, wet, or damaged.

STRANGE FACTS

- The instruction sheet found inside a box of Tampax Tampons states (in small type): "Remove used tampon before inserting a new one." That's not something you want to find out after going through an entire box.

- Marilyn Monroe said, "I don't mind living in a man's world as long as I can be a woman in it."

- The menstrual cycle lasts an average of twenty-eight days, but can range anywhere from twenty-one to forty days.

- When females live or work close together, their menstrual cycles begin to coincide, apparently triggered by the scent of each other's pheromones. The menstrual periods of women exposed to the scent of male pheromones seem to become shorter and more predictable.

- Euphemisms for menstruation include such ridiculous expressions as "the curse," "falling off the roof," "the monthly visitor," "the time of the month," "Aunt Flo," "on the rag," "carrying a flag," "female troubles," "having the painters in," "communists in the summer house," "wearing red shoes," "surfing the crimson wave," "taking Carrie to the prom," and "riding the cotton pony."

SIDE EFFECTS
BLOODSTAINS

ARM & HAMMER BAKING SODA
Mix Arm & Hammer Baking Soda with just enough water to make a paste, apply directly to the bloodstain, let it dry, and brush off.

CARNATION NONFAT DRY MILK and ORAL-B TOOTHBRUSH
Make a paste with equal parts Carnation NonFat Dry Milk and water, massage the mixture into the bloodstain (or brush with a clean, used toothbrush), and then rinse with water. The enzymes in the milk break down the protein in blood, dissolving the stain.

CHEEZ WHIZ
Smear Cheez Whiz over bloodstained clothing or sheets, let them sit for five minutes, then toss them in your regular wash. The enzymes in the Cheez Whiz help to clean the bloodstains from fabrics.

COCA-COLA
Saturate the bloodstain with Coca-Cola, let sit for five minutes, then launder as usual. Coke removes blood from clothing—even dried blood that has gone through the washing machine and dryer.

HYDROGEN PEROXIDE
Pouring hydrogen peroxide over a fresh bloodstain cleans the spot from clothing.

PARSONS' AMMONIA and ORAL-B TOOTHBRUSH
To remove bloodstains from clothes, mix two teaspoons Parsons' Ammonia in one cup water, pour the liquid over the stain, and scrub with a clean, used toothbrush.

TIDBITS ON LAY'S POTATO CHIPS

In 1932, Herman W. Lay, a dropout from Furman University living in Nashville, Tennessee, started using his 1929 Model A Ford to distribute potato chips made by a company in Atlanta, Georgia. By 1934, with six snack food routes, Lay was on his way to becoming a major distributor. In 1938, Lay bought the financially ailing company, changed its name to H.W. Lay & Company, and made Lay's Potato Chips the company's flagship product. H.W. Lay & Company became one of the largest snack and convenience food companies in the Southeast.

In 1961, Lay merged his company with the Frito Company of Dallas, Texas, to form Frito-Lay.

Frito Company founder Elmer Doolin, while working as an ice-cream maker in San Antonio, Texas, in 1932, stopped for lunch at a small San Antonio cafe, where he bought a plain package of corn chips made from corn dough. In 1938, Doolin tracked down the maker of the corn chips and for one hundred dollars bought the recipe and the manufacturing equipment— a converted hand-operated potato slicer. In 1945, the Frito Company, distributing Fritos Corn Chips across the Southwest, granted H.W. Lay & Company the right to manufacture and distribute Fritos Corn Chips in the Southeast.

IN 1853, George Crum, an American Indian working as a chef at Moon Lake Lodge in Saratoga Springs, New York, cooked up crisp, paper-thin French Fries to poke fun at a guest who kept sending his order of French fries back to the kitchen. The guest loved Crum's potato chips, which became known as Saratoga Chips on the menu and were soon packaged and distributed across New England.

LEGEND HOLDS that Elmer Doolin bought the original recipe for Fritos Corn Chips using one hundred dollars that he borrowed from his mother, who hocked her wedding ring to get it.

DOOLIN PRODUCED FRITOS CORN CHIPS in his mother's kitchen, making ten pounds of chips per hour, and sold them out of the back of his Model T Ford, earning as much as two dollars a day.

IN 1959, Vice President Richard Nixon took Fritos to Soviet leader Nikita Krushchev.

IN 1963, Bert Lahr, who played the Cowardly Lion in *The Wizard of Oz*, starred in commercials for Lay's Potato Chips, dressed as a devil and tempting viewers with the line, "Betcha can't eat just one."

TEX AVERY, the legendary animator who created Daffy Duck, Droopy, and a host of other characters, created the Frito Bandito.

IN 1965, Frito-Lay introduced Doritos.

A MEXICAN-AMERICAN GROUP threatened to sue the company over its advertising mascot, the Frito Bandito, for disparaging Mexicans.

IN 1968, Buddy Hackett starred in commercials for Lay's Potato Chips and told viewers, "You Can Eat a Million of 'em, but Nobody Can Eat Just One."

Muscle Pain

- **Alka-Seltzer.** Fill a bathtub with warm water and drop in six Alka-Seltzer tablets for a soothing bath to relieve sore muscles (unless you are allergic to aspirin, a key ingredient in Alka-Seltzer).

- **Arm & Hammer Baking Soda** and **Epsom Salt.** Add one cup Arm & Hammer Baking Soda and one cup Epsom Salt into running bath water. Soak your body to relax your muscles.

- **Ban Roll-On Deodorant** and **Therapeutic Mineral Ice.** Pry the top off an empty canister of Ban Roll-On Deodorant and wash out the bottle, roller ball, and lid. Fill the canister with Therapeutic Mineral Ice, replace the roller, and rub on achy muscles. The canister delivers the Mineral Ice with the benefit of a massage—without getting any hot salve on your hands.

- **Coppertone.** In a pinch, Coppertone sunscreen doubles as massage oil.

- **Epsom Salt.** Pour two cups Epsom Salt into a bath of warm water. Sit back and relax. The magnesium sulfate softens your skin while relaxing the kinks and stiffness in your muscles.

- **French's Mustard.** Rub a generous amount of French's Mustard into sore muscles, and then cover with a washcloth dampened with warm water as a soothing poultice.

- **Fruit of the Earth Aloe Vera Gel.** To treat muscle soreness, massage Fruit of the Earth Aloe Vera Gel into the sensitive area to cool, soothe, and tingle the stiffness and achiness.

- **Gatorade.** Drinking Gatorade quickly replenishes the body with carbohydrates, which the body converts into glycogen—a fuel for muscles.

- **Gold's Horseradish** and **Star Olive Oil.** Mix one tablespoon Gold's Horseradish in one-half cup Star Olive Oil. Let sit for thirty minutes. Apply as a massage oil to relieve sore muscles.

- **Heinz Apple Cider Vinegar.** Add three cups Heinz Apple Cider Vinegar to warm bath water to soak away sore muscles.

- **Johnson's Baby Powder.** Johnson's Baby Powder doubles as massage oil, lubricating the skin without the greasy mess of oil.

- **Land O Lakes Butter.** Land O Lakes Butter is an excellent massage oil substitute that also moisturizes the skin.

- **L'eggs Sheer Energy Panty Hose.** If you've pulled a tendon, wear a pair of panty hose as a substitute for an Ace bandage to reduce the swelling. You can cut off sections of the panty hose that you don't need, such as the other leg and the hose beneath the knee.

- **Skin-So-Soft.** Use Skin-So-Soft as a massage oil to alleviate the tightness of sore muscles.

- **Tabasco Pepper Sauce.** Rubbing the capsaicin-laced hot sauce onto the sore muscle numbs the pain. Capsaicin enters nerves and temporarily depletes them of the neurotransmitter that sends pain signals to the brain. If you feel a burning sensation on the skin, apply a thin coat of Colgate Toothpaste over the dried Tabasco Pepper Sauce. The glycerin in the toothpaste will reduce the burning discomfort and may also enhance the analgesia from the capsaicin. Do not apply Tabasco Pepper Sauce to an open wound.

- **Uncle Ben's Converted Brand Rice.** Pour two cups Uncle Ben's Converted Brand Rice into a microwave-safe container and heat in the microwave for one minute. Carefully pour or spoon the hot rice into a sock (not too compactly), tie a knot in the end, and place the warm sock over the afflicted area for ten minutes to relieve the pain. The sock conforms wherever applied.

- **Wilson Tennis Balls.** Put several Wilson Tennis Balls inside a sock and tie at the end, and have a friend roll this over your back. This technique is frequently used by labor coaches to massage the backs of women in labor.

- **Ziploc Freezer Bags.** Applying ice for ten minutes at a time relieves sore muscles. Fill a Ziploc Freezer Bag with water and freeze it or fill it with ice cubes. Wrap the ice pack in a paper towel before applying. For other ways to make and apply an ice pack, see page 198.

- **Ziploc Storage Bags.** Put a bag over your hand and use as a glove when applying BenGay or Therapeutic Mineral Ice to prevent getting the hot gel on your hands.

STRANGE FACTS

◆ The strongest muscles in the body are the two masseters on either side of the mouth, which control biting.

◆ The largest muscle in the human body is the gluteus maximus, better known as the buttock muscle.

◆ The human body has more than six hundred major muscles.

◆ The muscle Elvis Presley used to curl his lip is called the *levator labii superioris alaeque nasi*. It runs between the nostril and the upper lip.

◆ In the 1964 movie *Muscle Beach Party*, starring Frankie Avalon and Annette Funicello, handsome bodybuilders invade the gang's favorite beach.

◆ Muscle Beach is an actual beach in Los Angeles, California.

◆ "We are an intelligent species and the use of our intelligence quite properly gives us pleasure," wrote Carl Sagan in his 1979 book *Broca's Brain*. "In this respect the brain is like a muscle. When it is in use we feel very good. Understanding is joyous."

Nausea

- **Altoids Peppermints.** Sucking on two Altoids Peppermints calms an upset stomach. Peppermint is an antispasmodic, meaning it relaxes stomach muscles.

- **Canada Dry Ginger Ale.** Drink flat Canada Dry Ginger Ale to settle your upset stomach.

- **Coca-Cola.** Open a can of Coca-Cola, let it sit until it goes flat (roughly thirty minutes), then drink the defizzed real thing. Coca-Cola was originally invented as an elixir to cure upset stomachs, and it still works. Letting the bubbles out of the soda prevents the carbonation from further upsetting your stomach.

- **Gatorade.** Drinking Gatorade helps maintain the body's balance of electrolytes, which regulate the body's electrochemical balance, alleviating the queasiness of nausea.

- **Krispy Original Saltine Crackers.** If you're feeling hungry, start with bland foods such as Krispy Original Saltine Crackers, which you can easily digest.

- **Lipton Tea Bags.** Drinking hot Lipton Tea replaces vital bodily fluids and flushes impurities from your system.

- **Wonder Bread.** If you're feeling hungry, eat unbuttered toasted Wonder Bread. The carbohydrates will give you energy.

THE LOWDOWN ON PEPTO-BISMOL

At the beginning of the twentieth century, lower standards of hygiene and sanitation caused babies to come down with cholera infantum, a frightening disease that caused diarrhea and vomiting—sometimes resulting in death. There was no cure for the disease other than letting it run its course. At the time, one out of every five children died before the age of four.

To combat the symptoms of this awful disease, a doctor working at home in New York state combined pepsin, bismuth salicylate, zinc salts, salol, and oil of wintergreen, colored the mixture pink with food coloring, and called his formula Mixture Cholera Infantum. The mixture cured the diarrhea that accompanied the illness. Eventually, the widespread pasteurization of milk and public campaigns advocating hand washing to kill bacteria significantly reduced the number of cases of infant diarrhea.

Unable to make enough of the formula in his home to meet the overwhelming demand, the small-town doctor brought his formula to the Norwich Pharmacal Company in Norwich, New York. Norwich Pharmacal began manufacturing the mixture in twenty-gallon tubs and added the remedy to its catalog for medical professionals. Norwich Pharmacal refined the doctor's formula and advertised "Bismosal: Mixture Cholera Infantum" as an "elegant, pleasantly flavored" mixture suitable for children because it did not contain any opiates. In 1919, the company, hoping to market the product to adults as well as children, renamed the formula Pepto-Bismol, after the two main ingredients—pepsin and bismuth. Pepto-Bismol soon became Norwich's best-selling nonprescription drug. In 1982, Procter & Gamble acquired Norwich Eaton Pharmaceuticals.

CHOLERA INFANTUM was caused by a bacterial infection that can be treated with antibiotics.

DURING THE 1920S, Pepto-Bismol was sold at drugstore soda fountains.

THE ACTIVE INGREDIENT in Pepto-Bismol is bismuth subsalicylate.

PEPTO-BISMOL SOMETIMES DARKENS the tongue or stool. Small amounts of bismuth, the active ingredient in Pepto-Bismol, combine with trace amounts of sulfur in your saliva and gastrointestinal tract, forming a black-colored substance called bismuth sulfide. This temporary and harmless discoloration lasts until the Pepto-Bismol leaves your system, which —depending upon the regularity of your bowel movements, your age, and how much Pepto-Bismol you ingested—can take several days.

- **York Peppermint Pattie.** Eating a York Peppermint Pattie calms nausea. The peppermint calms stomach muscles.

STRANGE FACTS

- The word *nausea*, usually associated with seasickness, originates from the Greek root *naûs*, meaning "ship," and also the root for the words *nautical* and *navigation*.

- Nausea is when the stomach muscles gently contract, creating a feeling of queasiness.

- In German, the word for nausea is *übelkeit*.

- The expression "Eat humble pie," meaning "to learn a bitter lesson in humility," originated in Britain during the eleventh century and referred to a pie containing a stag's innards (known as "umbles"). Americans added the letter *h* to "umble pie."

- In his autobiography, novelist Charles Dickens wrote, "I have tried lately to read Shakespeare, and found it so intolerably dull that it nauseated me."

- In 1938, French existentialist Jean-Paul Sartre wrote a novel titled *La Nausée*.

- Nick Vermeulen of the Netherlands amassed the world's largest collection of airsick bags. As of May 1997, his collection numbered 2,112 different bags representing 470 airlines.

- The Chinese city of Guilin, best known for its huge limestone peaks jutting up from the horizon, is also the gastronomic capital of China, renowned for its chefs who prepare gourmet dishes made from wildcat, snake, bamboo rat, anteater, owl, and pangolin.

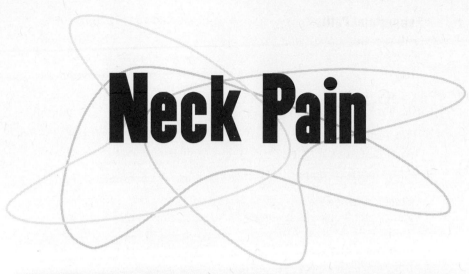

Neck Pain

- **L'eggs Sheer Energy Panty Hose.** To keep a soft neck brace clean, cut off the leg from a pair of clean, used L'eggs Sheer Energy Panty Hose, and wrap the neck brace inside it. The nylon cover will keep the neck brace clean.

- **Tabasco Pepper Sauce.** Rub the hot sauce into your neck. Tabasco Pepper Sauce contains capsaicin, a spicy alkaloid proven to numb pain when applied topically. Capsaicin enters nerves and temporarily depletes them of the neuro-transmitter that sends pain signals to the brain. If you feel a burning sensation on the skin, apply a thin coat of Colgate Toothpaste over the dried Tabasco Pepper Sauce. The glycerin in the toothpaste will reduce the burning discom-fort and may also amplify the analgesia from the capsaicin. Do not apply Tabasco Pepper Sauce to an open wound.

- **Ziploc Freezer Bags.** Placing an ice pack on your neck for ten minutes constricts the blood vessels, anesthetizing the pain. Fill a Ziploc Freezer Bag with water and freeze it or fill it with ice cubes to make an ice pack. Wrap the ice pack in a paper towel before applying. For other ways to make and apply an ice pack, see page 198.

STRANGE FACTS

- ◆ Mice, whales, elephants, giraffes, and humans all have seven neck vertebrae.

- On June 6, 1968, at the Smoky Mountain Raceway in Tennessee, the Dodge driven by Buddy Baker blew out a tire on the first turn and crashed into a concrete wall. Baker was strapped onto a rolling stretcher and put in an ambulance, but the ambulance driver neglected to latch the back door. As the ambulance pulled away, the back door opened, and the stretcher, with Baker strapped to it, rolled out and onto the racetrack where race cars headed straight toward him. Baker was rescued and taken safely to the hospital.

- The women of the Padaung or Karen tribe of Myanmar fit copper coils around their necks successively to extend the length of the neck. The longest neck extension on record measured 15.75 inches.

- A "pain in the neck" is a euphemism for an unbearable and persistent annoyance.

- Your neck supports up to eighteen pounds of weight. That's like carrying around a heavy bowling ball for sixteen hours a day.

- If Barbie were life size, she would stand seven feet, two inches tall and have a neck twice the length of a normal human's neck.

Nicotine Withdrawal

- **Alka-Seltzer.** Get short-term relief from nicotine withdrawal symptoms by drinking two Alka-Seltzer tablets dissolved in a glass of water at every meal (unless you're on a low-sodium diet, suffer from peptic ulcers, or are allergic to aspirin, a key ingredient in Alka-Seltzer).

- **Heinz White Vinegar.** Eliminate the odor of smoke in your home or office by filling a drinking glass halfway with Heinz White Vinegar and setting the glass on a shelf in the room. The vinegar absorbs the smell of the smoke.

- **Smirnoff Vodka.** Remove cigarette smoke from clothing by mixing one part Smirnoff Vodka to three parts water in a trigger-spray bottle. Spray the clothing, then launder and let dry. The vodka neutralizes the smell.

- **Tang.** Drinking several glasses of Tang eases the pangs of nicotine withdrawal. The ascorbic acid in Tang raises the acid level in your urine, clearing nicotine from the body faster.

- **Ziploc Storage Bags.** Keep carrot and celery sticks in a Ziploc Storage Bag so you have something healthy to put in your mouth whenever you get a craving for a cigarette.

STRANGE FACTS

◆ Aside from cancer and emphysema, smoking can cause bad breath, conception problems, gum disease, heart palpitations, impotence, indigestion, insomnia, memory problems, night blindness, poor blood circulation, and ulcers. Smoking can also trigger asthma, worsen bronchitis, exacerbate tinnitus (ringing in your ears), and turn white hair yellow.

◆ British Prime Minister Winston Churchill smoked fifteen cigars a day.

◆ Sigmund Freud, the father of psychoanalysis, smoked twenty cigars a day and developed cancer of the jaw and palate.

◆ Cigar smoker and novelist Mark Twain insisted that quitting the tobacco habit was easy. He had "done it 100 times."

◆ In 1997, the Liggett Group, the fifth-largest tobacco company in the United States, admitted that smoking is addictive and causes health problems (including lung cancer, heart and vascular disease, and emphysema), and that the tobacco companies have sought for years to sell their products to children as young as fourteen.

◆ In 1997 alone, according to the American Cancer Society, an estimated 160,400 Americans died from lung cancer.

Nosebleed

- **Afrin.** Soak a cotton ball with Afrin Nasal Spray and insert it in the nostril. The nasal spray clots the blood.

- **Bag Balm** and **Q-Tips Cotton Swabs.** Once you've stopped the bleeding, apply a thin coat of Bag Balm with a Q-Tips Cotton Swab inside the nostril to kill bacteria, ease healing, and prevent itching.

- **Heinz White Vinegar.** Dampen a cotton ball with Heinz White Vinegar and plug the bleeding nostril. The acetic acid cauterizes the wound.

- **Jell-O.** Place one tablespoon any flavor Jell-O powder on the tongue and press the Jell-O against the roof of the mouth, letting it slowly dissolve. The gelatin stops the nosebleed by clotting the wound.

- **Q-Tips Cotton Swabs.** After you stop the bleeding, dip a Q-Tips Cotton Swab in water and use it to clean the inside of your nostrils.

- **Vaseline Petroleum Jelly** and **Q-Tips Cotton Swabs.** Once you've stopped the bleeding, use a Q-Tips Cotton Swab to apply a thin coat of Vaseline inside the nostril to kill bacteria, ease healing, and prevent itching.

- **Ziploc Freezer Bags.** Placing an ice pack over your nose for ten minutes constricts the blood vessels, reducing bleeding. Fill a Ziploc Freezer Bag with water and freeze it or fill it with ice cubes. Wrap the ice pack in a paper towel before applying. For other ways to make and apply an ice pack, see page 198.

Nose your way to a doctor if bleeding lasts more than fifteen to thirty minutes, you feel weak or faint, or you've lost a lot of blood.

STRANGE FACTS

◆ In his 1835 short story "The Nose," Russian satirist Nikolai Gogol tells the story of a man who wakes up one morning to discover that his nose, no longer on his face, has run away, and he proceeds to chase after it.

◆ In England, tapping your nose with your forefinger gestures secrecy or confidentiality. In Italy, the same gesture means "Be careful."

◆ The medical term for nosebleed is *epistaxis*, a word derived from the Greek prefix *epi* (meaning "dripping") and the Greek root *stag* (meaning "drop").

◆ The trunk of the average adult elephant measures roughly five feet long and can hold up to 1.5 gallons of water.

◆ In French, "nosebleed" is *saignement du nez*.

◆ The thin wall of cartilage and bones that separates the two nostrils inside the nose is called the septum. The mucous membrane lining a curved septum (known as a deviated septum) is more apt to become dry from the air being inhaled and exhaled through the nose, resulting in nosebleeds when irritated.

◆ The nasal passages lead from the nostrils back to the upper part of the throat.

◆ Giraffes can close their nostrils completely to prevent sand and dust from getting inside.

Pet Problems

BATHING AND DEODORIZING:

- **Alberto VO5 Conditioning Hairdressing.** Detangle and shine a dog's coat by brushing in a small amount of Alberto VO5 Conditioning Hairdressing.

- **Arm & Hammer Baking Soda.** For body odor, sprinkle some baking soda on the cat or dog, work it in, then brush it off. This dry shampoo leaves your pet smelling fresh.

- **Bounce.** To get rid of the smell of a wet dog, wipe down the animal with Bounce dryer sheets, making the dog springtime fresh.

- **Carnation NonFat Dry Milk.** Wash your dog with powdered milk. Add two cups Carnation NonFat Dry Milk to the bathwater to neutralize bad smells and soften the dog's coat.

- **Clean Shower.** Clean Shower removes pet odors from carpets and floors. Simply spray the spot, let it sit for a few minutes, blot up with a damp sponge, then dry with a paper towel.

- **Kingsford's Corn Starch.** For a dry shampoo, rub Kingsford's Corn Starch into the dog or cat's fur, and then brush it out.

- **Mrs. Stewart's Liquid Bluing.** Whiten white pet fur by adding a couple of drops of Mrs. Stewart's Liquid Bluing to the rinse water while bathing your pet.

- **Wesson Corn Oil.** Give your dog's coat a shine by simply adding a teaspoon of Wesson Corn Oil to each food serving.

DISEASES AND INJURIES:

- **Accent Flavor Enhancer.** End coprophagy by adding one teaspoon Accent Flavor Enhancer to the pet's food twice daily for three days. Accent Flavor Enhancer is monosodium glutamate, a digestive enzyme that prevents a pet from eating its own feces.

- **Bag Balm.** Quicken healing of cuts, scratches, skin irritations, and paw abrasions by rubbing on Bag Balm, the salve created to relieve cracking in cow udders.

- **Mrs. Stewart's Liquid Bluing.** Reduce the algae growth in garden lily ponds, fish ponds, and feeding troughs of farm animals. Simply add a few drops of Mrs. Stewart's Liquid Bluing. Mrs. Stewart's Liquid Bluing contains a nontoxic amount of a pH balancer and a biocide to prevent the buildup of algae and bacteria.

- **Wesson Corn Oil.** To eliminate ear mites in cats, put a few drops of Wesson Corn Oil into your cat's ear, massage, then clean with a cotton ball. Repeat daily for three days. The oil soothes the cat's sensitive skin, smothers the mites, and promotes healing.

FLEAS:

- **Dawn.** To kill fleas on a dog, use a few drops of Dawn Dishwashing Liquid in the dog's bath to shampoo the dog thoroughly. Rinse well to avoid irritating the dog's skin.

- **McCormick Garlic Powder.** To prevent fleas, sprinkle your dog's food with garlic powder every day. Many pet owners claim that the resulting scent released from your dog's skin repels fleas.

- **Skin-So-Soft.** After bathing the dog, rinse the animal with two ounces of Skin-So-Soft per gallon of water. Skin-So-Soft repels fleas and ticks, and also gives the dog a shiny coat.

HAIRBALLS:

- **Alberto VO5 Conditioning Hairdressing.** Prevent cat hairballs by rubbing in a little Alberto VO5 Conditioning Hairdressing into the feline's coat. (The cat can still lick its fur without any harm. Alberto VO5 Conditioning Hairdressing is natural and nontoxic.)

- **Vaseline Petroleum Jelly.** To prevent hairballs, apply a dollop of Vaseline Petroleum Jelly to the cat's nose. The cat will lick off the jelly, which lubricates hair in the stomach, letting it pass through the animal's digestive system.

- **Wesson Corn Oil.** Putting a teaspoon of Wesson Corn Oil on your cat's food once a week helps hair pass through your cat's digestive system, preventing hairballs.

HORSES:

- **Alberto VO5 Conditioning Hairdressing.** Detangle a horse's mane and tail by rubbing in a dollop of Alberto VO5 Conditioning Hairdressing before brushing.

- **Bag Balm.** Soften hardened, dry, pinched, or contracted horse hoofs and quarter cracks. Simply rub in Bag Balm.

- **Bounce.** Repel insects from a horse by tying a sheet of unscented Bounce to the brow band of the horse's bridle.

- **Heinz Apple Cider Vinegar.** Pour one-quarter cup Heinz Apple Cider Vinegar into a sixteen-ounce trigger-spray bottle, fill the rest of the bottle with water, shake well, and spray the horse with this harmless mixture to repel flies.

- **Scope Cool Peppermint Mouthwash** and **Johnson's Baby Oil.** Mix equal parts Scope Cool Peppermint Mouthwash with Johnson's Baby Oil in a sixteen-ounce trigger-spray bottle, and spray it on your horses to repel flies.

LITTER BOXES:

- **Arm & Hammer Baking Soda.** Deodorize a cat litter box by covering the bottom of the litter box with one-quarter inch Arm & Hammer Baking Soda, then add the litter as usual.

- **Bounce.** Deodorize a cat litter box by using one or two sheets of Bounce as air filters in the top of the box.

- **20 Mule Team Borax.** Deodorize a cat litter box by mixing 1.5 cups 20 Mule Team Borax to every five pounds cat box filler to reduce and control odor in the cat box.

SKUNK:

- **Campbell's Tomato Juice.** Pour Campbell's Tomato Juice over your afflicted pet, massage the juice thoroughly into his coat, and leave it on for fifteen minutes. Then rinse and shampoo your pet with pet shampoo. But be warned: Tomato juice can temporarily dye a white dog pink. For more tips on washing the smell of skunk from dogs and cats, see page 286.

STICKERS AND BURRS:

- **Crisco All-Vegetable Shortening.** A dab of Crisco All-Vegetable Shortening over the burr helps the sticker slide out of fur easily.

- **Pam Cooking Spray.** Spray the sticker or burr with Pam Cooking Spray, then brush your pet. The vegetable oil helps ease the cocklebur from fur.

- **WD-40.** In a pinch, a spritz of WD-40 helps remove burrs from any animal's hair. Once you've pulled off the burr, wash off the WD-40 with pet shampoo.

TOENAILS:

- **Kingsford's Corn Starch.** If you clip your dog's toenail too short and it starts bleeding, pack cornstarch into the nail bed to clot the blood.

TRAINING:

- **Listerine.** Fill a trigger-spray bottle with equal parts Listerine and water. When the dog misbehaves, spray the solution in the dog's mouth (avoiding the dog's eyes) and say "No!" The side benefit? The solution eliminates doggy breath.

- **Maxwell House Coffee.** To prevent a cat from having a love affair with your houseplants, add used Maxwell House Coffee grounds to the top of the potting soil. Kitty will be turned off by that nasty scent. The coffee grounds, filled with nutrients, also fertilize the plants.

- **McCormick Black Pepper.** To keep dogs or cats out of your flowerbed or vegetable garden, sprinkle the garden beds with McCormick Black Pepper. Dogs and cats have a keen sense of smell, and the scent of pepper repels them.

- **ReaLemon.** To train a dog to stop barking, squirt some ReaLemon lemon juice in the dog's mouth and say "Quiet."

- **Reynolds Wrap.** Keep dogs and cats off sofas and upholstered chairs by placing sheets of Reynolds Wrap on the furniture. The sound of rustling foil frightens pets.

SIDE EFFECTS
BATHING AND DEODORIZING

ARM & HAMMER BAKING SODA

After blotting up the urine and cleaning it with club soda (see below), let the spot dry completely, cover it with Arm & Hammer Baking Soda, let it sit for one hour, and then vacuum it up. The baking soda will remove the smell of urine.

CANADA DRY CLUB SODA

After blotting up as much urine as possible, pour Canada Dry Club Soda over the stained area and immediately blot it up.

HEINZ WHITE VINEGAR

If you don't want to recarpet or put the house up for sale, all you need is Heinz White Vinegar. After blotting up the stain, mix one cup vinegar and one cup water in a sixteen-ounce trigger-spray bottle (or use the vinegar full strength), and saturate the spot on the carpet. It's going to smell like urine and vinegar for about three days, but once it dries, the vinegar will completely deodorize the stain. You won't smell a thing.

HUGGIES BABY WIPES

To clean cat vomit from the carpet, rub the stain with a Huggies Baby Wipe.

PAMPERS

Place a Pampers disposable diaper over the urine stain, sit several heavy books on top of the diaper to keep it pressed flat against the stain, and let it sit for one hour. The absorbent diaper will soak up most of the urine.

PARSONS' AMMONIA

After blotting up the puddle of urine and cleaning the spot with club soda (see above), dampen a cloth with Parsons' Ammonia and rub the spot. The ammonia deodorizes the urine, and the lingering scent (imperceptible to people) prevents the cat from urinating in that spot again.

20 MULE TEAM BORAX

To neutralize the smell of pet stains in carpeting, dampen the spot with water, rub in 20 Mule Team Borax, let it dry, then vacuum or brush it clean.

• **Tabasco Pepper Sauce.** Prevent cats from scratching wood furniture by rubbing the furniture with a cloth dampened with Tabasco Pepper Sauce. The faint smell of the spicy sauce repels cats.

STRANGE FACTS

◆ On their wedding night, French Empress Joséphine's dog, convinced that Napoleon was attacking her in bed, bit him.

- Abraham Lincoln said, "No matter how much cats fight, there always seem to be plenty of kittens."

- Neutering a cat extends the feline's life span by two to three years.

- A person who fears cats is called an ailurophobe.

- Every year, Americans spend more on dog food than on baby food.

- Cats can make more than one hundred vocal sounds. Dogs make roughly ten.

- Dogs and cats consume more than eleven billion dollars worth of pet food a year. That's more than the gross national products of Botswana, Chad, and Rwanda *combined*.

- The word *mutt* is short for "muttonhead," early English slang for a dimwit or dullard. The word did not refer to dogs until early in the twentieth century.

- Terry, the female cairn terrier that played Toto in the 1939 movie *The Wizard of Oz*, was paid 125 dollars a week. Judy Garland earned five hundred dollars a week for playing Dorothy.

- Volney, the roaring lion in the MGM logo, lived at the Memphis Zoo. Volney's hide is now on display in the McPherson Museum located in McPherson, Kansas.

- Four out of ten dog and cat owners carry photographs of their pets in their wallets.

- On the night of November 12, 1974, Mrs. Hollis Sharpe of Los Angeles, California, walked her miniature poodle and cleaned up after him with a piece of newspaper and a plastic bag. A mugger came up from behind, grabbed the bag, pushed Mrs. Sharpe to the ground, hopped in a car, and drove off.

- The average cat-food meal is the equivalent of five mice.

- Millie, the Bush family dog, earned more money in 1991 than President George Bush did.

- The most popular name for a dog is Brandy. The most popular name for a cat is Kitty.

A WALK WITH MILK-BONE

In the late 1800s, the owner of a London butcher shop who also made baked goods tried to create a new recipe for tea biscuits to sell to his customers. Deciding that his new batch of biscuits tasted awful, he tossed one to his dog, who quickly gobbled up the treat, inspiring the butcher with a new idea. Dog owners throughout the city were soon clamoring to buy this new canine treat now shaped like a bone and packaged specifically for dog owners.

In 1908, American businessman F. H. Bennett bought the recipe from the butcher, and the F. H. Bennett Biscuit Co. was soon marketing the dog biscuit under the brand name Malatoid, receiving a trademark in 1911. Since milk was a primary ingredient in the biscuit, the company changed the name to Milk-Bone in 1915.

The Nabisco Biscuit Company acquired Milk-Bone dog biscuits, the only dog biscuit commercially available to the public for fifty years. Initially, Nabisco advertised the treat strictly as an indulgence for dogs. Eventually, the company began to tout the fact that Milk-Bone biscuits clean a dog's teeth, improve a dog's breath, and nutritionally supplement a dog's regular diet.

IN 1955, Milk-Bone sponsored *Rin Tin Tin*, the serialized radio show on the Mutual radio network.

ON AN EPISODE of the television comedy series *Cheers*, Norm enters the bar, prompting Woody to ask, "How's it going, Mr. Peterson?" Norm replies, "It's a dog-eat-dog world, Woody, and I'm wearing Milk-Bone underwear."

RACHAEL LEIGH COOK, who starred as Josie in the 2001 movie *Josie and the Pussycats*, starred in the 1999 movie *She's All That*, and costarred with Sylvester Stallone in the 2000 movie *Get Carter*, appeared as a model on the cover of Milk-Bone boxes.

♦ Spraying a dog with WD-40 cures mange, getting rid of parasitic mites, according to *USA Today*. However, the WD-40 Company, feeling that the potential misuse of the product—which is made from petroleum distillates—is too great, refuses to condone using WD-40 to cure mange on animals.

Pizza Burn

- **Carnation NonFat Dry Milk.** Did piping hot pizza burn the roof of your mouth? Mix one teaspoon Carnation NonFat Dry Milk in two ounces water. Swish the thick milk solution around your mouth until the burning sensation subsides.

- **Cool Whip.** If you burn your mouth or tongue, eat a tablespoon of Cool Whip and, using your tongue, press the nondairy dessert topping against the roof of your mouth to coat the lesion.

- **Domino Sugar.** To relieve a tongue burned by hot pizza, steaming soup, or hot coffee or tea, sprinkle a pinch of Domino Sugar on the tongue. The pain should subside quickly.

- **Morton Salt.** Dissolve one teaspoon Morton Salt in a glass of warm water and rinse your mouth with the solution frequently to speed healing after burning your tongue or the roof of your mouth.

- **Popsicle.** Sucking on an ice-cold Popsicle and pressing it against the burn soothes the pain just like an ice pack would. Of course, unlike an ice pack, a Popsicle actually tastes good.

- **Reddi-wip.** Soothe the pizza burn on the roof of your mouth by grabbing a can of Reddi-wip and filling your mouth with whipped cream. With your tongue, press the Reddi-wip against the roof of your mouth to coat the lesion.

STRANGE FACTS

- In 1958, two brothers about to graduate from college in Wichita, Kansas, borrowed six hundred dollars from their mother, purchased some secondhand equipment, rented a small building at 254 Hayville Road, and called their restaurant Pizza Hut. They had to give away pizzas to generate interest in the fledgling business.

- In 1960, college dropout Thomas Monaghan, a former Marine who had been raised in an orphanage and several foster homes, borrowed nine hundred dollars and bought DomiNick's (named after original owners Dom and Nick), a failed pizza parlor at 2121 Grove Street in Ypsilanti, Michigan, which he ran with his brother James. A year later, Monaghan traded a Volkswagen Beetle for his brother's half of the company, which he renamed Domino's in 1965.

- In 1969, Pizza Hut adopted the trademark red roof for its restaurants, and within two years, Pizza Hut became the number one pizza restaurant chain in the world in both sales and number of restaurants.

- In 1975, Amstar Corporation (maker of Domino Sugar) sued Domino's Pizza for trademark infringement. Domino's Pizza won the legal battle.

- Domino's founder Thomas Monaghan invented the corrugated pizza box and insulated bags to transport pizzas.

- In 1989, commercials for Domino's Pizza, showing employees battling the Noid, a gremlin who delays deliveries and carries a gun that can turn a pizza ice cold, provoked twenty-two-year-old Kenneth Noid to walk into a Domino's Pizza shop in Chamblee, Georgia, with a .357 magnum revolver and take two employees hostage. When police arrived, Noid demanded $100,000 in cash, a getaway car, and a copy of *The Widow's Son*, a 1985 novel about secret societies in an eighteenth-century Parisian prison. After five hours, Noid surrendered to police. No one was hurt.

- In 1991, Pizza Hut delivered pizza to Russian president Boris Yeltsin and his supporters, who prevailed over an attempted political coup.

When food supplies dwindled in the Russian Parliament Building, Yeltsin called Pizza Hut delivery.

◆ In 1995, Pizza Hut sold more than $5.3 billion worth of food. That's equal to buying two slices of pizza for every man, woman, and child in Somalia every day for a year.

◆ In 1995, Domino's Pizza used more than two million cases of pizza sauce (requiring more than 170 million pounds of tomatoes), 110 million pounds of part-skim mozzarella cheese, and 108 million pounds of flour. That's enough ingredients to make a pizza the size of Utah.

◆ *Mockba*, the favorite Pizza Hut pizza in Russia, is topped with sardines, tuna, mackerel, salmon, and onions.

◆ There are three Domino's Pizza stores in Medellín, Colombia, considered the most dangerous city in the world—suggesting that drug lords may like their pizza delivered hot and fresh within thirty minutes just like everyone else.

◆ In Thailand, the Pizza Hut menu features Spicy Shrimp Pizza in Thai traditional Tom Yam style (topped with fresh shrimp and mushrooms with galingale, lemongrass, and chili plus a slice of lime).

◆ Toppings at the Domino's stores in India include pickled ginger, minced mutton, and tofu.

◆ Domino's had to change its first marketing slogan in the United Kingdom from "One Call Does It All." In the U.K., a "call" refers to a personal visit (particularly from a call girl).

Poison Ivy

- **Adolph's Meat Tenderizer.** Relieve the itch of poison ivy by making a paste of meat tenderizer and water and applying the mixture over the affected area as a liniment. The enzymes in meat tenderizer break down the proteins in urushiol oil (the oil in poison ivy that rapidly penetrates the skin and combines with skin proteins to trigger an allergic reaction) while simultaneously numbing the skin.

- **Arm & Hammer Baking Soda.** Make a paste of Arm & Hammer Baking Soda and water and apply it to the affected area.

- **Balmex.** To relieve poison ivy, apply Balmex to the affected area. The diaper rash ointment relieves the burning pain and dries any oozing sores.

- **Carnation NonFat Dry Milk.** Mix one cup Carnation Nonfat Dry Milk and 2.5 cups water in a Rubbermaid container. Fill the rest of the container with ice cubes, and then sprinkle two tablespoons salt over the ice. Saturate a washcloth (or a Stayfree Maxi Pad) in the ice-cold milky solution and apply to the affected area three or four times daily.

- **Cascade.** Fill your cupped palm with a handful of Cascade and scrub affected areas in the shower. The phosphates in the dishwashing powder cleanse the urushiol oil from skin and dry the inflammation.

- **Cheerios.** Pour two cups Cheerios in a blender and grind them into a fine powder on medium-high speed. Put the powdered Cheerios into a warm bath and soak in the oats for thirty minutes. It's a soothing oatmeal bath that relieves the itching from poison ivy. Use a plastic or mesh drain cover to avoid clogging your pipes when you empty the tub.

- **Clorox.** Immediately wash with soap and water, then mix equal parts Clorox and water, saturate a cotton ball with the liquid, and dab it on affected areas. The bleach removes urushiol oil and treats the resulting rash. If the bleach begins to irritate the skin, shower it off.

- **Cutex Nail Polish Remover.** Within thirty minutes of contact with poison ivy, wash the contaminated skin with soap and water, then use a cotton ball to apply Cutex Nail Polish Remover to the area. According to the *New York Times*, the acetone in the nail polish remover will remove some of the urushiol oil, reducing the severity of the itching and possibly preventing a rash altogether.

- **Dickinson's Witch Hazel.** Apply Dickinson's Witch Hazel to the affected skin to soothe the itching.

- **Heinz White Vinegar** and **Morton Salt.** Pour Heinz White Vinegar over the affected area. Then sprinkle lightly with Morton Salt, let dry, and brush clean. Repeat if itching recurs or if the rash begins oozing. The vinegar and salt treatment should dry up the rash within two days.

- **Kiwi White Liquid Shoe Polish.** Apply white shoe polish over the affected area. The pipe clay and zinc oxide in the shoe polish soothes the rash and prevents oozing sores from erupting.

- **Listerine.** Douse the affected area with Listerine. This antiseptic treatment will sting but should stop the itching immediately.

- **Nestea.** Fill a bathtub with warm water, empty in an entire jar of Nestea powder, mix well, then take the Nestea Plunge for fifteen minutes. The tannic acid in the tea soothes the itching and dries up the poison ivy rash.

- **Parsons' Ammonia.** Within thirty minutes of contact with poison ivy, wash the contaminated skin with soap and water, then pour Parsons' Ammonia over the area to remove the urushiol oil before the rash occurs.

- **Phillips' Milk of Magnesia.** The alkalinity of Phillips' Milk of Magnesia relieves the itch of poison ivy. Simply use a cotton ball to dab it on the affected areas.

- **Preparation H.** Applying Preparation H to poison ivy relieves the burning and swelling and clears up the rash.

- **Quaker Oats** and **L'eggs Sheer Energy Panty Hose.** Using a blender, grind one cup Quaker Oats into a fine powder. Cut off the foot from a clean, used pair of L'eggs Sheer Energy Panty Hose, fill it with the powdered oats, and tie a knot in the nylon. Hang the "oatmeal tea bag" from the spigot in the bathtub, fill the tub with warm water, and soak for thirty minutes for an inexpensive and soothing oatmeal bath. The oatmeal sack can be used as a gentle washcloth.

- **ReaLemon.** Applying ReaLemon lemon juice over poison ivy soothes itching and alleviates the rash.

- **Right Guard.** Spraying deodorant on your skin can protect you from getting poison ivy in the first place. The aluminum chlorohydrate in the deodorant prevents the urushiol oil in poison ivy from irritating the skin.

- **Smirnoff Vodka.** Pouring vodka over the affected areas immediately will remove the urushiol oil from the skin.

Don't go itching for trouble! If your blisters are weeping honey-colored fluid, the itching is severe and keeps you up at night, or the rash occurs on your face (especially near your eyes), see your doctor.

STRANGE FACTS

- ◆ The active ingredient in poison ivy and poison oak is urushiol oil, one of the most potent external toxins known to man.

- ◆ The average person breaks out in a rash after coming into contact with just one ten-millionth of a gram of urushiol oil.

- ◆ Less than one-quarter ounce of urushiol oil could give a rash to every person on earth.

- ◆ Urushiol oil is similar to carbolic acid.

- The Japanese painted urushiol lacquer over the gold leaf upon restoring the Golden Temple in Kyoto. If anyone attempts to steal the gold, they will literally be caught red-handed.

- The 1959 hit song "Poison Ivy," written by Paul Gibson and recorded by the Coasters, warns "You're gonna need an ocean of calamine lotion" if you get involved with a certain girl named Ivy.

- In the 1997 movie *Batman and Robin*, actress Uma Thurman co-stars as villain Poison Ivy, a former botanist who had her blood replaced with aloe, her skin infused with chlorophyll, and her lips filled with venom—making her kisses deadly.

Pregnancy

- **Canada Dry Ginger Ale.** To calm the nausea of morning sickness, drink Canada Dry Ginger Ale to settle your upset stomach.

- **Gatorade.** To relieve morning sickness, drink Gatorade to help maintain the body's balance of electrolytes, which regulate the body's electrochemical balance.

- **Huggies Baby Wipes.** After an episiotomy, use unscented Huggies Baby Wipes instead of toilet paper. These wet wipes are gentle enough for a baby and perfect after an operation on the more sensitive areas of your body.

- **Krispy Original Saltine Crackers.** To relieve morning sickness, eat a few Krispy Original Saltine Crackers first thing in the morning to absorb the excess fluids in your stomach and ease nausea.

- **Wilson Tennis Balls.** Fill a sock with three or four Wilson Tennis Balls and tie a knot to seal the open end of the sock. Have a partner roll the sock over your back to ease your achy muscles, particularly when you go into labor.

- **Wonder Bread.** Eat a toasted piece of Wonder Bread to absorb the excess fluids in your stomach and relieve morning sickness.

Baby yourself! If morning sickness and backaches become severe or persist despite your self-care efforts, talk to your doctor.

• **Ziploc Storage Bags.** Keep several gallon-size Ziploc Storage Bags on hand (in your purse, desk drawer, or glove compartment) for morning sickness. Afterward, simply zip the bag shut and toss it into the nearest trash can.

Strange Facts

◆ Ancient Greek physician Hippocrates (circa 460–377 B.C.E.), considered the father of modern medicine, incorrectly claimed that the sex of an unborn child could be determined based on which one of the mother's breasts became larger.

◆ Ancient Scandinavian mothers told their children that storks brought new babies because storks nested on chimney stacks of homes, returning to the same chimney every year. In the nineteenth century, Danish writer Hans Christian Andersen popularized the myth through his fairy tales.

◆ Some pregnant women who are eager to induce labor drink castor oil mixed with orange juice to initiate contractions, but doctors strongly advise against this practice. Castor oil can often stimulate labor in a woman ready to give birth by irritating the intestine into contractions (creating a corresponding reflex contraction in the uterine muscles). However, castor oil can also cause uncontrolled uterine activity, spasmodic and painful contractions, and hyperstimulation of the uterus, which can result in fetal distress, the passage of meconium into the uterus, and increased risk of intervention.

◆ In Mexico, Parker Pen's advertising agency translated the phrase "won't leak in your pocket and embarrass you" by using the Spanish verb *embarazar* incorrectly, which made the phrase read, "won't leak in your pocket and make you pregnant."

◆ The two most common surgeries are biopsies and cesarean sections.

◆ An armadillo's egg cell always splits into four quarters when fertilized, resulting in perfect quadruplets.

◆ The African elephant is pregnant for 640 days. That's more than twenty-one months.

- In 1986, bookstores received copies of *First Love: A Young People's Guide to Sexual Information* by popular radio sex adviser Dr. Ruth Westheimer. Three months later, the publisher, Warner Books, discovered that the book incorrectly told readers that a woman will not get pregnant if she has intercourse during the week before ovulation. In fact, a woman having intercourse during this time is most likely to get pregnant. Warner Books recalled the 115,000 copies in distribution and issued a corrected edition with a different color cover. Surprisingly, no lawsuits resulted from any readers who became pregnant.

- The first white wedding dress for pregnant brides was unveiled at the bridal fair in 1995 in Harrogate, England.

- Kangaroos are not the only animals that carry their young in pouches. Other animals with pouches include the anteater, koala, opossum, sea horse, and Tasmanian devil.

Psoriasis

- **Arm & Hammer Baking Soda.** Mix one-third cup Arm & Hammer Baking Soda in a gallon of water. Soak a washcloth in the solution, wring it out, and apply it as a compress to the affected area.

- **Bag Balm.** Apply a dab of Bag Balm (the salve created to relieve cracking in cow udders) to the dry or cracked skin.

- **Carnation NonFat Dry Milk.** Add one handful Carnation NonFat Dry Milk to a bathtub of warm water and soak for fifteen minutes. The lactic acid in the milk moisturizes dry skin.

- **Crisco All-Vegetable Shortening.** After bathing and while still dripping wet, coat the affected area with Crisco All-Vegetable Shortening to seal in the moisture.

- **Heinz Apple Cider Vinegar.** Add one cup Heinz Apple Cider Vinegar to a bathtub of cold water for a refreshing bath to help soothe the itching.

- **Lubriderm.** Immediately after getting out of the shower or bath, rub Lubriderm over the affected area to help your skin retain water.

- **Pam Cooking Spray.** After rehydrating your skin with a shower or bath, spray the psoriasis sores with Pam Cooking Spray to moisturize the skin.

- **Saran Wrap.** Apply cortisone cream to the lesions, and, using tape, cover with a piece of Saran Wrap no larger than a half dollar to seal in the moisture and inhibit proliferation.

- **Star Olive Oil.** Before toweling yourself dry after a bath or shower, rub olive oil into the affected areas as a moisturizer.

- **Vaseline Petroleum Jelly.** Before toweling yourself dry after getting out of the shower or bath, coat the affected areas of your skin with Vaseline Petroleum Jelly to seal in the moisture.

- **Wesson Corn Oil.** Add a couple of capfuls of Wesson Corn Oil to a warm bath.

- **Ziploc Freezer Bags.** Placing an ice pack over the affected skin soothes psoriasis. Fill a Ziploc Freezer Bag with water and freeze it or fill it with ice cubes. Wrap the ice pack in a paper towel before applying. For other ways to make and apply an ice pack, see page 198.

STRANGE FACTS

◆ No one knows what causes psoriasis nor do doctors know how to cure it.

◆ Scientists theorize that psoriasis results from an accelerated division of skin cells on the outer skin layer. These poorly developed cells cannot shed fast enough. Instead, they pile up, forming white scales that cover thick, itchy patches that leave the skin red and inflamed.

◆ American author Ernest Hemingway suffered from psoriasis.

◆ In 1942, Admiral William F. "Bull" Halsey Jr. was hospitalized in Hawaii to treat a severe flare-up of psoriasis, preventing him from commanding the United States fleet at the battle of Midway in the Pacific Ocean during World War II. Instead, Rear Admiral Raymond A. Spruance took command.

◆ In "God (A Play)," published in his 1972 book *Without Feathers*, Woody Allen names the characters Trichinosis, Diabetes, and Hepatitis—but fails to include Psoriasis.

◆ Television commercials coined the unusual phrase "eczema, seborrhea, and heartbreak of psoriasis."

- In the 1972 movie *Last Tango in Paris*, Marlon Brando chases after a man having an affair with his wife and wrestles him to the ground. The man pleads with Brando, explaining that his own wife has skin like a fish—an allusion, in all likelihood, to psoriasis.

- In the 1978 movie *Grease*, Olivia Newton-John tells her friends she is no stranger to heartbreak. DeeDee Conn replies, "Why? You got psoriasis?"

- On the television show *The Wonder Years*, the eldest son, Wayne, is rejected for the army because he has psoriasis.

Rash

- **Arm & Hammer Baking Soda.** Dissolve one-half cup Arm & Hammer Baking Soda in a tepid bath. Soak in the bath for fifteen minutes.

- **French's Mustard.** Rub French's Mustard over the rash, or empty a bottle of French's Mustard into a bathtub filled with warm water, mix well, and soak in the mustard bath for fifteen minutes.

- **Heinz Apple Cider Vinegar.** Splash Heinz Apple Cider Vinegar on the rash to soothe the skin.

- **Johnson's Baby Powder.** To relieve the itching of a rash, pat Johnson's Baby Powder onto the affected area.

- **Kingsford's Corn Starch.** Sprinkle Kingsford's Corn Starch on the rash to absorb moisture and relieve the itching.

- **Neutrogena Body Moisturizer.** Prevent rashes by moisturizing arms and legs with Neutrogena Body Moisturizer.

- **Quaker Oats** and **L'eggs Sheer Energy Panty Hose.** Pour one cup Quaker Oats in a blender and blend into a powder. Cut off the foot from a clean, used pair of L'eggs Sheer Energy Panty Hose and fill with the powdered Quaker Oats. Tie a knot in the nylon, hang it from the tub's spigot, and fill the tub with warm water. Soak in the tub for thirty minutes for an inexpensive and soothing oatmeal bath. Use the oatmeal sack as a washcloth.

- **SueBee Honey.** Apply a thin coat of SueBee Honey over the affected skin to heal the rash. Honey is a disinfectant ointment.

- **Ziploc Freezer Bags.** Placing an ice pack over a rash soothes the itching. Fill a Ziploc Freezer Bag with water and freeze it or fill it with ice cubes. Wrap the ice pack in a paper towel before applying. For other ways to make and apply an ice pack, see page 198.

Strange Facts

◆ The Bible contains the verse "Be not rash with thy mouth" (Ecclesiastes 5:2).

◆ In the 18th century, Scottish poet Robert Burns wrote:
    Green grow the rashes O;
    Green grow the rashes O;
    The sweetest hours that e'er I spend,
    Are spent among the lasses O!

◆ When Walt Disney released the movie *Son of Flubber* in 1963, Hassenfeld Brothers, a Rhode Island toy company known today as Hasbro, sold more than four million packages of a tie-in product: Flubber, a mixture of rubber and mineral oil somewhat like Silly Putty. When the Flubber caused minor rashes in hundreds of children, Hasbro recalled the product and commissioned a city dump to burn the substance. When the burning substance created a huge cloud of black smoke, the city ceased the operation. The Coast Guard then gave Hasbro permission to dump the Flubber at sea. The globules resurfaced all over Narragansett Bay. Local fishermen helped round up the Flubber, which was then buried—either in a landfill or, as legend holds, under the parking lot of a Hasbro factory.

◆ Aside from referring to a skin irritation, the word *rash* also means "brash" and "impulsive."

Runny Nose

- **Campbell's Chicken Noodle Soup.** Sipping a bowl of hot Campbell's Chicken Noodle Soup actually helps decongest nasal passages while simultaneously rehydrating and reenergizing the body with essential salts.

- **Gatorade.** Drinking a quart of liquid, such as Gatorade, daily replaces vital bodily fluids and keeps the mucous lining moist so the cilia at the back of the nose and throat can clear your nasal passages. Gatorade rehydrates the body and replaces electrolytes.

- **Gold's Horseradish.** Gold's Horseradish is a natural remedy for a congested nose. Eat some horseradish on saltine crackers.

- **Lipton Tea Bags, ReaLemon,** and **SueBee Honey.** Drinking hot tea with lemon and honey replaces vital bodily fluids, flushes impurities from your system, and helps decongest your sinuses. (Honey should not be fed to infants under one year of age.)

- **McCormick Garlic Powder.** Spice your foods with McCormick Garlic Powder. Garlic contains a chemical that makes mucus less sticky, clearing the sinuses.

- **Morton Salt.** Clear congested sinuses by mixing one-half teaspoon Morton Salt in one cup warm water. Fill an aspirator or an eyedropper with the saline solution, insert it in your nostril, hold your head back so you're facing the ceiling, and inhale the liquid. Blow your nose thoroughly. Repeat several times. (You can make an impromptu eyedropper with a Glad

Flexible Straw, too—just insert the straw into the liquid, cover the open end of the straw with your finger, and lift. The liquid will stay in the straw until you release your finger.)

- **Tabasco Pepper Sauce** and **Campbell's Tomato Juice.** Mix ten to twenty drops Tabasco Pepper Sauce in a glass of tomato juice. Drink several of these decongestant tonics daily to help relieve congestion in the nose, sinuses, and lungs. Or gargle with ten to twenty drops Tabasco Pepper Sauce mixed in a glass of water to clear out the respiratory tract. The capsaicin spurs the nerve fibers, working like a natural decongestant.

- **Vaseline Petroleum Jelly** and **Q-Tips Cotton Swabs.** When your nose gets sore from too much blowing, apply a thin coat of Vaseline Petroleum Jelly around your nostrils, using a Q-Tips Cotton Swab.

- **Ziploc Storage Bags.** Keep a large Ziploc Storage Bag on hand so you can dispose of used tissues and seal the bag to avoid spreading germs.

STRANGE FACTS

- ◆ The mucous membrane responsible for your sense of smell is the size of a dime.

- ◆ When people say they "smell rain," they actually smell the chemicals on the inside of plant cells. The low-pressure system that precedes a rainstorm causes plants to open, enabling us to better smell them.

- ◆ Ancient Greek physician Galen (circa 130–200 B.C.E.) wrongly insisted that the brain—not the sinus passages—manufactures phlegm.

- ◆ In 1530, Dutch author Erasmus of Rotterdam wrote his popular book of manners, *On Civility in Children*, including the advice: "You should not offer your handkerchief to anyone unless it has been freshly washed. Nor is it seemly, after wiping your nose, to spread out your handkerchief and peer into it as if pearls and rubies might have fallen out of your head."

- ◆ The word *snot* also means "brat" and the adjective *snotty* means "arrogant."

- The 1970s television sitcom *Welcome Back, Kotter*, starring Gabe Kaplan and John Travolta, popularized the meaningless catchphrase "Up your nose with a rubber hose."

- If your nose is congested and you close your eyes, you will be unable to differentiate between the taste of an apple and a potato, or red wine and coffee (if served at the same temperature).

- Mucus is composed primarily of a compound of protein and sugar.

- In German the word for mucus is *Nasenschleim*, which literally means "nose slime."

- Comedian Jimmy Durante had a huge, bulbous nose, which earned him the nickname "Schnozolla."

Shampoo

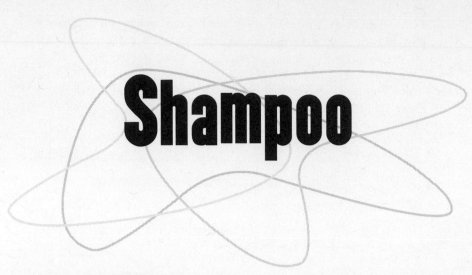

- **Arm & Hammer Baking Soda.** To remove conditioner and styling gel buildup from hair, wash hair once a week with one tablespoon Arm & Hammer Baking Soda mixed with your regular shampoo. Rinse thoroughly, then condition and style as usual.

- **Budweiser.** The king of beers makes a terrific shampoo for oily hair, although shampooing your hair too frequently with beer can eventually dry out your scalp and lead to dandruff.

- **Comet.** To strip styling gel and hair spray build-up from hair, dissolve one tablespoon Comet (without bleach) in two cups water, pour the solution through hair, and let set for three minutes. Shampoo and condition as usual.

- **Country Time Lemonade.** The citric acid in Country Time Lemonade cuts through sebum oil in hair when used as shampoo.

- **Dawn.** To cut through grease and grime in hair, use a few drops of Dawn dishwashing liquid as shampoo. The detergent in Dawn thoroughly cleanses hair.

- **Epsom Salt.** Mix three tablespoons Epsom Salt in one-half cup shampoo, and use one tablespoon of this mixture to shampoo oily hair. Massage in well, and then rinse with cool water. The Epsom Salt absorbs the oil from hair.

- **Heinz Apple Cider Vinegar.** Add one tablespoon Heinz Apple Cider Vinegar to a twelve-ounce bottle of shampoo and shake it well. The vinegar thickens the shampoo (so you use less), helps rinse styling gel and hair spray buildup from your hair, and restores natural acids.

- **Listerine.** If you have oily hair, use a cotton ball to apply Listerine to your scalp after shampooing. The mouthwash, being both an antiseptic and an astringent, will slow down oil secretions.

- **ReaLemon.** For oily hair, mix equal parts ReaLemon lemon juice and water, and, after using your regular shampoo, rinse your hair with the lemon solution.

- **Smirnoff Vodka.** Add one jigger Smirnoff Vodka to a twelve-ounce bottle of shampoo. The alcohol cleanses the scalp, removes toxins from hair, and stimulates the growth of healthy hair.

- **Tang.** Pour one tablespoon Tang drink mix into the cupped palm of your hand, add enough water to make a paste, then wash your hair with the first drink mix to go to the moon. The citric acid in Tang cuts through sebum oil in hair.

- **Woolite.** Wash your hair with a capful of Woolite to gently strip hair spray and styling gel buildup and soften your hair at the same time. Avoid getting the Woolite in your eyes.

STRANGE FACTS

- ◆ The scalp releases sebum oil into the hair, which in turn causes dirt to stick to the hair.

- ◆ Ancient Egyptians used water and citrus juice to effectively wash the sebum oil from hair.

- ◆ During the Middle Ages, Europeans boiled water and soap with potash, unwittingly giving the cleansing formula an abundance of negatively charged hydroxyl ions—much like modern-day shampoos.

- ◆ British hairdressers coined the word *shampoo* from the Hindu *champoo* ("to massage") to refer to hair cleansing formulas made from water, soap, and potash.

◆ In the 1890s, German chemists discovered the detergents that would wash sebum oil from hair.

◆ Soap cannot be used to shampoo hair because soap scum remains behind.

◆ In the 1975 movie *Shampoo*, Warren Beatty stars as a hedonistic Beverly Hills hairdresser seeking intimate relationships with no strings attached.

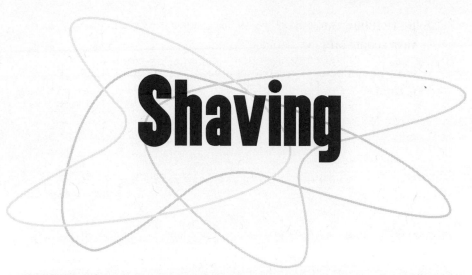

Shaving

- **Absorbine Jr.** To prevent skin irritations in the bikini area from shaving, apply Absorbine Jr. to the skin afterward. The Absorbine Jr. burns momentarily, but it does prevent itching and red bumps.

- **Alberto VO5 Conditioning Hairdressing.** Soothe your legs after shaving by rubbing a dollop of Alberto VO5 Conditioning Hairdressing into your skin to make your legs feel velvety smooth.

- **Arm & Hammer Baking Soda.** For an effective aftershave lotion to minimize razor burn, mix one tablespoon Arm & Hammer Baking Soda in one cup water.

- **Baby Magic Baby Powder.** Prevent friction burns when shaving your legs with an electric razor by dusting legs lightly with Baby Magic Baby Powder before shaving.

- **Cheez Whiz.** If you run out of shaving cream, slather on Cheez Whiz. The oils in the Cheez Whiz lubricate the skin, giving you a remarkably close shave and an alluring aroma.

- **Clairol Herbal Essences Conditioner.** Cream rinse makes an excellent substitute for shaving cream. The emollients in Clairol Herbal Essences Conditioner leave the skin feeling soft and help to prevent rashes and bumps.

- **Clean Shower.** Spray the safety razor blade with Clean Shower after each use, then rinse it thoroughly to triple the life of the razor.

- **Close-Up Red Gel Toothpaste.** If you have sensitive skin, Close-Up Red Gel Toothpaste doubles as a nonallergenic shaving cream, giving a close, smooth shave that leaves the skin feeling slightly anesthetized.

- **Cool Whip.** Apply Cool Whip to wet skin as a substitute for shaving cream. The oils in Cool Whip moisturize the skin for a close shave.

- **Jif Peanut Butter.** Choosy shavers choose Jif. In a pinch, you can shave with peanut butter. In fact, this little tidbit was discovered by former United States senator Barry Goldwater while on a camping trip. Just slather Jif Peanut Butter on your face or legs, and shave as you normally would. The oils in the peanut butter lubricate the skin for a smooth shave. Just be sure you use the creamy, not the chunky.

- **Johnson's Baby Oil.** Slathering Johnson's Baby Oil on skin before shaving raises hair stubs for a clean shave, lubricates the razor, moisturizes sensitive skin, and prevents the safety razor blade from rusting.

- **Land O Lakes Butter.** If you run out of shaving cream, slather Land O Lakes Butter on wet skin for a silky, smooth shave.

- **Listerine.** Disinfect and extend the life of your safety razor blades by washing them with Listerine after each use.

- **Lubriderm.** In a pinch, this moisturizing cream doubles as a luxurious shaving cream.

- **Miracle Whip.** To avoid a rash from shaving your bikini area, use Miracle Whip as a substitute for shaving cream. Miracle Whip hydrates the skin, preventing razor burn.

- **Noxzema.** This cold cream doubles as shaving cream in a pinch, lubricating the skin.

- **Oral-B Toothbrush.** Use a clean, used Oral-B Toothbrush to clean all the gunk out of your safety razor blades.

- **Pam Cooking Spray.** This aerosol oil goes on easily at the push of a button, lubricating the skin for a smooth, no-stick shave.

- **Reddi-wip.** Apply Reddi-wip to wet skin, let sit for two minutes, then shave. This tasty substitute for shaving cream also moisturizes the skin while you shave.

SIDE EFFECTS

NICKS AND CUTS

AFRIN

If you cut yourself shaving, squirt some Afrin nasal spray on the cut and the bleeding will stop within seconds. Afrin helps the blood clot quickly.

CHAPSTICK

Dab on some ChapStick to stop a shaving nick from bleeding.

DICKINSON'S WITCH HAZEL and Q-TIPS COTTON SWABS

Use a Q-Tips Cotton Swab to dab some Dickinson's Witch Hazel on a shaving nick. This astringent causes the blood vessels to shrink and contract.

McCORMICK ALUM

To stop a shaving nick from bleeding, dab on a pinch of McCormick Alum. Alum is the active ingredient in styptic pencils.

- **Smirnoff Vodka.** Prolong the life of razors by filling a cup with Smirnoff Vodka and letting your safety razor blade soak in the alcohol after shaving. The vodka disinfects the blade and prevents rusting.

- **Vaseline Petroleum Jelly.** Dipping your safety razor blade in Vaseline Petroleum Jelly after each use prevents the blade from rusting.

- **WD-40.** Extend the life of your safety razor blades by spraying them with WD-40. The water-displacement formula prevents the blades from rusting.

STRANGE FACTS

- ◆ According to archaeologists, men shaved their faces as far back as the Stone Age. Prehistoric men shaved with clam shells, shark teeth, sharpened pieces of flint, and knives.

- ◆ Archaeologists have discovered gold and copper razors in Egyptian tombs dating back to the fourth century B.C.E. A golden razor found in King Tut's tomb was still sharp enough to be used.

- Ancient Egyptians shaved their eyebrows to mourn the deaths of their cats.

- In 500 B.C.E., Histiaeus wrote a secret message on the shaved head of a slave, waited for his hair to grow back, and then sent the slave across enemy lines. When the slave's head was shaved, the message was revealed.

- Ancient Egyptians shaved their faces and heads during hand-to-hand combat so the enemy had less to grab.

- In 1895, American King Camp Gillette invented the modern safety razor with a replaceable blade.

- In 1931, former United States Army colonel Jacob Schick—having mortgaged his home and gone into serious debt—introduced the world's first electric razor. In his first year, Schick sold three thousand razors at twenty-five dollars each—in the heart of the Depression. By reinvesting his money in advertising, he sold nearly two million shavers in 1937 alone.

- Aerosol cans to deliver shaving cream were introduced in the mid-1950s.

- Shaving in the shower wastes an average of ten to thirty-five gallons of water. To conserve water, fill the sink basin with an inch of water and vigorously rinse your razor often in the water after every second or third stroke.

- The longest beard, according to *Guinness World Records*, measured 17.5 feet long and was presented to the Smithsonian Institution in 1967.

- The first shaving creams specifically targeted to women were introduced in 1986.

- Pfizer, the company that makes Barbasol Shaving Cream, also makes Viagra.

- Seventy percent of women rate clean-shaven men as sexy.

A CLOSE SHAVE WITH GILLETTE

In 1895, while shaving with a straight razor at home in Brookline, Massachusetts, King C. Gillette, traveling salesman and author of the 1894 book *The Human Drift*, decided to develop a disposable razor blade. For the next six years, Gillette sought investors and toolmakers to develop the technology to manufacture paper-thin steel blades. Finally, in 1901, MIT professor William Nickerson teamed up with Gillette to perfect the safety razor, and with the financial support of some wealthy friends, the two men formed the American Safety Razor Company. In 1903, Gillette sold fifty-one sets of safety razors and 168 disposable razors. Americans bought 90,844 sets in 1904, and two years later, sales reached 300,000 razors and over half a million blades. Gillette retired as president of the company in 1931, ironically the same year that Jacob Schick invented the electric razor.

DURING WORLD WAR I, the United States government bought 3.5 million Service Set shaving kits from Gillette for the armed forces, totaling more than thirty-six million blades.

IN THE 1920S, Gillette distributed free razors through boxes of Wrigley's gum and a "Shave and Save" plan at banks.

GILLETTE IS THE WORLD'S number one seller of blades and razors.

THE STRENGTH OF EARLY LASERS was measured in Gillettes—the number of blue razor blades a given beam could puncture.

IN 1975, the very first broadcast of *Saturday Night Live* mocked Gillette's Trac II razor with a parody commercial for a three-bladed razor. In 1998, Gillette got the last laugh, unveiling the Mach 3, the world's first three-bladed razor.

Shingles

- **Bayer Aspirin** and **Cutex Nail Polish Remover.** Using a mortar and pestle, crush two Bayer Aspirin tablets into powder, and mix with two tablespoons Cutex Nail Polish Remover. Apply the mixture to the affected area with a cotton ball and let dry for immediate relief that lasts for several hours. Do not use if you are allergic to aspirin.

- **Kingsford's Corn Starch.** Toss a handful of corn starch into the bathtub and fill with warm water for a soothing twenty-minute bath to relieve the itching.

- **Phillips' Milk of Magnesia.** Use a cotton ball to dab Phillips' Milk of Magnesia on the blisters to cool and soothe the sores and speed healing.

- **Quaker Oats** and **L'eggs Sheer Energy Panty Hose.** In a blender, grind one cup Quaker Oats into a fine powder. Cut off the foot from a clean, used pair of L'eggs Sheer Energy Panty Hose, then pour the oat powder into the panty hose foot. Tie a knot in the nylon, hang the sachet from the spigot in the bathtub, and fill the tub with warm water. Soak in the soothing oatmeal bath for thirty minutes, then use the oatmeal sack as a washcloth.

- **Tabasco Pepper Sauce.** Spread the hot sauce along the line of blisters to decrease the burning pain. Tabasco Pepper Sauce contains the alkaloid capsaicin, a spicy compound proven to numb pain when applied topically. Capsaicin enters nerves and temporarily depletes them of the neurotransmitter that sends pain signals to the brain. If you feel a burning sensation on the skin, apply a thin coat of Colgate Toothpaste over the dried Tabasco Pepper

Sauce. The glycerine in the toothpaste will reduce the burning discomfort and may also amplify the analgesia from the capsaicin.

- **Ziploc Storage Bags.** After the blisters have healed, if you still have pain, fill a Ziploc Storage Bag with ice cubes, wrap it in a paper towel, and use it to rub down the afflicted skin.

Save your skin! See a doctor if shingles occur near your eyes, are widespread and painful, or if you are over sixty years old.

STRANGE FACTS

◆ Shingles are caused by the *Varicella* virus, the bug lying dormant in your nerves ever since you had the chicken pox as a child. A weakened immune system awakens the virus, causing a line of blisters to break out on one side of the body. The blisters scab within two weeks, and the accompanying itching and pain subsides after a maximum of six weeks.

◆ The word *shingles* originates from the Latin word *cingulum*, meaning "girdle."

◆ Shingles are more commonly the thin pieces of slate or wood laid in overlapping rows to cover the roof or walls of a building. This word *shingles*, however, is derived from the Latin word *scindula*, meaning "to cut."

◆ A shingle is hung outside a place of business as a signboard.

◆ The phrase "hang out your shingle" means to go into business.

◆ In the United States Army, chipped beef on toast is referred to as "S.O.S.," the acronym for "something" on a shingle.

Skunk Odor

- **Arm & Hammer Baking Soda, Hydrogen Peroxide,** and **Dawn.** In a bucket, mix the contents of one small box Arm & Hammer Baking Soda, two cups hydrogen peroxide, one teaspoon Dawn Dishwashing Liquid, and one gallon warm water. Use a scrub brush to wash with this solution.

- **Campbell's Tomato Juice.** Empty two one-quart cans tomato juice into a bucket and sponge the juice full strength all over your body, face, and through your hair while sitting in a bathtub with the drain plugged. Fill the bathtub with water and soak in the diluted tomato juice for fifteen minutes, then rinse clean. To deodorize a pet, pour Campbell's Tomato Juice over the animal and rub it in. Sponge it over the pet's face. Rinse and repeat. The acids from the tomatoes neutralize the skunk smell.

- **Coca-Cola.** Pour four two-liter bottles Coke into a bucket, sponge yourself down in the shower, and rinse clean. The acids in the Coca-Cola kill skunk odor.

- **Listerine.** Applying Listerine full strength to the affected areas removes the smell of skunk spray on humans and dogs. (Avoid getting Listerine in eyes or ears.) Then wash with soap and water, and rinse. The antiseptic in Listerine neutralizes the skunk odor.

- **Massengill Disposable Douche.** The ingredients in Massengill Disposable Douche neutralize skunk odor. Simply wash yourself or a sprayed animal with this feminine hygiene product, then rinse well.

- **Playtex Living Gloves.** If you're washing the smell of skunk from a child or a family pet, be sure to wear Playtex Living Gloves to avoid getting the skunk smell all over yourself.

- **ReaLemon.** You'll need several bottles of ReaLemon lemon juice to wash down your body or your pet, but the acids in lemon juice eliminate skunk odor—reportedly better than tomato juice.

STRANGE FACTS

- In nearly every Pepe LePew cartoon, Pepe the skunk falls in love with a black cat that accidentally gets a white stripe painted down its back.

- In an episode of *The Partridge Family*, a skunk stows away aboard the Partridge family's bus. Mr. Kincaid forces America's grooviest television family to bathe in tomato juice to get rid of the smell.

- The skunk cabbage, a plant that grows in low swamps in eastern and central North America, is named for its unpleasant odor.

- John Waters' 1981 movie *Polyester*, starring Divine and Tab Hunter, was filmed in "Odorama." Viewers experienced the movie's various smells—including vomit and excrement—with a scratch-and-sniff card.

- In the 1989 movie *Troop Beverly Hills*, starring Shelley Long, the troop wins a race at a Wilderness Girls Jamboree because they are running away from a skunk.

- On the animated television series *Rugrats*, Chuckie Finster, having been sprayed by a skunk, tries every possible remedy, but cannot get rid of the smell—until he jumps into a pot of borscht.

- The skunk sprays its foul-smelling musk up to twelve feet. The odor remains for several days.

- Before spraying, a skunk stamps its front feet and hisses or growls.

Snoring

- **Band-Aid Bandages.** Open nasal passages by adhering a Band-Aid Bandage across your nose to breathe easier.

- **Pam Cooking Spray.** Spray one quick burst of Pam Cooking Spray in a snorer's throat before going to bed. The cooking spray lubricates the back of the throat just like expensive de-snoring sprays.

- **Silly Putty.** Some doctors prescribe Silly Putty to patients as ear plugs, although this use is discouraged by the manufacturer. If you share a bedroom with someone who snores, make a small ball of Silly Putty (about the size of a nickel) and smush it over the opening to your ear, without getting deep inside the ear canal.

- **Tampax Tampons.** In an emergency, you can use two appropriate-size Tampax Tampons as earplugs.

- **Wilson Tennis Balls.** Sew a pocket on the back of your pajama top or T-shirt, adding a Velcro flap to seal the pocket shut. Place a Wilson Tennis Ball inside the pocket, seal it shut, and wear the garment to bed. The majority of people who snore do so when sleeping on their backs. If you have a tennis ball in your back, you'll roll over on your own without any prodding from a loved one.

STRANGE FACTS

◆ Doctors have yet to discover a cure for snoring.

◆ In *The Tempest*, William Shakespeare wrote: "Thou dost snore distinctly. There's meaning in thy snores."

◆ In *Tom Sawyer Abroad*, Mark Twain wrote: "There ain't no way to find out why a snorer can't hear himself snore."

◆ United States presidents George Washington, Abraham Lincoln, and Theodore Roosevelt all snored.

◆ The United States Patent and Trademark Office has issued more than three hundred patents for antisnoring devices.

◆ Snoring is caused by breathing through the mouth while asleep. The exhaled air vibrates the soft palate in the roof of the mouth near the throat, causing the rough sound.

◆ In the nineteenth century, doctors tried to cure snoring by surgically removing the uvula—the pink flap that hangs from the roof of the mouth in the back of the throat. It did not work.

◆ According to *Guinness World Records*, Sweden's Örebro Regional Hospital recorded sleep-apnea sufferer Kåre Walkert of Kumala, Sweden, snoring at a peak level of ninety-three decibels on May 24, 1993. That's louder than the sound of a motorcycle engine being revved at full throttle.

Sore Throat

- **Arm & Hammer Baking Soda.** Dissolve one tablespoon Arm & Hammer Baking Soda in a glass of water and sip the solution throughout the day to soothe a sore throat.

- **Aunt Jemima Original Syrup.** Take two teaspoons Aunt Jemima Original Syrup to coat and soothe the irritated throat.

- **BenGay.** Relieve the discomfort of a sore throat by applying BenGay on your neck as a liniment.

- **Coca-Cola.** Gargle with Coca-Cola. The carbonation in the cola helps loosen phlegm.

- **Cutty Sark Scots Whiskey** and **SueBee Honey.** An old Scottish remedy calls for mixing four tablespoons Cutty Sark Scots Whiskey with four table-spoons SueBee Honey. Warm the mixture in a microwave oven. Gargle with the solution, and then swallow it. (Obviously, do not administer this alcoholic remedy to a child.)

- **French's Mustard, Morton Salt, SueBee Honey,** and **ReaLemon.** Mix two tablespoons French's Mustard, one tablespoon Morton Salt, one table-spoon SueBee Honey, two teaspoons ReaLemon lemon juice, and 1.5 cups boiling water. Cover and let the mixture cool for fifteen minutes, then gargle with it.

- **Gatorade.** Drinking as much Gatorade as possible rehydrates the body so your body can moisturize your throat naturally.

- **Gold's Horseradish, SueBee Honey,** and **McCormick Ground Cloves.** Mix one tablespoon Gold's Horseradish, one teaspoon SueBee Honey, and one teaspoon McCormick Ground Cloves in a glass of warm water, and stir. Sip slowly, continually stirring to prevent the horseradish from settling. (Honey should not be fed to infants under one year of age—nor should horseradish, for obvious reasons.)

- **Heinz Apple Cider Vinegar.** Mix one teaspoon Heinz Apple Cider Vinegar in one cup warm water. Whenever you feel a sore throat coming on, gargle with the mixture, and then swish and swallow it.

- **Hershey's Syrup.** Take two teaspoons of Hershey's Syrup to coat and soothe a sore throat.

- **Hydrogen Peroxide.** To kill the bacteria causing a sore throat, gargle with hydrogen peroxide, then spit out.

- **Life Savers.** Sucking on Life Savers hard candy helps the body create more saliva to moisturize your dry throat.

- **Lipton Tea Bags, ReaLemon,** and **SueBee Honey.** Brew a cup of Lipton tea, add one teaspoon ReaLemon lemon juice and one teaspoon SueBee Honey, and slowly sip the liquid to relieve a sore throat. (Honey should not be fed to infants under one year of age.)

- **McCormick Black Pepper** and **SueBee Honey.** Mix one-eighth teaspoon McCormick Black Pepper, one teaspoon SueBee Honey, and just enough hot water to dissolve the honey to drink it quickly. (Honey should not be fed to infants under one year of age.)

- **McCormick Garlic Powder.** Spice your foods with McCormick Garlic Powder. Garlic is a natural antibiotic and antiseptic.

- **Morton Salt.** Dissolve one teaspoon Morton Salt in one cup warm water and gargle with the solution once an hour to soothe your throat.

- **Popsicles.** Sucking on a nice, cold Popsicle brings instant relief to a sore throat. The sugars help coat the throat and give you energy.

- **ReaLemon.** Mix one teaspoon ReaLemon lemon juice in a glass of water and gargle with the solution every hour. The citric acid in the lemon juice helps kill bacteria in the throat.

- **Smirnoff Vodka.** Add one tablespoon Smirnoff Vodka to a glass of warm water and gargle. The alcohol helps numb the sore throat.

- **Star Olive Oil.** Take two teaspoons Star Olive Oil to soothe and coat a dry, scratchy throat.

- **SueBee Honey.** Take one teaspoon SueBee Honey at bedtime, letting the soothing liquid trickle down your throat. (Honey should not be fed to infants under one year of age.)

- **Tabasco Pepper Sauce** and **Campbell's Tomato Juice.** Mix ten to twenty drops Tabasco Pepper Sauce in a glass of tomato juice. Drink several of these decongestant tonics daily to help relieve congestion in the nose, sinuses, and lungs. Or gargle with ten to twenty drops Tabasco Pepper Sauce mixed in a glass of water to clear out the respiratory tract.

- **Tang.** Mix two teaspoons Tang in a glass of water and drink the orange beverage to fight a sore throat. The vitamin C in Tang helps your body fight the germs invading your throat.

STRANGE FACTS

- ◆ The hyoid bone in your throat is the only bone in the body not attached to another bone.

- ◆ Eleanor Roosevelt once said, "A woman is like a tea bag. You don't know how strong it is until it gets into hot water."

- ◆ Giraffes have no vocal cords.

- ◆ The infamous 1972 X-rated pornographic movie *Deep Throat* starred Linda Lovelace, who, in her 1980 autobiography *Ordeal* revealed that she had been forced to appear in the film by her abusive husband and had never been paid for her role. Lovelace became an anti-pornography campaigner, lecturing to women's groups and testifying before congressional committees investigating pornography.

- ◆ While investigating the Watergate scandal, *Washington Post* reporters Bob Woodward and Carl Bernstein referred to an anonymous Nixon administration source as Deep Throat. To this day, no one knows who Deep Throat was.

COLD FACTS ABOUT POPSICLES

On a cold winter night in 1905, eleven-year-old Frank Epperson left a glass of lemonade with a spoon in it outside on the porch. In the morning, he pulled on the spoon and out came the world's first Epsicle. The enterprising young man began selling his ice pop to his school friends. Eighteen years later, in 1923, Epperson, who ran a lemonade stand at an amusement part in Alameda, California, applied for a patent for "frozen ice on a stick," which his children renamed Popsicle. By 1928, Epperson had earned royalties on more than sixty million Popsicles.

During the Depression, Epperson created the twin Popsicle so two children could split it for a nickel. Epperson also invented the Fudgsicle, Creamsicle, and Dreamsicle. In the 1950s, when Popsicles boxed in a multipack were introduced to grocery stores, sales skyrocketed into the billions. As of 2002, there are more than thirty variations on the original Popsicle.

POPSICLE STICKS are made from birchwood.

DURING WORLD WAR II, the Eighth Air Force unit chose the Popsicle as a symbol of American life.

THERE HAVE BEEN MORE THAN one hundred different Popsicle flavors.

THE MOST POPULAR Popsicle flavors are orange, cherry, and grape.

IT TAKES 275 WRITERS to come up with the riddles printed on Popsicle sticks.

IF ALL THE STICKS FROM POPSICLES eaten in one year were laid end to end, they would circle the earth three times.

IN 1997, AMERICANS ATE MORE THAN 1.2 billion Popsicles. That's 2,220 Popsicles every minute.

THE COMPANY'S STATE-OF-THE ART PLANT in Sikeston, Missouri, can produce 1.2 million Popsicles every day.

◆ In French, the word for throat is *gorge*. In English, a gorge is a small, steep canyon, usually with a stream running through it.

◆ In an episode of the television sitcom *Full House*, when Danny Tanner, played by comedian Bob Saget, gets laryngitis, the members of his extended family pretend to understand what his lips are saying, but intentionally express the opposite idea to infuriate him.

Splinters

- **DAP Caulk.** Coat the splinter with a drop of DAP Caulk, wait for it to dry, then peel off the dried caulk in the opposite direction that the splinter entered the skin. The splinter should be stuck to the dried caulk.

- **Elmer's Glue-All.** Pour a drop of Elmer's Glue-All over the splinter, let it dry, then peel the dried glue off the skin. The splinter should stick to the dried glue.

- **Orajel.** Coat the splinter with Orajel to anesthetize the skin while removing the splinter with tweezers or a needle.

- **Scotch Packaging Tape.** Place Scotch Packaging Tape over the splinter and gently peel off the tape in the opposite direction that the splinter went in. The splinter should come off with the tape.

- **Wesson Corn Oil.** Soak the splintered skin in Wesson Corn Oil for a few minutes to soften it before trying to remove the splinter with a needle or tweezers.

STRANGE FACTS

- ◆ A splinter is also called a sliver.

- ◆ In one of *Aesop's Fables*, "The Lion and the Mouse," a mouse pulls a painful thorn from a lion's paw, earning the lion's gratitude, protection, and friendship for the rest of his life.

◆ In the children's fairy tale "Sleeping Beauty," as told in Charles Perrault's 1697 book, a princess discovers a spinning wheel in a remote section of the castle on her eighteenth birthday and gets a poison splinter of flax, putting her in a deep sleep.

◆ The word *splinter* means "to detach" or "to break away."

◆ A splinter group is a group of people who break away from a larger group because of a difference of opinion or to be more effective as a smaller body.

◆ In French, a splinter is an *éclat*, which also means "a burst," "brilliance," "radiance," or "glamour."

Stress

- **Arm & Hammer Baking Soda, Epsom Salt,** and **Morton Salt.** Fill a bathtub with warm water and add one handful Arm & Hammer Baking Soda, one handful Epsom Salt, and one handful Morton Salt. Soak in the warm, relaxing bath to soothe muscles and relieve stress.

- **BenGay.** Rub a dab of BenGay into your temples and massage gently to relieve tension throughout your body. Avoid getting the BenGay in your eyes.

- **Bubble Wrap.** Pop the bubbles in a sheet of Bubble Wrap to relieve tension and provide a harmless outlet for your anxiety and aggression.

- **Crayola Crayons.** If you're experiencing stress or tension, pick up a box of Crayola Crayons and draw a picture to express your feelings. Your anxieties, frustrations, or fears will come out in your drawing and your choice of colors—giving you surprising insight into your emotions.

- **Gold Medal Flour.** To make a stress ball, stretch a balloon a few times, insert a funnel into the neck of the balloon, and fill the balloon with Gold Medal Flour. Tie a knot and squeeze the flour-filled balloon to relieve stress.

- **McCormick Vanilla Extract.** Soak a cotton ball in McCormick Vanilla Extract and place on a saucer as aromatherapy to calm your nerves.

- **Silly Putty.** Playing with Silly Putty has therapeutic value in reducing emotional pressure and calming nerves.

- **Slinky.** Bounce a Slinky between two hands to calm your nerves and help tension disappear. Be sure to keep a Slinky in your glove compartment to relieve stress when you're stuck in bumper-to-bumper traffic.

- **Wilson Tennis Balls.** Fill a sock with three or four Wilson Tennis Balls and tie a knot to seal the open end of the sock. Have a partner roll the sock over your back. This technique is frequently used by labor coaches to massage the backs of pregnant women in labor.

STRANGE FACTS

◆ Stress, tension, and anxiety cause your adrenal glands to pump out stress hormones, such as adrenaline and cortisol, to deal with the situation. If your adrenal glands produce too many of these hormones, taxing your heart and weakening your immune system, you become susceptible to disease.

◆ The best-selling prescription drug in the United States is Valium, a tranquilizer used to relieve stress.

◆ Trying to cope with stress by drinking coffee or alcohol can actually raise the levels of stress hormones in the blood, making you more tense and anxious.

◆ On March 29, 1990, the woodworking class of Shakamak High School in Jasonville, Indiana, launched a yo-yo measuring six feet in diameter and weighing 820 pounds from a 160-foot crane. It "yo-yoed" twelve times. The word *yo-yo* means "come-come" in Filipino, and the toy purportedly originated in the Philippines as a weapon.

◆ Opossums do not actually "play possum." In reality, they pass out from sheer terror.

◆ The biggest human fear is speaking before a group.

Stuck Ring

- **Alberto VO5 Conditioning Hairdressing.** To remove a ring stuck on a finger, rub on a dab of Alberto VO5 Conditioning Hairdressing, hold your hand up toward the ceiling to drain the blood from the area, and slide off the ring.

- **ChapStick.** Coat the ring finger with ChapStick, and gently ease off the ring.

- **Crisco All-Vegetable Shortening.** Use a dab of Crisco All-Vegetable Shortening and the ring will glide off the finger. This slippery stuff got its name from the Greek word for "grease" combined with the abbreviation for "company."

- **Jif Peanut Butter.** Famous agronomist George Washington Carver created more than three hundred products from the peanut, including axle grease. The oils in Jif Peanut Butter can lubricate that stuck ring enough to slide it off a finger.

- **Johnson's Baby Oil.** A few drops of Johnson's Baby Oil will help that ring slip off your finger.

- **Land O Lakes Butter.** Smear some Land O Lakes Butter over the ring and it will slide right off.

- **Lubriderm.** Apply Lubriderm—the moisturizing lotion originally developed in 1948 by Texas Pharmacal for Texas dermatologists as a base for their own formulations—around the ring band and slide off the ring.

- **Miracle Whip.** During the Depression, when mayonnaise became a luxury item, Kraft developed Miracle Whip—a spoonable dressing that combined the best features of both mayonnaise and boiled dressing. Smear the dressing first introduced at the 1933 Chicago World's Fair over the finger and slide off the ring.

- **Oral-B Mint Waxed Floss.** Tuck one end of a piece of floss through the ring, and then wrap the floss around the ring finger, spiraling from the ring to the fingertip. Unwrap the floss starting at the base and the ring will slowly and gently work itself off the finger.

- **Pam Cooking Spray.** Lubricate the finger with this cooking spray containing lecithin dissolved in an organic solvent.

- **Preparation H.** Coat the finger with Preparation H to reduce swelling, and the ring will slide right off.

- **Vaseline Petroleum Jelly.** Explorer Robert Peary took Vaseline Petroleum Jelly to the North Pole to protect his skin from chapping and his mechanical equipment from rusting. Had a ring gotten stuck on his finger, he would have been prepared for that emergency.

- **WD-40.** Several medical journals claim that WD-40 is the perfect remedy for a toe stuck in the bathtub faucet, a finger stuck in a soda bottle, or a ring stuck on a finger.

- **Windex.** This blue liquid not only cleans windows, but the modest soap content makes a finger slippery enough that a tight ring will slip right off.

- **Wish-Bone Thousand Island Dressing.** In 1945, the Wish-Bone Restaurant opened in Kansas City, Missouri, serving salad dressing made from a recipe brought by the owner's mother from her native country, Italy. Little did she know that the salad dressing could be used to remove a ring stuck on a finger.

STRANGE FACTS

◆ Around 34,000 B.C.E., prehistoric people living in what is now France made rings from ivory.

BUTTERING UP LAND O LAKES

In 1921, a group of small, farmer-owned dairy cooperatives banded together to form the Minnesota Cooperative Creameries Association in Arden Hills, Minnesota, to distribute butter produced by the cooperatives. In 1924, the association decided to package their butter—made from fresh, sweet cream and sold in one-pound boxes with four individually wrapped sticks—under one brand name.

The co-op ran a contest, offering five hundred dollars in gold to the person who named the golden butter. Two contestants, Mrs. E. B. Foss and Mr. George L. Swift, offered the winning name—Land O Lakes, a nickname for Minnesota, famous for having over 15,000 lakes.

The co-op imposed strict standards for butter quality and helped implement grading regulations for the industry. In 1926, the association changed its corporate name to Land O Lakes Creameries, Inc.

ANCIENT ROMANS USED BUTTER as a hairdressing cream and as a skin cream.

PEOPLE STARTED MAKING BUTTER as early as 2000 B.C.E., when people in India began making it from the milk of water buffaloes.

AROUND THE SAME TIME the co-op was searching for a brand name, the Land O Lakes Indian Maiden was created, based on the legends of Hiawatha and Minnehaha, who were native to Minnesota and Wisconsin. In 1928, Land O Lakes received a painting of an Indian maiden holding a carton of butter, inspiring a new design for the butter carton. In 1939, na-tionally renowned illustrator Jess Betlach updated the Indian Maiden. Betlach's distinctive design, with only minor changes, continues to grace Land O Lakes products to this day.

IN AN EPISODE OF *SEINFELD*, Kramer uses butter as a substitute for shaving cream and tanning oil.

BUTTER WAS PROBABLY DISCOVERED by accident. When milk is transported in containers, the agitation naturally makes the cream congeal.

THE NATURAL COLOR OF BUTTER varies from pale to deep yellow, depending on the breed of cow and what it was fed. Cows eating fresh green grass produce a deep yellow butter; cows eating grain or hay produce a paler butter. Butter makers usually add food coloring to make butter more attractive.

BUTTER LASTS UP TO TWO WEEKS in the refrigerator.

BUTTER CAN BE MADE from the milk of cows, goats, horses, reindeer, sheep, yaks, and other animals.

WISCONSIN PRODUCES MORE BUTTER than any other state, followed by California and Minnesota.

IN THE UNITED STATES, people use twice as much margarine as butter. Margarine, made from vegetable oil, costs less than butter and contains less cholesterol—a fatty substance that many scientists believe causes arteriosclerosis in human beings, a disease that can lead to a heart attack.

◆ Around 2800 B.C.E., the first recorded wedding ring—signifying the eternity of marriage—was used in the Third Dynasty of the Old Kingdom of Egypt.

◆ Early Hebrews placed the wedding ring on the index finger, and Jewish wedding ceremonies follow that tradition to this day.

◆ In India, married couples wore the wedding ring on the thumb.

◆ In the third century B.C.E., Greek physicians believed a "vein of love" ran from the finger next to the pinkie directly to the heart, making this finger the logical home for a wedding ring.

◆ Christians adapted the practice of wearing the wedding ring on the second-to-last finger by having the groom place the ring over his bride's index finger "in the name of the Father," then place it on the middle finger "in the name of the Son," and then finally on the ring finger "in the name of the Holy Spirit."

◆ In 860 C.E., Pope Nicholas I decreed that a man intending to marry a woman must give her an engagement ring made from a precious metal, ideally gold, requiring a financial sacrifice to demonstrate the seriousness of his intent. Whoever broke off the engagement gave up the ring.

◆ In 1477, Maximilian I, who would later become the Holy Roman Emperor, gave Mary of Burgundy the first known diamond engagement ring.

◆ In 1518, upon the birth of the dauphin of France, son of King Francis I, a tiny diamond engagement ring was presented on his behalf to two-year-old Princess Mary, daughter of Henry VIII, to seal their engagement in the hopes of allying France and England.

◆ Beatle Ringo Starr, born with the name Richard Starkey, was nick-named Ringo for the many rings he wore on his fingers.

Sunburn

- **Afta.** Dabbing Afta after shave lotion on sunburned skin relieves sunburn pain promptly.

- **Arm & Hammer Baking Soda.** Dissolve one-half cup Arm & Hammer Baking Soda in a tepid bath. Soak for fifteen minutes, then let the powdered solution dry on your skin.

- **Carnation NonFat Dry Milk.** Fill a bathtub with warm water and add four handfuls Carnation NonFat Dry Milk. Soak in the milk bath for twenty minutes to ease the pain.

- **Cheerios.** Pour two cups Cheerios in a blender and blend into a fine powder on medium-high speed. Put the powdered Cheerios into a warm bath and soak in the oats for thirty minutes. The soothing oatmeal bath relieves the pain of sunburn. Use a plastic or mesh drain cover to avoid clogging your pipes.

- **Cool Whip.** Spread Cool Whip on the sunburn, let sit for twenty minutes, and then rinse off with lukewarm water.

- **Crisco All-Vegetable Shortening.** After soaking in a cool bath, seal the moisture into your skin by coating the sunburned area with Crisco All-Vegetable Shortening.

- **Dannon Yogurt.** Spread Dannon Yogurt (any flavor you please) on the sunburn, let sit for twenty minutes, and then rinse clean with lukewarm water.

- **Desitin.** Coat the sunburn with Desitin diaper rash ointment to reduce the pain and redness.

- **Dickinson's Witch Hazel.** Moisten a washcloth with Dickinson's Witch Hazel and apply it to the burn.

- **French's Mustard.** Rub French's Mustard on the sunburn to stop the stinging and prevent blistering. Let the mustard dry on the skin.

- **Fruit of the Earth Aloe Vera Gel.** Coat the sunburned skin with Fruit of the Earth Aloe Vera Gel to soothe and relieve the pain.

- **Heinz White Vinegar.** Saturate a washcloth with Heinz White Vinegar and use it as a compress to cover the sunburn, pressing down lightly. Or add two cups vinegar to cool bathwater and soak.

- **Kingsford's Corn Starch.** Add enough water to Kingsford's Corn Starch to make a paste, and apply directly to the burn.

- **Lipton Tea Bags.** Pat the sunburn with wet Lipton Tea Bags. The tannic acid in the tea relieves sunburn pain.

- **Lubriderm.** After soaking or using compresses, moisturize the skin with a generous coat of Lubriderm.

- **Miracle Whip.** Slather Miracle Whip liberally over the sunburn to relieve the pain and moisturize the skin.

- **Nestea.** Empty a jar of Nestea powdered iced tea mix into a bathtub, fill the bath with warm water, and soak in it. It may sound like an unusual way to take the Nestea Plunge, but the tannic acid in the tea relieves sunburn pain.

- **Niagara Spray Starch.** To soothe sunburned skin, spray Niagara Spray Starch on the affected area. The spray starch sizzles and cools the skin.

- **Phillips' Milk of Magnesia.** Coat the sunburned skin with Milk of Magnesia, let dry, and leave on overnight. The milk of magnesia keeps the skin cool all night and relieves the sunburn pain.

- **Preparation H.** Rub Preparation H into the sunburned skin immediately to quell the burning sensation and reduce the redness.

- **Quaker Oats** and **L'eggs Sheer Energy Panty Hose.** Using a blender, grind one cup Quaker Oats into a fine powder. Cut off the foot from a clean, used pair of L'eggs Sheer Energy Panty Hose, fill it with the powdered oats, and tie a knot in the nylon. Tie the oatmeal sack to the spigot, letting it dangle in the flow of water as the tub fills with warm water. Soak for thirty minutes in this inexpensive and soothing oatmeal bath, using the oatmeal sack as a mild washcloth.

- **Ziploc Freezer Bags.** An ice pack can relieve mildly burned skin. Fill a Ziploc Freezer Bag with water and freeze it or fill it with ice cubes. Wrap the ice pack in a paper towel before applying. For other ways to make and apply an ice pack, see page 198.

Play it cool! See your doctor if your sunburn begins to blister or you feel ill.

Strange Facts

◆ Contrary to popular belief, you can get a sunburn on a cloudy day. Ultraviolet rays from the sun penetrate clouds, no matter how overcast the sky may be.

◆ Turnips turn green when sunburned.

◆ Pigs, walruses, and light-colored horses can be sunburned.

◆ The place with the most hours of possible sunshine is Yuma, Arizona, where the chance of sunshine during the day is 91 percent.

◆ Starting on February 9, 1967, St. Petersburg, Florida, recorded 768 consecutive days of sunshine, ending on March 17, 1969.

◆ To avoid getting a sunburn, apply sunscreen thirty minutes before going outside.

◆ To figure out how many hours of protection you can expect from a sunscreen, take the number of minutes it takes your skin to start burning without sunscreen, multiply by the sun protection factor

(SPF) printed on the bottle of Coppertone, and divide the result by sixty. For instance, if you usually burn in thirty minutes, an SPF 8 lotion should protect you for approximately four hours.

◆ The higher the SPF of a sunscreen, the higher the price.

◆ The higher in the sky the sun is, the higher the SPF number you need. Also, the closer to the equator you are, the stronger the sunscreen you need.

◆ Never use a sunscreen that is more than a year old. Abide by the expiration dates.

Swimmer's Ear

- **ConAir Pro Style 1600 Hairdryer.** Whenever your ears get wet, set your ConAir Pro Style 1600 Hairdryer on warm, hold it a foot away from your ear, and aim into the opening for thirty seconds to dry the moisture inside. The bacteria and fungi that cause swimmer's ear thrive in moist conditions.

- **Heinz White Vinegar** and **Glad Flexible Straws.** Insert a Glad Flexible Straw in a bottle of Heinz White Vinegar, cover the open end of the straw with your finger, and lift. The liquid will stay in the straw until you release your finger. Put a few drops of the vinegar into the affected ear several times daily for three days to kill the bacteria and fungi.

- **Johnson's Baby Oil.** Before swimming, use an eardropper or Glad Flexible Straw (see above) to put a few drops of Johnson's Baby Oil in your ears to prevent bacteria and fungi from making a home in your ears.

- **Silly Putty.** When you go swimming or take a shower, use Silly Putty as earplugs to prevent water from getting inside your ears. Make a small ball of Silly Putty (about the size of a nickel) and smush it over the opening to your ear, without getting deep inside the ear canal. Some doctors prescribe Silly Putty to patients as ear plugs, although this use is discouraged by the manufacturer. Keeping your ears dry inhibits infection.

- **Smirnoff Vodka.** Use an eardropper or Glad Flexible Straw (see above) to put a few drops of Smirnoff Vodka in the affected ear several times daily for three days to kill the bacteria and fungus.

Don't play it by ear! If you have severe pain or swelling, a fever, or drainage, contact your doctor for professional treatment.

Strange Facts

◆ In 1972, American swimmer Mark Spitz won seven gold medals in a single Olympics, setting a world record.

◆ On July 29, 1978, American Penny Dean swam across the English Channel in seven hours, forty minutes, setting a world record. Dean swam from Dover in Great Britain to Cap Gris-Nez in France.

◆ Olympic gold-medal diver Greg Louganis, considered to be the best diver in the world, is the first person to ever win double gold medals for diving in two consecutive Olympics.

◆ All dogs instinctively know how to dog paddle.

◆ Polar bears swim in the icy waters of the Arctic Ocean.

◆ Every year on January 1, the members of Polar Bear Clubs in cities across America go swimming in frigid lakes, rivers, and oceans.

◆ Undergraduates at Cornell University must swim four laps across a pool in Teagle Gym in order to qualify for graduation.

Tartar and Plaque

- **Arm & Hammer Baking Soda.** Wet your toothbrush, dip it in Arm & Hammer Baking Soda to coat the bristles with a thick layer of powder, and brush your teeth, concentrating along the gum line. Plain baking soda is a gentle abrasive that cleans like the strongest toothpaste. The baking soda neutralizes the acidic bacterial waste while simultaneously deodorizing your mouth and polishing your teeth.

- **Dentyne.** If you can't brush your teeth after a meal, chew a piece of Dentyne sugarless gum for twenty minutes. The act of chewing gum causes your mouth to salivate, washing your teeth and neutralizing the acid in the plaque.

- **Easy Cheese.** According to studies done by the Dow Institute for Dental Studies at the University of Iowa, eating five grams of cheddar cheese (less than an ounce) before meals eliminates the acid production of plaque.

- **Fruit of the Earth Aloe Vera Gel.** Brushing your gums with a dab of Fruit of the Earth Aloe Vera Gel on a toothbrush helps your gums heal and helps reduce plaque.

- **Hydrogen Peroxide.** Rinsing your mouth with a solution of equal parts hydrogen peroxide (3 percent solution) and water for thirty seconds inhibits bacteria. Be sure not to swallow.

- **Lipton Tea Bags.** Scientists at Washington University in St. Louis, Missouri, discovered that black tea inhibits the bacteria that cause plaque, possibly because of the natural fluoride in tea. The April 1986 issue of *Dentistry* also urged readers to drink more tea to prevent plaque. Drink tea made by brewing a Lipton Tea Bag in a cup of water for at least six minutes (to extract the most fluoride possible). You can also use tea as a mouthwash.

- **Listerine.** Listerine is the only over-the-counter brand of mouthwash clinically proven to help prevent and reduce supragingival plaque accumulation and gingivitis when used in a conscientiously applied program of oral hygiene and regular professional care.

- **MasterCard.** Scraping your tongue several times from back to front with the edge of a MasterCard credit card removes the bacteria and toxins festering in your mouth.

- **McCormick Food Coloring.** To spot plaque on your teeth, put ten drops red food coloring into a glass, add one teaspoon water, and swirl it around. Pour the red solution into your mouth, swish it around well, and then spit it out. Fill the glass with clean water and rinse your mouth well. The remaining red stains on your teeth are plaque. Brush these areas well.

- **Vegemite.** In a pinch, you can brush your teeth with Vegemite, a favorite Australian sandwich spread. Vegemite is a mild abrasive.

Strange Facts

◆ As early as 3000 B.C.E., Egyptians brushed their teeth with a "chew stick," a twig with a frayed end of soft fibers that was rubbed against the teeth to clean them. Ancient Egyptians also invented dental floss, using thread.

◆ In 1498, the Chinese originated the first bristled toothbrush, made from bristles plucked from the backs of hogs' necks and fastened to bamboo or bone handles.

◆ Traders from the Orient introduced Europeans to the practice of brushing their teeth, and the few Europeans who adopted the practice opted for horsehair toothbrushes, though most preferred the Roman toothpick.

- In 1876, Johnson & Johnson received the first patent for a woven silk dental floss, but the company waited twenty years before making dental floss commercially available—in waxed and unwaxed silk.

- In 1937, the United States imported 1.5 million pounds of hog bristles for toothbrushes.

- After DuPont chemists invented nylon in the 1930s, the company marketed the first nylon-bristle toothbrush in 1938.

- In 1945, Grand Rapids, Michigan, became the first city in the United States to fluoridate its water.

- Maine, home to Forster Toothpicks, is the toothpick capital of the world.

- In 1961, the Squibb Company introduced the first electric toothbrush, and a year later, General Electric introduced the battery-operated, rechargeable cordless electric toothbrush.

- Colgate-Palmolive introduced a toothpaste in France called Cue, unwittingly using the name of a notorious French pornography magazine.

- Listerine should not be swallowed or administered to children under twelve years of age because it contains 26.9 percent pharmaceutical-grade alcohol.

- Tooth enamel is the hardest substance in the human body.

- Thirteen percent of Americans brush their teeth from side to side.

- Women tend to floss their teeth more often than men.

- The most common noncontagious disease in the world is gingivitis, caused by excessive buildup of plaque on teeth and gums.

- According to the American Dental Association, 80 percent of all Americans fail to replace their toothbrushes until after the bent bristles are no longer fit for cleaning teeth.

- Consumers buy more than 10.5 billion feet of dental floss every year. That's enough dental floss to reach to the moon and back at least four times.

SIDE EFFECTS

THE BRUSH-OFF

EFFERDENT

To sanitize a toothbrush, fill a glass with water, drop in two Efferdent tablets, and let the toothbrush sit in the solution overnight. Then rinse the toothbrush clean.

Q-TIPS COTTON SWABS

A Q-Tips Cotton Swab can actually be used as a substitute toothbrush.

TAMPAX TAMPONS

In a pinch, a Tampax Tampon can be used as a toothbrush.

Toothache

- **Colgate Toothpaste.** Temporarily reglue a loose crown by putting a dab of Colgate Toothpaste inside the crown and pressing it back in place. Then see your dentist as soon as possible.

- **Fruit of the Earth Aloe Vera Gel.** Dissolve one teaspoon Fruit of the Earth Aloe Vera Gel in one cup water and use the mixture as a mouth rinse to soothe toothache pain.

- **Lipton Tea Bags.** Relieve a toothache or stop gums from bleeding by pressing a dampened Lipton Tea Bag against the cavity or sore gums. The tannic acid in the tea numbs the spot and clots blood.

- **Listerine.** Swishing a mouthful of Listerine around the cavity, lost filling, or broken tooth relieves a toothache temporarily. Listerine is an analgesic, instantly relieving the pain of an exposed nerve for a considerable length of time.

- **McCormick Black Pepper** and **Mr. Coffee Filters.** Add one-quarter teaspoon McCormick Black Pepper to one cup boiling water, stir, cover, and simmer on a low heat for seven minutes. Remove from the heat, let sit for fifteen minutes, then strain through a Mr. Coffee Filter. While the liquid is still warm, take small sips and swish it through your mouth, concentrating on the affected area. Repeat as needed.

- **McCormick Vanilla Extract.** To relieve a toothache, saturate a cotton ball with McCormick Vanilla Extract and place it against the sore spot. The high alcohol content dulls the pain.

- **Morton Salt.** Add one teaspoon Morton Salt to a glass of warm water and rinse your mouth with the solution to help soothe and anesthetize the pain.

- **Popsicle.** Sucking on an ice-cold Popsicle and pressing it against the gum soothes the pain just like an ice pack.

- **Smirnoff Vodka.** Take a shot of Smirnoff Vodka and swish it over the tooth, allowing your gums to absorb some of the alcohol and numb the pain. Swallow or spit out the rest.

- **Tabasco Pepper Sauce.** Apply a dab of Tabasco Pepper Sauce to the gum. Made from a variety of pepper called *Capsicum frutescens*, Tabasco Pepper Sauce contains an alkaloid called capsaicin that has been proven to numb pain when applied topically.

- **Ziploc Freezer Bags.** Applying an ice pack to your jaw can relieve toothache pain. Fill a Ziploc Freezer Bag with water and freeze or fill it with ice cubes. Wrap the ice pack in a paper towel before applying. For other ways to make and apply an ice pack, see page 198.

Don't let a toothache put the bite on you. If you experience swelling, pain when you bite, a foul-tasting discharge, or redness, see your dentist as soon as possible.

STRANGE FACTS

- ◆ The tooth is the only part of the human body that cannot repair itself.

- ◆ Rhazes, a tenth-century Persian doctor, first recommended filling cavities. He drilled teeth slowly (and painfully) with a handheld bit and filled the holes with a solidifying paste made from alum and mastic.

- ◆ For some four hundred years, beginning in the fourteenth century, barber-surgeons in Europe whitened teeth with a solution of nitric acid, which destroyed the enamel, causing cavities.

- ◆ Fifteenth-century physician Marcellus incorrectly insisted that magnets could be used to cure toothaches.

- In 1578, England's Queen Elizabeth endured several weeks of excruciating dental pain until the bishop of London persuaded her to have the offending tooth pulled—by voluntarily having one of his good teeth extracted to show her that the pain was bearable.

- In 1685, while suffering from the agony of a tooth infection, French King Louis XIV revoked religious freedom.

- Brother Giovanni Battist Orsenigo of Rome, Italy, who practiced dentistry from 1868 to 1904, saved all the teeth he extracted. By 1903, he had collected more than two million teeth.

- Porpoise teeth have been used as money.

- "To a person with a toothache," wrote George Bernard Shaw, "even if the world is tottering, there is nothing more important than a visit to the dentist."

- The human tooth contains approximately fifty-five miles of canals.

- On March 31, 1990, in Paris, France, Belgian Walter Arfeuille lifted 621 pounds of weights 6.75 inches off the ground using his teeth.

- A pack-a-day smoker will lose approximately two teeth every ten years.

- On July 21, 1992, in Shcherbinka, Russia, Robert Galstyan of Masis, Armenia, used his teeth to pull two railroad cars coupled together, weighing a total of 483,197 pounds, a distance of twenty-three feet.

- Over thirty million Americans have diastema—a gap between two front teeth.

- In the 2001 movie *Cast Away*, Tom Hanks, stranded on a deserted island in the South Pacific, cures a toothache by knocking out his tooth with the blade of an ice skate.

Ulcer

- **Canada Dry Ginger Ale.** Drink Canada Dry Ginger Ale to calm the stomach. Ginger helps promote smooth digestion.

- **Dannon Yogurt.** Eating between one and four cups of yogurt with active cultures daily prevents the ulcer-causing bacteria in the stomach from thriving. The *Lactobacillus acidophilus* in yogurt act like an antibiotic in the stomach, and the lactose in yogurt breaks down into lactic acid in the stomach, aiding digestion.

- **Pepto-Bismol.** Take Pepto-Bismol according the directions on the bottle. Bismuth, one of the ingredients in Pepto-Bismol, kills the bacteria in your stomach that may be responsible for causing ulcers. (Please note that the Federal Drug Administration has not approved Pepto-Bismol as an ulcer remedy.)

- **Phillips' Milk of Magnesia.** When you feel the symptoms of an ulcer, take one teaspoon Phillips' Milk of Magnesia. The antacid helps relieve the symptoms.

STRANGE FACTS

- ◆ Open sores in the stomach lining are called gastric ulcers. Open sores in the lining of the upper part of the small intestine are called duodenal ulcers.

- Ancient Greek physician Galen (circa 130-200 C.E.) wrongly insisted that ulcers are caused by an excess of black bile.

- Ancient Roman doctors cured ulcers by having their patients eat cabbage—a modern day herbal remedy.

- While doctors once believed that ulcers resulted from stress and bad eating habits, research has shown that in most cases a bacterium called *Helicobacter pylori* seems to weaken the mucous tissue in the stomach, making it vulnerable to digestive acids.

- Duodenal ulcers are caused by an abundance two digestive juices: hydrochloric acid and pepsin.

- Pepsi Cola is named for the digestive enzyme pepsin.

- Patients confined to bed or a wheel chair frequently get decubitus ulcers, better known as bedsores.

- The Beatles never wrote a song containing the word *ulcer*.

Urinary Tract Infection

- **Alka-Seltzer.** Treat urinary tract infections by dissolving two Alka-Seltzer tablets in a glass of water and drinking it at the onset of any symptoms. Alka-Seltzer begins eliminating urinary tract infection almost instantly.

- **Arm & Hammer Baking Soda.** Mix one teaspoon Arm & Hammer Baking Soda in a glass of water and drink the solution once a day for three days. (Sodium bicarbonate relieves the pain quickly, but read the instructions on the side of the box carefully before proceeding.)

- **Dannon Yogurt.** Women who have fewer yeast infections tend to have fewer bouts with bladder infections. The March 1992 issue of the *Annals of Internal Medicine* reported that daily consumption of yogurt containing *Lactobacillus acidophilus* cultures results in a threefold decrease in the incidence of yeast infections.

- **Ocean Spray Cranberry Juice Cocktail.** Inflammation of the urinary bladder caused by bacteria can be treated by abstinence from sexual intercourse and drinking two or more glasses of Ocean Spray Cranberry Juice Cocktail every day until the pain subsides. Cranberry juice flushes bacteria from the bladder either by increasing the acidity in the bladder or by preventing bacteria from clinging to bladder walls.

 Don't burn yourself out! If you suspect that you have a urinary tract infection and the symptoms don't clear up within two days, see a doctor.

A SPLASH OF OCEAN SPRAY

In 1930, three cranberry growers determined to expand the market for their crops formed an agricultural cooperative, naming their organization Ocean Spray. President Marcus L. Urann, a lawyer and cranberry grower who had perfected a shelf-stable cranberry sauce, urged the cooperative to develop innovative products made from cranberries. That same year, the cooperative introduced Ocean Spray Cranberry Juice Cocktail, becoming the world's first producer of cranberry juice drinks. In 1963, Ocean Spray introduced Cran-Apple Cranberry Apple Juice Drink, the juice industry's first juice blend, revolutionizing the business. The overwhelming success of the blend prompted the cooperative to add new flavors to the line, including a variety of low-calorie cranberry juice blends.

In 1976, grapefruit growers from Florida's Indian River region joined the Ocean Spray cooperative. The group introduced Ocean Spray Grapefruit Juice, which quickly became the best-selling bottled grapefruit juice in the United States, followed by Ocean Spray Pink Grapefruit Juice Cocktail, the first citrus blend of its kind. In 1991, the cooperative launched Ocean Spray Ruby Red Grapefruit Juice Drink, followed by Premium 100% Ruby Red Grapefruit Juice, and grapefruit juice drinks blended with strawberries, tangerines, and mangoes.

OCEAN SPRAY IS THE NUMBER ONE BRAND of canned and bottled juice drinks in the United States.

IN 1995, Ocean Spray introduced Craisins —sweetened, dried cranberries similar to raisins.

OCEAN SPRAY PRODUCTS are available in nearly fifty countries around the world.

IN 1999, Ocean Spray introduced Cranberry Juice Cocktail with Calcium, a supercharged version of its classic juice drink.

STRANGE FACTS

- Women are twenty-five times more likely than men to get bladder infections.

- By the age of twenty-five, one out of every four women has had a urinary tract infection.

- Urinary tract infections, technically called cystitis, are caused by a bacterium called E. coli—better known for causing food poisoning.

- Cranberries are sorted for ripeness by being bounced. A fully ripened cranberry can be dribbled like a basketball.

- Cranberry Jell-O Brand Gelatin Dessert is the only Jell-O flavor that comes from real fruit, not artificial flavoring.

- Ancient Romans used urine as mouthwash and as an ingredient in toothpaste—convinced that urine whitened teeth.

- Urine was used as an active ingredient in toothpastes and mouthwashes until the eighteenth century. The active ingredient in urine was ammonia, later used in modern toothpastes.

Varicose Veins

- **Bayer Aspirin.** Taking one Bayer Aspirin a day thins the blood and seems to prevent blood from clotting in superficial veins, in some cases making varicose veins virtually disappear. (All heart patients should get their doctor's approval before taking any medication, including aspirin, on a daily basis.)

- **L'eggs Sheer Energy Panty Hose.** If you don't have support hose, put on a pair of L'eggs Sheer Energy Panty Hose to provide relief from pain. The nylon hose helps prevent blood from collecting in veins closest to the skin, pushing it back into the veins.

- **McCormick Bay Leaves, Star Olive Oil**, and **Mr. Coffee Filters.** Place three McCormick Bay Leaves and four teaspoons Star Olive Oil in a saucepan and warm over a low heat without letting the oil burn or smoke. Let the mixture cool, then strain through a Mr. Coffee Filter. Apply to the affected area.

- **Preparation H.** Reduce spider veins by rubbing a dab of Preparation H into the skin. Preparation H is a vasoconstrictor, reducing swelling.

STRANGE FACTS

◆ Ancient Greek physician Hippocrates (circa 460–377 B.C.E.), considered the father of modern medicine, incorrectly claimed that bald people who get varicose veins regain their hair.

- Women are four times as likely as men to get varicose veins.

- Pregnant women frequently get varicose veins from increased pelvic pressure exerted by the uterus and growing fetus and decreased blood return from the lower body and limbs.

- Male infertility can be caused by varicose veins in the scrotum.

- Veins have walls that are thinner, less elastic, and less muscular than the walls of arteries.

- Arteries carry blood away from the heart to all parts of the body. Veins return blood back to the heart.

- The human body contains approximately 100,000 miles of blood vessels.

- The word *varicose* means "abnormally enlarged or swollen."

Vomiting

- **Canada Dry Ginger Ale.** Drink Canada Dry Ginger Ale to calm the stomach. Ginger helps ease nausea.

- **Coca-Cola.** Open a can of Coca-Cola, let it sit until it goes flat (roughly thirty minutes), then drink the defizzed real thing. Coca-Cola was originally invented as an elixir to cure upset stomachs, and it still works. Drinking the soda flat prevents the carbonation from further upsetting your stomach.

- **Domino Sugar, Morton Salt,** and **ReaLemon.** Drinking plenty of fluids during a bout of vomiting is essential to avoiding dehydration. To make your own rehydration solution, mix three teaspoons sugar, one teaspoon salt, and two teaspoons lemon juice in a tall glass of water. Drink the entire solution to replace the glucose, minerals, and vitamin C being flushed out of your body.

- **Gatorade.** To settle your stomach after a bout of vomiting and to prevent dehydration, drink Gatorade to replace the electrolytes flushed out by vomiting.

- **Jell-O.** When you're ready to start eating again, begin with clear, soft foods like Jell-O to give your bowels a rest until your symptoms improve.

- **Krispy Original Saltine Crackers.** When you're feeling ready for food again, start with bland foods like Krispy Original Saltine Crackers, which you can easily digest.

THE POWER OF TIDE

In the 1920s, Americans used soap flakes to clean their laundry. The flakes performed poorly in hard water, leaving a ring in the washing machine, dulling colors, and turning whites gray. In the 1930s, scientists at Procter & Gamble discovered synthetic surfactants that extracted dirt and grease from clothes and then suspended them until they could be washed away. In 1933, Procter & Gamble introduced Dreft detergent, which, made with surfactants, could only clean lightly soiled clothes. A decade later, Procter & Gamble scientists discovered special chemical compounds called "builders" that help surfactants penetrate clothes fibers more deeply, allegedly "making them (the surfactants) more effective than soap flakes, even on tough greasy stains."

In 1943, Procter & Gamble invented Tide, the first heavy-duty detergent made from a combination of synthetic surfactants and builders. Three years later, Procter & Gamble introduced Tide to test markets as the "New Washday Miracle." Within weeks, Tide outsold every other brand, forcing store owners to limit the number of boxes each customer could buy. Over the next twenty-one years, Procter & Gamble improved Tide twenty-two times.

TIDE IS THE BEST-SELLING heavy-duty laundry detergent in the United States today.

***CONSUMER REPORTS* CLAIMS** "No laundry detergent will completely remove all common stains" and reports very little difference in performance between major brand-name powdered detergents.

EVERY YEAR, researchers for Procter & Gamble duplicate the mineral content of water from all parts of the United States and wash 50,000 loads of laundry to test Tide detergent's consistency and performance.

- **Lipton Tea Bags.** Drink plenty of Lipton tea. The tannin in tea helps stop the muscular contractions in the intestines, and the tea itself replaces fluids lost by the body.

- **Mott's Apple Sauce.** When you have the energy to eat, Mott's Apple Sauce makes a great starter food that the body can easily digest.

- **Uncle Ben's Converted Brand Rice.** Eating plain Uncle Ben's Original Converted Brand Rice will help cure diarrhea.

SIDE EFFECTS
CLEANING UP THE MESS

ARM & HAMMER BAKING SODA

After cleaning a vomit stain from the carpet, cover the spot with Arm & Hammer Baking Soda to remove the smell, let sit for one hour, then vacuum it up.

BARBASOL SHAVING CREAM

To clean the stain from the carpet, squirt some Barbasol Shaving Cream on the spot, scrub, wash with water, and blot dry.

CANADA DRY CLUB SODA

Apply Canada Dry Club Soda to the stain, rub it in, wait a few minutes, and blot.

CLEAN SHOWER

Spray Clean Shower on the stain, rub with a wet sponge, and let dry.

HUGGIES BABY WIPES

To clean the stain from the carpet, wipe the spot with Huggies Baby Wipes. The baby wipes absorb vomit from carpet without leaving a stain behind.

MORTON SALT

Dampen the stain with water, blot well, then pour Morton Salt to cover the stain. The salt will absorb the remaining liquids. Then sweep up the salt and vacuum.

MURPHY'S OIL SOAP

Mix one-quarter cup Murphy's Oil Soap to one gallon water. Use a brush to scrub the spot with the soap mixture, blot with a towel, rinse, and repeat if needed.

PAMPERS

Blot up liquid from carpet by spreading a Pampers disposable diaper over the spot. Place several heavy books on the top of the diaper, and let it sit for one hour. The water-retaining polymers in Pampers disposable diapers absorb liquids thoroughly.

PARSONS' AMMONIA

Scrub the stain with a mixture of two cups Parsons' Ammonia in one gallon warm water, then blot it dry.

SHOUT

Spray Shout on the stain, let sit for five minutes, then wipe clean with a clean, wet rag.

SMIRNOFF VODKA

Spray Smirnoff Vodka on the stain, scrub with a brush, then blot dry.

STP CARB SPRAY CLEANER

Use STP carburetor cleaner on the stain to remove the spot from the carpet. Let sit ten minutes, then wash with water and blot dry.

TIDE and HEINZ WHITE VINEGAR

Scrub the stain with a mixture of one cup Tide and two cups Heinz White Vinegar. Rinse with cool water, blot, and let dry.

20 MULE TEAM BORAX

After cleaning up the stain, sprinkle 20 Mule Team Borax over the spot, let dry, and vacuum. (Before treating, make sure the carpet dye is color-fast by testing an unexposed area with a paste of 20 Mule Team Borax and water.)

WINDEX

Apply Windex Glass Cleaner to the stain, rub it in with a sponge, wait five minutes, then blot up.

- **Ziploc Storage Bags.** Keep several gallon-size Ziploc Storage Bags nearby (in your pocket, desk drawer, purse, or glove compartment) to use as vomit bags. Afterward, simply zip the bag shut and toss it into the nearest trash can.

STRANGE FACTS

- The Book of Proverbs in the Bible includes the verses "If you find honey, eat just enough—too much of it, and you will vomit" (25:16) and "As a dog returns to its vomit, so a fool repeats his folly" (26:11).

- In the biblical book of Jonah, God commands the great fish and "it vomited Jonah onto dry land" (Jonah 2:10).

- In 1530, Dutch author Erasmus of Rotterdam wrote his popular book of manners, *On Civility in Children*, including the advice: "Do not be afraid of vomiting if you must; for it is not vomiting but holding the vomit in your throat that is foul."

- In January 1992, President George Bush, attending a state dinner in Tokyo, Japan, and suffering from an intestinal flu, vomited into the lap of prime minister Kiichi Miyazawa and then collapsed on him— giving birth to the Japanese word Bushuru ("to vomit publicly").

- Horses and rabbits cannot vomit.

- Euphemisms for vomiting include such colorful expressions as "tossing your cookies," "feeding the fish," "losing your lunch," "blowing chow," "barfing," "upchucking," and "praying to the porcelain god."

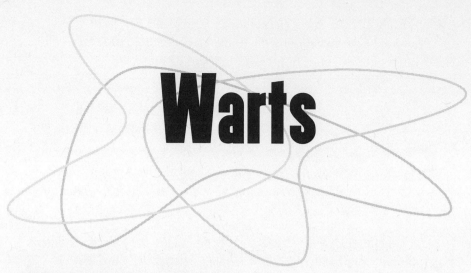

Warts

- **Band-Aid Bandages** and **Morton Salt.** Moisten the gauze in the center of a Band-Aid Bandage, sprinkle it liberally with Morton Salt, and adhere the salted bandage over the wart. Repeat for several weeks until the wart disappears. The Band-Aid keeps the wart moist while the salt keeps the wart irritated.

- **Bayer Aspirin.** Dampen a Bayer Aspirin tablet, place it over the wart, and tape it in place (unless you are allergic to aspirin). Repeat until the wart falls off. Salicylic acid, the main ingredient in aspirin, is also the main ingredient in wart removal liquids like Compound W and Wart-Off.

- **Blistex.** Cover the wart with Blistex medicated lip balm for several days until it magically disappears.

- **Castor Oil.** Apply a drop of plain castor oil to the wart twice a day and then cover it snugly with a piece of first aid adhesive tape. Or mix a thick paste of castor oil and baking soda, apply to the wart a couple of times a day, and cover with a bandage, glove, or sock.

- **Clorox.** Using a Q-Tips Cotton Swab, apply a dab of Clorox directly to the wart—without getting any on the surrounding skin. Repeat for several days until the wart dissolves.

- **Crayola Chalk.** Rub the wart with the side of a piece of white chalk to create a good buildup of chalk on the wart. Repeat for several days until the wart vanishes.

- **Elmer's Glue-All.** Cover the wart with Elmer's Glue-All, let it dry (which usually takes about twenty minutes), then peel the dried glue from the skin. Repeat two or three times a day until the wart disappears.

- **Fruit of the Earth Aloe Vera Gel** and **Band-Aid Bandages.** To obliterate a wart, saturate a cotton ball with Fruit of the Earth Aloe Vera Gel, place it over the wart, and cover with a Band-Aid to hold it in place. Repeat daily until the wart disappears.

- **Heinz Apple Cider Vinegar.** Combine one part Heinz Apple Cider Vinegar and one part glycerin to create a lotion. Apply daily to the wart until it dissolves.

- **Hydrogen Peroxide.** Dab hydrogen peroxide on the wart and let it dry, repeating several times a day for several days until the wart dissolves.

- **Maybelline Crystal Clear Nail Polish.** Paint the wart with a thick coat of Maybelline Crystal Clear Nail Polish to make an airtight seal, suffocating the virus. Repeat for several days until the wart washes off with soap and water.

- **ReaLemon** and **Q-Tips Cotton Swabs.** Apply a dab of ReaLemon lemon juice directly to the wart using a Q-Tips Cotton Swab. Repeat for several days until the acids in the lemon juice dissolve the wart.

- **Tang** and **Band-Aid Bandages.** Make a paste from Tang and water, apply it to the wart, and cover with a Band-Aid. The ascorbic acid can kill the wart-producing virus and, together with the citric acid in the Tang, may slowly dissolve it.

- **Vaseline Petroleum Jelly.** Before applying Compound W or any other salicylic acid solution to remove a wart, coat the skin surrounding the wart with Vaseline Petroleum Jelly to prevent the acid from burning this skin.

STRANGE FACTS

- ◆ Warts are caused by the human papillomavirus.

- ◆ Children get warts more often than adults do.

- ◆ While toads have warty skin, touching a toad does not cause warts on people. However, if touched, warts on toads can exude a thick, toxic liquid that, if rubbed in the eye or nose, causes the mucous membranes to burn.

◆ The warthog, an African pig with large curved tusks, gets its name from the three pairs of large wartlike protrusions on its face.

◆ Plantar warts grow on the soles of the feet and feel like sharp tacks.

◆ In Walt Disney's 1937 animated movie *Snow White and the Seven Dwarfs*, when the wicked queen turns herself into an old hag, she has a wart on the tip of her nose.

◆ In the 2001 movie *Spy Kids*, starring Antonio Banderas, young Juni Cortez has warts on his hands from being scared all the time.

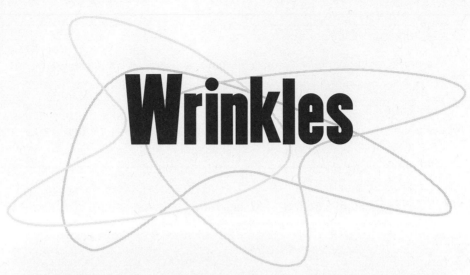

Wrinkles

- **Alberto VO5 Conditioning Hairdressing.** Rub a little Alberto VO5 Conditioning Hairdressing in the area around your eyes to help prevent dry lines.

- **Castor Oil.** Before going to bed, rub castor oil around your eyes to help prevent wrinkles.

- **Coppertone.** Using sunscreen with a sun protection factor of at least 15 whenever you go out in the sun can prevent wrinkling, discoloration, pronounced blood vessels, and cancerous lesions that may be caused by prolonged exposure to the sun. Be sure to apply Coppertone thirty minutes before going outside.

- **Crisco All-Vegetable Shortening.** Many plastic surgeons tell their patients recovering from a face-lift to apply Crisco All-Vegetable Shortening as a salve to prevent scarring and speed healing. Crisco works as an excellent skin moisturizer, keeping skin healthy. Use it on your face every night before going to bed.

- **Preparation H.** Preparation H can not only shrink hemorrhoids, but also moisturize skin, shrink puffiness around your eyes, and reduce fine wrinkles around the eyes.

- **Star Olive Oil** and **Heinz Apple Cider Vinegar.** To prevent wrinkles, mix one tablespoon Star Olive Oil and one-half tablespoon Heinz Apple Cider Vinegar. Rub the ointment into your skin.

STRANGE FACTS

◆ In the eighth century, Chinese herbal practitioner Liu Pi concocted an anti-aging medicine and presented it to Tang emperor Hsien Tsung. The emperor drank it and died.

◆ Spanish explorer Ponce de León searched Florida for the mythical Fountain of Youth, a spring whose waters would reputedly make old people young and heal the sick. He did find a spring in St. Augustine that he thought would give him eternal youth, and today you can visit the Fountain of Youth at 155 Magnolia Street and admire a statue of Ponce de León that does not age.

◆ In Canto I of his 1812 poem *Childe Harold's Pilgrimage,* Lord Byron wrote:
>What is the worst of woes that wait on age?
>What stamps the wrinkle deeper on the brow?
>To view each loved one blotted from life's page,
>And be alone on earth as I am now.

◆ "Life would be infinitely happier," wrote American novelist Mark Twain, "if we could only be born at the age of eighty and gradually approach eighteen."

◆ Groucho Marx said, "A man is only as old as the woman he feels."

◆ "When your friends begin to flatter you on how young you look," wrote Mark Twain, "it's a sure sign you're getting old."

Yeast Infection

- **ConAir Pro Style 1600 Hairdryer.** After toweling yourself dry, set a blow dryer on low warm, hold it a foot away from your crotch, and let the warm air dry your pubic hair to prevent recurring yeast infections. Eliminating moisture helps prevent yeast from growing.

- **Dannon Yogurt.** The March 1992 issue of the *Annals of Internal Medicine* reports that daily consumption of yogurt containing *Lactobacillus acidophilus* cultures results in a threefold decrease in the incidence of candidal vaginitis (yeast infections).

- **Dannon Yogurt.** Use a turkey baster to insert Dannon Plain Yogurt into the vagina. The *Lactobacillus acidophilus* cultures in yogurt kill the *Candida albicans* in the vagina. Some women use yogurt as a sexual lubricant. (Do not use yogurt in the vagina unless you know for certain that you have a yeast infection. Other bacterial infections thrive on yogurt, making the problem worse.)

- **Dawn.** Kill the *Candida albicans* fungus in your panties by putting a few drops of Dawn Dishwashing Liquid on the crotch and scrubbing it with water before throwing the garments in your regular wash.

- **Heinz White Vinegar.** Douche with four teaspoons Heinz White Vinegar to one pint warm water to adjust the pH balance in the vagina, making a less hospitable environment for the yeast to proliferate.

- **McCormick Cinnamon.** Bring four cups water to boil, add eight to ten broken cinnamon sticks, then simmer for five minutes. Remove from heat, cover, and let steep for forty-five minutes. When lukewarm, use the solution as a douche to reduce *Candida albicans*. In 1974, the *Journal of Food Science* reported that cinnamon inhibits the growth of aflatoxins.

- **McCormick Garlic Powder.** Flavoring your food with garlic helps get rid of a yeast infection. Garlic boosts immunity and is both an antibacterial and an antifungal.

- **Morton Salt** and **Heinz White Vinegar.** Fill a bathtub with six inches warm water, add one-half cup salt and one-half cup vinegar, and sit in the water, knees apart, for fifteen minutes. The salt content of the water matches the natural saline level of your body, and the vinegar helps rebalance your vagina's pH level to roughly 4.5.

If the Yeast Beast hasn't ceased in the least after one week of self-treatment, contact your doctor.

STRANGE FACTS

- ◆ Seventy-five percent of all women get at least one yeast infection during their lives.

- ◆ *Candida albicans*, the bacteria most often responsible for causing yeast infections, usually migrates from the intestinal tract to the vagina.

- ◆ Bakers add yeast to dough to make it rise. In bread making, the yeast converts the sugar in the flour into alcohol and carbon dioxide. Bubbles of gas get trapped by the gluten in the dough, and as the gas expands, the bread rises. Baking destroys the yeast and causes the alcohol to evaporate from the bread. Before yeast began being produced commercially in the 1880s, bread makers prepared dough and left it uncovered so that airborne yeast plants landed on it and began the fermentation process.

◆ The yeast used to ferment alcoholic beverages is actually a fungus. Members of the same fungus family (*Asomycetes*) produce the antibiotics penicillin and streptomycin.

◆ In 1876, French scientist Louis Pasteur first reported that yeasts were living cells.

◆ In September 1972, two founders of the Federation of Feminist Women's Health Centers, Carol Downer and Colleen Wilson, were arrested at their Los Angeles Women's Self-Help Clinic and charged with practicing medicine without a license. Downer had inserted yogurt into the vagina of a women's center staff member. The trial, known as "The Great Yogurt Conspiracy," became a crucial turning point in the women's health movement. Downer was found not guilty by arguing that applying yogurt as a home remedy for an ordinary yeast infection is not practicing medicine.

# **Acknowledgments**

At Rodale, I am grateful to my editor, Ellen Phillips, for her passion, enthusiasm, and excitement for this book. I am also deeply indebted to Tami Booth, Barb Newton, Stephanie Tade, Andrew Gelman, Karen Bolesta, Tara Long, Linda Rutenbar, Kris Siessmayer, Linda Smith, Jennifer Bright, Ann Gossy, Shea Zukowski, and Kathy Dvorsky.

A very special thanks to my agent, Jeremy Solomon; my manager, Barb North; my Web site partner, Michael Teitelbaum; and to the hundreds of people who constantly visit my Web site and send me their ingenious ideas.

Above all, all my love to Debbie, Ashley, and Julia.

The Fine Print

SOURCES

- *All-New Hints from Heloise* by Heloise (New York: Perigee, 1989)
- *America's Stupidest Business Decisions* by Bill Adler (New York: Quill, 1997)
- *Another Use For* by Vicki Lansky (Deephaven, Minnesota: Book Peddlers, 1991)
- *Ask Anne & Nan* by Anne Adams and Nancy Walker (Brattleboro, Vermont: Whetstone, 1989)
- *The Bag Book* by Vicki Lansky (Deephaven, Minnesota: Book Peddlers, 2000)
- *Baking Soda Bonanza* by Peter A. Ciullo (New York: HarperPerennial, 1995)
- *The Blunder Book* by M. Hirsh Goldberg (New York: Quill, 1984)
- *The Book of Lists* by David Wallechinsky, Irving Wallace, and Amy Wallace (New York: William Morrow, 1977)
- *The Book of Lists 2* by Irving Wallace, David Wallechinsky, Amy Wallace, and Sylvia Wallace (New York: William Morrow, 1980)
- *The Book of 1,001 Home Health Remedies* by the editors of *Natural Healing Newsletter* (Peachtree City, Georgia: FC&A, 1993)
- *Can You Trust a Tomato in January?* by Vince Staten (New York: Simon & Schuster, 1993)
- *Cat Owner's Home Veterinary Handbook* by Delbert G. Carlson, James M. Giffin, Lisa Carlson (Hungry Minds, 1995)
- *A Dash of Mustard* by Katy Holder and Jane Newdick (London: Chartwell Books, 1995)
- *Dictionary of Trade Name Origins* by Adrian Room (London: Routledge & Kegan Paul, 1982)
- *The Doctors Book of Food Remedies* by Selene Yeager and the editors of *Prevention Health Books (Emmaus, Pennsylvania: Rodale, 1998)*
- *The Doctors Book of Home Remedies* by editors of *Prevention* Magazine (Emmaus, Pennsylvania: Rodale, 1990)
- *The Doctors Book of Home Remedies II* by Sid Kirchheimer and the editors of *Prevention* Magazine (Emmaus, Pennsylvania: Rodale, 1993)
- *Encyclopedia of Pop Culture* by Jane and Michael Stern (New York: HarperCollins, 1992)
- *Famous American Trademarks* by Arnold B. Barach (Washington, D.C.: Public Affairs Press, 1971)
- *The Film Encyclopedia* by Ephraim Katz (New York: Perigee, 1979)

🖖 The Fine Print

- *"Food for Thought—and Your Face"* by Leslee Komaiko, *Los Angeles Times*, February 20, 2001, p. E1–3
- *The Food Pharmacy: Dramatic New Evidence That Food Is Your Best Medicine* by Jean Carper (New York: Bantam, 1988)
- *"The Frito"* by Nicholas Lemann, *Texas Monthly* Magazine, May 1982
- *The Guinness Book of World Records* (New York: Bantam, 1998)
- *The Healing Foods: The Ultimate Authority on the Curative Power of Nutrition* by Patricia Hausman and Judith Benn Hurley (Emmaus, Pennsylvania: Rodale, 1989)
- *Heinerman's Encyclopedia of Healing Herbs & Spices* by John Heinerman (West Nyack, New York: Parker Publishing, 1996)
- *Hints from Heloise* by Heloise (New York: Arbor House, 1980)
- *A History of American Foreign Policy*, second edition, by Alexander DeConde (New York: Charles Scribner's Sons, 1971)
- *Home Remedies from the Country Doctor* by Jay Heinrichs, Dorothy Behlen Heinrichs, and the editors of *Yankee* Magazine (Emmaus, Pennsylvania: Rodale, 1999)
- *Home Remedies: What Works* by the editors of *Prevention* Health Books (Emmaus, Pennsylvania: Rodale, 1998)
- *Hoover's Company Profile Database* (Austin, Texas: The Reference Press, 1996)
- *Hoover's Guide to Private Companies 1994–1995* (Austin, Texas: The Reference Press, 1995)
- *Household Hints & Formulas* by Erik Bruun (New York: Black Dog and Leventhal, 1994)
- *Household Hints & Handy Tips* by *Reader's Digest* (Pleasantville, New York: Reader's Digest Association, 1988)
- *Household Hints for Upstairs, Downstairs, and All Around the House* by Carol Reese (New York: Henry Holt and Company, 1982)
- *How the Cadillac Got Its Fins* by Jack Mingo (New York: HarperCollins, 1994)
- *"Hypocholesterolemic Effect of Yogurt and Milk,"* by G. Hepner, et al. (*American Journal of Clinical Nutrition*, January 1979), pp. 19–24
- *It's Your Body: A Woman's Guide to Gynecology* by Niels Lauersen, M.D., and Steven Whitney (New York: Berkley Books, 1977)
- *Kitchen Medicines* by Ben Charles Harris (Barre, Massachusetts: Barre, 1968)
- *Laughing with Hugh Troy: World's Greatest Practical Joker* by Con Troy (Wyomissing, Pennsylvania: Trojan Books, 1983)
- *Make It Yourself* by Dolores Riccio and Joan Bingham (Radnor, Pennsylvania: Chilton, 1978)
- *Mary Ellen's Best of Helpful Hints* by Mary Ellen Pinkham (New York: Warner/B. Lansky, 1979)
- *Mary Ellen's Greatest Hints* by Mary Ellen Pinkham (New York: Fawcett Crest, 1990)
- *Medical Blunders* by R. M. Youngston (New York: New York University Press, 1996)
- *Nature's Medicines* by Gale Maleskey and the editors of *Prevention* Magazine (Emmaus, Pennsylvania: Rodale, 1999)

- "Obituaries," *Los Angeles Times*, January 25, 2000
- *Oops!* by Paul Kirchner (Los Angeles, General Publishing Books, 1996)
- "Oops! A Horribly Regrettable Mix-up," *Time*, March 31, 1980
- *The Origins of Everyday Things* by the editors of *Reader's Digest* (London: Reader's Digest, 1999)
- *Our Story So Far* (St. Paul, Minnesota: 3M, 1977)
- *The Oxford Companion to English Literature*, fourth edition, edited by Sir Paul Harvey (Oxford: Clarendon Press, 1973)
- *Panati's Extraordinary Origins of Everyday Things* by Charles Panati (New York: HarperCollins, 1987)
- *Practical Problem Solver* by *Reader's Digest* (Pleasantville, New York: Reader's Digest, 1991)
- *Prevention Food Cures* by the editors of *Prevention* Magazine (Emmaus, Pennsylvania: Rodale, 2001)
- *Reader's Digest Book of Facts* (Pleasantville, New York: Reader's Digest, 1987)
- *Rodale's Book of Hints, Tips & Everyday Wisdom* by Carol Hupping, Cheryl Winters Tetreau, and Roger B. Yepsen, Jr. (Emmaus, Pennsylvania: Rodale, 1985)
- *Scientific Blunders* by R. M. Youngston (New York: Carroll & Graf, 1998)
- *So Who the Heck Was Oscar Meyer?* by Doug Gelbert (New York: Barricade Books, 1996)
- *Solve Your Child's Sleep Problems* by Richad Ferber, M.D. (New York: Simon & Schuster, 1985)
- *Strange Stories, Amazing Facts* (Pleasantville, New York: Reader's Digest, 1976)
- *Strawberry Fields Forever: John Lennon Remembered* by Vic Garbarini and Brian Cullman with Barbar Graustark (New York: Bantam, 1980)
- *Symbols of America* by Hal Morgan (New York: Viking, 1986)
- *Time Almanac Reference Edition 1994*, (Washington, D.C.: Compact Publishing, 1994)
- *The 20th Century* by David Wallechinsky (New York: Little, Brown, 1995)
- *The WD-40 Book* by Jim and Tim—the Duct Tape Guys (Roseville, Minnesota: Bad Dog Press, 1997)
- *Who Cut the Cheese: A Cultural History of the Fart* by Jim Dawson (Berkeley, California: Ten Speed Press, 1998)
- *Why Did They Name It . . . ?* by Hannah Campbell (New York: Fleet, 1964)
- *The Woman's Day Help Book* by Geraldine Rhoads and Edna Paradis (New York: Viking, 1988)
- *The World Almanac and Book of Facts 1993* (Mahwah, New Jersey: World Almanac Books, 1993)
- *The World Almanac and Book of Facts 1998* (Mahwah, New Jersey: World Almanac Books, 1998)
- *The World Almanac and Book of Facts 2000* (Mahwah, New Jersey: World Almanac Books, 2000)
- *The World Book Encyclopedia* (Chicago: World Book, 1985)

 **Trademark Information**

"A.1." is a registered trademark of Nabisco, Inc.

"Accent Flavor Enhancer" is a registered trademark of The Pillsbury Company.

"Adolph's" is a registered trademark of Lipton, Inc.

"Afrin" is a registered trademark of Schering-Plough HealthCare Products, Inc.

"Ajax" is a registered trademark of Colgate-Palmolive Company.

"Alberto VO5" is a registered trademark of Alberto-Culver USA, Inc.

"Alka-Seltzer" is a registered trademark of Bayer Corporation. Bayer Corporation does not endorse any uses for Alka-Seltzer other than those indicated on the package label.

"Altoids" is a registered trademark of Callard & Borser-Suchard, Inc.

"Aqua Net" is a registered trademark of Faberge USA, Inc.

"Arm & Hammer" is a registered trademark of Church & Dwight Co., Inc. Church & Dwight Co., Inc., does not recommend uses of Arm & Hammer Pure Baking Soda not described on the package or in current company brochures.

"Aunt Jemima" is a registered trademark of The Quaker Oats Company.

"Baby Magic" is a registered trademark of Playtex Products, Inc.

"Bag Balm" is a registered trademark of Dairy Association Co, Inc.

"Balmex" is a registered trademark of Macsil Inc.

"Ban" is a registered trademark of Chattem, Inc.

"Band-Aid" is a registered trademark of Johnson & Johnson.

"Bar Keepers Friend" is a registered trademark of SerVaas Laboratories.

"Barbasol" and "Beard Buster" are registered trademarks of Pfizer Inc. Pfizer Inc. does not recommend or endorse any use of Barbasol Thick & Rich Shaving Cream beyond those indicated on the usage instructions on the package label.

"Bayer" is a registered trademark of Bayer Corporation. Bayer Corporation does not endorse any use for Bayer Aspirin other than those listed on the product label.

"Bazooka" is a registered trademark of The Topps Company, Inc.

"BenGay" is a registered trademark of Pfizer Inc.

"Betty Crocker" and "Potato Buds" are registered trademarks of General Mills, Inc.

"Bioré" is a registered trademark of The Andrew Jergens Company.

"Blistex" is a registered trademark of Blistex Inc.

"Bounce" is a registered trademark of Procter & Gamble. Procter & Gamble does not recommend or endorse any use of Bounce beyond those for which this product has been tested as indicated in the usage instructions on the package label.

"Bounty" is a registered trademark of Procter & Gamble.

"Bubble Wrap" is a registered trademark of Sealed Air Corporation.

"Budweiser" is a registered trademark of Anheuser-Busch, Inc.

"Cadbury" is a registered trademark of Cadbury Limited Company.

Trademark Information

"Campbell" is a registered trademark of Campbell Soup Company. Campbell Soup Company does not endorse or recommend any use of Campbell's products beyond those for which the products have been tested as indicated in the usage instructions on the label.

"Canada Dry" is a registered trademark of CadburySchweppes.

"Carnation" is a registered trademark of Nestlé.

"Cascade" is a registered trademark of Procter & Gamble. Procter & Gamble does not recommend or endorse any use of Cascade Dishwasher Detergent beyond those for which this product has been tested as indicated in the usage instructions on the product label.

"ChapStick" is a registered trademark of A. H. Robins Company.

"Charmin" is a registered trademark of Procter & Gamble.

"Cheerios" is a registered trademark of General Mills, Inc.

"Cheez Whiz" is a registered trademark of Kraft Foods Holdings, Inc.

"Clairol" and "Herbal Essences" are registered trademarks of Clairol, Inc.

"Clean Shower" is a registered trademark of Clean Shower, LP.

"Clorox" is a registered trademark of The Clorox Company.

"Close-Up" is a registered trademark of Chesebrough-Ponds USA.

"Coca-Cola" and "Coke" are registered trademarks of the Coca-Cola Company. The Coca-Cola Company does not endorse any use of Coca-Cola other than as a soft drink.

"Colgate" is a registered trademark of Colgate-Palmolive Company. Colgate-Palmolive Company does not recommend or endorse any use of Colgate toothpaste other than those uses indicated on the package label.

"Comet" is a registered trademark of Procter & Gamble.

"ConAir" and "Pro Style" are registered trademarks of Conair Corporation. The Conair Corporation does not endorse the use of a hairdryer other than for drying hair.

"Cool Whip" is a registered trademark of Kraft Foods Holdings, Inc.

"Coppertone" is a registered trademark of Schering-Plough HealthCare Products, Inc.

"Cortaid" is a registered trademark of Pharmacia & Upjohn Company.

"Country Time" and "Country Time Lemonade" are registered trademarks of Kraft Foods Holdings, Inc.

"CoverGirl" and "Nailslicks" are registered trademarks of Noxell Corporation.

"Crayola" is a registered trademark of Binney & Smith.

"Crest" is a registered trademark of Procter & Gamble.

"Crisco" is a registered trademark of Procter & Gamble. Procter & Gamble does not recommend or endorse any use of Crisco All-Vegetable Shortening beyond those for which this product has been tested as indicated in the usage instructions on the product label.

"Cutex" is a registered trademark of MedTech Products Inc.

"Cutty Sark" is a registered trademark of Berry Bros. & Rudd Ltd.

"Dannon" is a registered trademark of The Dannon Company, Inc. The Dannon Company, Inc. does not support usage of its yogurt products in any manner other than for normal dairy food and dairy consumption.

"DAP" is a registered trademark of DAP, Inc.

"Dawn" is a registered trademark of Procter & Gamble. Procter & Gamble does not recommend or endorse any use of Dawn Concentrated Dish Liquid beyond those for which this product has been tested as indicated in the usage instructions on the product label.

"Dentyne" is a registered trademark of Warner-Lambert Company.

"Desitin" is a registered trademark of Pfizer Inc.

"Dial" is a registered trademark of The Dial Corporation.

"Dickinson's" is a registered trademark of Dickinson Brands Inc.

"Dixie" is a registered trademark of Georgie-Pacific.

"Domino" is a registered trademark of Domino Foods, Inc.

"Dorito's" is a registered trademark of Frito-Lay, Inc.

"Downy" is a registered trademark of Procter & Gamble. Procter & Gamble does not recommend or endorse any use of Downy beyond those for which this product has been tested as indicated in the usage instructions on the product label.

"Dr. Bronner's" is a registered trademark of All-One-God-Faith, Inc.

"Dreft" is a registered trademark of Procter & Gamble.

"Easy Cheese" is a registered trademark of Nabisco.

"Easy-Off" is a registered trademark of Reckitt & Colman Inc.

"Efferdent" is a registered trademark of Warner-Lambert Company. Warner-Lambert Company does not endorse any use of Efferdent denture cleanser other than those indicated in the usage instructions on the package label.

"Elmer's" and "Glue-All" and Elmer the Bull are registered trademarks of Elmer's Products, Inc.

"Endust" is a registered trademark of Sara Lee Corporation.

"Fantastik" is a registered trademark of S.C. Johnson & Son, Inc.

"Febreze" is a registered trademark of Proctor & Gamble.

"Formula 409" is a registered trademark of The Clorox Company.

"Forster" is a registered trademark of Diamond Brands Incorporated.

"French's" is a registered trademark of Reckitt & Colman Inc.

"Fritos" is a registered trademark of Frito-Lay, Inc.

"Fruit of the Earth" is a registered trademark of Fruit of the Earth, Inc.

"Gatorade" is a registered trademark of Stokely-Van Camp, Inc..

"Gillette" is a registered trademark of The Gillette Company.

"Glad" is a registered trademark of The Glad Products Company.

"Gold Medal" is a registered trademark of General Mills, Inc.

"Gold's Horseradish" is a registered trademark of Gold Pure Food Products Co. Inc.

"Green Giant" is a registered trademark of The Pillsbury Company.

"Halls" and "Mentho-Lyptus" are registered trademarks of Warner-Lambert Company.

"Hartz" and "2 in 1" are registered trademarks of The Hartz Mountain Corporation.

"Heinz" is a registered trademark of H.J. Heinz Company.

"Hershey's" is a registered trademark of Hershey Foods Corporation.

"Huggies" is a registered trademark of Kimberly-Clark Corporation.

"Hunt's" is a registered trademark of Conagra Grocery Products Company.

"Ivory" is a registered trademark of Procter & Gamble. Procter & Gamble does not recommend or endorse any use of Ivory Soap beyond those for which this product has been tested as indicated in the usage instructions on the product label.

"Jell-O" is a registered trademark of Kraft Foods Holdings, Inc. Kraft Foods does not endorse any use of its products other than the intended use which is indicated on the package label.

"Jet-Puffed" is a registered trademark of Nabisco, Inc.

"Jif" is a registered trademark of Procter & Gamble. Procter & Gamble does not recommend or endorse any use of Jif peanut butter beyond those for which this product has been tested as indicated in the usage instructions on the product label.

"Johnson & Johnson" and "Johnson's" are registered trademarks of Johnson & Johnson.

Trademark Information

"Joy" is a registered trademark of Procter & Gamble.

"Karo" is a registered trademark of CPC International Inc.

"Kellogg's" is a registered trademark of Kellogg Company.

"Kikkoman" is a registered trademark of Kikkoman Corporation.

"Kingsford" is a registered trademark of The Kingsford Products Company.

"Kingsford's" and the Kingsford logo are registered trademarks of CPC International Inc.

"Kiwi" is a registered trademark of Sara Lee Corporation.

"Kleenex" is a registered trademark of Kimberly-Clark Corporation.

"Kodak" is a registered trademark of Eastman Kodak Company.

"Kool-Aid" is a registered trademark of Kraft Foods Holdings, Inc. Kraft Foods does not endorse any use of its products other than the intended use which is indicated on the package label.

"Kraft" is a registered trademark of Kraft Foods Holding, Inc.

"Krazy Glue" is a registered trademark of Borden, Inc. The company accepts no liability for any use of Instant Krazy Glue that is not specifically endorsed on the product's packaging and labeling.

"L'eggs" and "Sheer Energy" are registered trademarks of Sara Lee Corporation.

"Land O Lakes" is a registered trademark of Land O'Lakes, Inc.

"Lay's" is a registered trademark of Frito-Lay, Inc.

"Life Savers" is a registered trademark of Nabisco, Inc.

"Lipton," "The 'Brisk' Tea," and "Flo-Thru" are registered trademarks of Thomas J. Lipton, Inc.

"Listerine" is a registered trademark of Warner-Lambert Company. The Warner-Lambert Company does not endorse any use of Listerine mouthwash other than those indicated in the usage instructions on the package label.

"Lubriderm" is a registered trademark of Warner-Lambert Company. The Warner-Lambert Company does not endorse any use of Lubriderm Dry Skin Lotion other than those indicated in the usage instructions on the package label.

"Lysol" is a registered trademark of Reckitt & Colman Inc.

"M&M's" is a registered trademark of Mars, Incorporated.

"Maalox" is a registered trademark of Novartis Consumer Health, Inc.

"Massengill" is a registered trademark of GlaxoSmithKlein.

"MasterCard" is a registered trademark of MasterCard International Incorporated.

"Maxwell House" and "Good to the Last Drop" are registered trademarks of Kraft Foods Holding, Inc. Kraft Foods does not endorse any use of its products other than the intended use which is indicated on the package label.

"Maybelline" and "MoistureWhip" are registered trademarks of Maybelline, LLC. Maybelline, LLC. does not recommend or endorse any use of Maybelline Crystal Clear Nail Polish other than as a nail polish.

"McCormick" is a registered trademark of McCormick & Company, Inc. McCormick & Company, Inc. does not endorse any use of its products other than as seasonings in foods.

"Mennen" and "Afta" are registered trademarks of The Mennen Company.

"Milk-Bone" is a registered trademark of Kraft Foods Holdings, Inc.

"Miracle Whip" is a registered trademark of Kraft Foods Holding, Inc.

"Morton" and the Morton Umbrella Girl are registered trademarks of Morton International, Inc.

"Mott's" is a registered trademark of Mott's Inc.

"Mountain Dew" is a registered trademark of PepsiCo, Inc.

"Mr. Coffee" is a registered trademark of Sunbeam Products, Inc.

"Mrs. Stewart's" is a registered trademark of Luther Ford & Company.

"Murphy" is a registered trademark of Colgate-Palmolive Company. Colgate-Palmolive Company does not recommend or endorse any use of Murphy's Oil Soap other than those uses indicated on the package label.

"Mylanta" is a registered trademark of Johnson & Johnson Merck Consumer Pharmaceuticals Co.

"Neosporin" is a registered trademark of Warner-Lambert Company.

"Nestea" and "Nestlé" are registered trademarks of Nestlé.

"Neutrogena" is a registered trademark of Neutrogena Corporation.

"Niagara" is a registered trademark of CPC International Inc.

"Noxzema" is a registered trademark of Procter & Gamble.

"Ocean Spray" is a registered trademark of Ocean Spray Cranberries, Inc.

"Orajel" is a registered trademark of Del Laboratories, Inc.

"Oral-B" is a registered trademark of Oral-B Laboratories.

"Orville Redenbacher's Gourmet" is a registered trademark of Conagra Grocery Products Company.

"Palmolive" is a registered trademark of Colgate-Palmolive Company. Colgate-Palmolive Company does not recommend or endorse any use of Palmolive dish washing liquid other than those uses indicated on the package label.

"Pam" is a registered trademark of International Home Foods. The company does not endorse any use of Pam Original Cooking Spray other than those indicated on the label.

"Pampers" is a registered trademark of Procter & Gamble. Procter & Gamble does not recommend or endorse any use of Pampers beyond those for which this product has been tested as indicated in the usage instructions on the product label.

"Parsons'" is a registered trademark of Church & Dwight Co., Inc.

"Paul Mitchell" is a registered trademark of John Paul Mitchell Systems.

"Pepto-Bismol" is a registered trademark of Procter & Gamble. Procter & Gamble does not recommend or endorse any use of Pepto-Bismol beyond those for which this product has been tested as indicated in the usage instructions on the product label.

"Phillips'" is a registered trademark of Bayer Corporation. Bayer Corporation does not endorse any uses of Phillips' Milk of Magnesia other than those indicated on the package label.

"Pine-Sol" is a registered trademark of The Clorox Company.

"Playtex," "Gentle Glide," "Living," and "Made Strong to Last Long" are registered trademarks of Playtex Products, Inc.

"Pledge" is a registered trademark of S.C. Johnson & Son, Inc.

"Popsicle" is a registered trademark of Good Humor-Breyers Ice Cream.

"Post-it" is a registered trademark of 3M.

"Preparation H" is a registered trademark of Whitehall-Robbins.

"Purell" is a registered trademark of Gojo Industries.

"Q-Tips" is a registered trademark of Chesebrough-Pond's USA Co.

"Quaker Oats" is a registered trademark of The Quaker Oats Company.

"ReaLemon" is a registered trademark of Eagle Family Foods, Inc.

"Reddi-wip" is a registered trademark of ConAgra Brands, Inc. The company does not recommend or accept liability for any use of Reddi-wip Whipped Light Cream other than for food topping.

"Resolve" is a registered trademark of Reckitt & Colman Inc.

Trademark Information

"Reynolds Wrap" is a registered trademark of Reynolds Metals.

"Right Guard" is a registered trademark of The Gillette Company.

"Rolaids" is a registered trademark of Warner-Lambert Company.

"Rubbermaid" is a registered trademark of Rubbermaid Home Products.

"S.O.S." is a registered trademark of The Clorox Company.

"Saran" is a registered trademark of S.C. Johnson & Son, Inc.

"Scope" is a registered trademark of Procter & Gamble.

"Scotch-Brite," "Scotch" "Scotchgard," and "3M" are registered trademarks of 3M.

"Scott" is a registered trademark of Kimberly-Clark Corporation.

"Selsun Blue" is a registered trademark of Abbott Laboratories.

"7-Up" is a registered trademark of Dr Pepper/Seven-Up, Inc.

"Shout" is a registered trademark of S.C. Johnson & Son, Inc.

"Silly Putty" is a registered trademark of Binney & Smith Inc.

"Skin-So-Soft" is a registered trademark of Avon Products, Inc.

"Slinky" is a registered trademark of James Industries.

"Smirnoff" is a registered trademark of United Vintners & Distributors.

"Smith Brothers" is a registered trademark of Warner-Lambert Company.

"Smucker's" is a registered trademark of The J.M. Smucker Co.

"Speed Stick" is a registered trademark of The Mennen Company.

"Spic and Span" is a registered trademark of Procter & Gamble.

"Spray 'n Wash" is a registered trademark of Reckitt Benckiser, Inc.

"Star" is a registered trademark of Star Fine Foods.

"Static Guard" is a registered trademark of Alberto-Culver USA, Inc.

"Stayfree" is a registered trademark of McNeil-PPC, Inc.

"STP" is a registered trademark of STP Products Company.

"SueBee" is a registered trademark of Sioux Honey Assocation.

"Sun-Maid" is a registered trademark of Sun-Maid Growers of California.

"Sunshine Krispy" is a registered trademark of Sunshine Biscuits, Inc.

"Sure-Jell" is a registered trademark of Kraft Foods Holdings, Inc.

"Tabasco" is a registered trademark of McIlhenny Company.

"Tang" is a registered trademark of Kraft Foods Holdings, Inc. Kraft Foods does not endorse the use of any of its products other than the intended use which is indicated on the package label.

"Tide" is a registered trademark of Procter & Gamble.

"Tidy Cats" is a registered trademark of the Ralston Purina Company.

"Trojan" is a registered trademark of Carter-Wallace, Inc.

"Tums" is a registered trademark of SmithKlineBeecham.

"Turtle Wax" is a registered trademark of Turtle Wax, Inc.

"20 Mule Team" is a registered trademark of United States Borax Inc.

"Twinkies" is a registered trademark of Interstate Bakeries Corporation.

"Uncle Ben's" and "Converted" are registered trademarks of Uncle Ben's, Inc.

"USA Today" is a registered trademark of Gannett Co, Inc.

"Vaseline" is a registered trademark of the Chesebrough-Pond's USA, Co.

"Vegemite" is a registered trademark of Kraft Foods Holdings, Inc.

"Velcro" is a registered trademark of Velcro Industries B.V.

Trademark Information

"Vicks" and "VapoRub" are registered trademarks of Procter & Gamble. Procter & Gamble does not recommend or endorse any use of Vicks VapoRub beyond those for which this product has been tested as indicated in the usage instructions on the product label.

"Visine" is a registered trademark of Pfizer Inc.

"WD-40" is a registered trademark of the WD-40 Company.

"Wesson" is a registered trademark of Conagra Grocery Products Company.

"Wilson" is a registered trademark of Wilson Sporting Goods Co.

"Windex" is a registered trademark of S. C. Johnson & Son, Inc.

"Wish-Bone" is a registered trademark of Thomas J. Lipton, Inc.

"Wonder" is a registered trademark of Interstate Brands Corporation.

"Woolite" is a registered trademark of Reckitt & Colman Inc.

"Wrigley's," "Juicy Fruit," and "Wrigley's Spearmint" are registered trademarks of Wm. Wrigley Jr. Company.

"York" is a registered trademark of Hershey Foods Corporation.

"Ziploc" is a registered trademark of S.C. Johnson & Son, Inc.

Index

A

A.1. Steak Sauce, for treating insect bites, 204
Absorbine Jr., for preventing shaving skin
    irritations, 279
Accent Flavor Enhancer, for preventing pet
    coprophagy, 252
Acne treatments, 1–3
Adolph's Meat tenderizer, for treating
  backache, 20
  bee and wasp stings, 32
  foot ache, 158
  insect bites, 204
  jellyfish stings, 213
  poison ivy, 261
Afrin Nasal Spray, for treating
  nosebleed, 249
  shaving cuts, 281
Afta aftershave lotion, for treating sunburn, 302
Air fresheners, 5–6
Ajax cleansing powder, as hair lightener, 175
Alberto VO5 Conditioning Hairdressing
  for bandage removal, 95
  for bathing and deodorizing pets, 251
  for detangling horse's mane, 253
  for manicure, 140
  for ring removal from finger, 298
  for skin protection while dyeing hair, 175
  for treating
    chafing, 67
    chapped lips, 69
    dry hair, 112
    dry skin and windburn, 118
    flyaway hair, 114
    foot ache, 158
    pets' hairballs, 252
    wrinkles, 329
Alka-Seltzer
  for cleaning toilets, 111
  for treating
    bad breath, 23
    flu, 151
    foot ache, 158
    foot odor, 161
    hangover, 182
    indigestion, 201

    insect bites, 204
    muscle pain, 239
    nicotine withdrawal, 247
    urinary tract infection, 317
Allergy treatments, 8–9
Altoid Peppermints, for treating
  allergies, 8
  colds, 78
  cough, 90
  flatulence, 146
  flu, 151
  menstrual problems, 235
  nausea, 242
Ammonia. *See* Parson's Ammonia
Aphrodisiac, 227
Aqua Net Hairspray
  as insecticide, 35
  for treating lice, 221
Arm & Hammer Baking Soda
  as aftershave lotion, 279
  as air freshener, 5
  for bathing and deodorizing pets, 251
  in baths, 26, 210, 235, 239, 296
  for cleaning
    bloodstains, 237
    contact lenses, 85
    dentures and retainers, 102
    food-coloring stains on hands, 179
    hair brushes, combs, and curling irons, 170
    skunk spray odor, 286
    smelly diapers, 105
    urine odors, 31, 255
    vomit odors, 324
  for deodorizing cat litter box, 253
  for earwax removal, 126
  as facial, 136
  as hair shampoo, 116, 276
  for manicure and pedicure, 140
  for treating
    acne, 1
    athlete's foot, 15
    bad breath, 23
    bee and wasp stings, 32
    body odor, 42
    boils, 46

Arm & Hammer Baking Soda (cont.)
  for treating (cont.)
    burns, 56
    canker sores, 65
    chicken pox, 71
    cold sores, 76
    dental tartar and plaque, 308
    diaper rash, 104
    dry skin and windburn, 118
    flatulence, 146
    flu, 151
    foot ache, 158
    foot odor, 161
    green hair, 166
    indigestion, 201
    insect bites, 204
    insomnia, 210
    jellyfish stings, 213
    menstrual odors, 235
    muscle pain, 239
    poison ivy, 261
    psoriasis, 268
    rashes, 271
    smelly clothes, 43
    smelly shoes and socks, 16
    sore throat, 290
    stress, 296
    sunburn, 302
    urinary tract infection, 317
Arthritis treatments, 11–12
Aspirin. See Bayer Aspirin
Asthma treatments, 13, 13
Athlete's foot treatments, 15, 17
Aunt Jemima Original Syrup
  as insecticide, 35
  for treating
    burns, 56
    dry hair, 112
    headache, 184
    insomnia, 210
    sore throat, 290

B

Baby care tips and treatments, 18–19
Baby Magic Baby Powder
  as hair shampoo, 116
  for shaving with electric razor, 279
  for treating
    cast itches, 51
    dry skin and windburn, 118, 121
    hemorrhoids, 189
    smelly shoes and socks, 16
Baby oil. See Johnson's Baby Oil
Baby wipes. See Huggies Baby
    Wipes
Backache treatments, 20–22
Bad breath treatments, 23–24

Bag Balm, for treating
  chapped lips, 69
  cuts and scrapes, 92
  diaper rash, 104
  dry horse hooves, 253
  dry skin and windburn, 118
  eczema, 129
  nosebleed, 249
  pets' cuts and scrapes, 252
  psoriasis, 268
  sore nipples, 48
Baking soda. See Arm & Hammer Baking Soda
Balmex, for treating
  cold sores, 76
  poison ivy, 261
Ban Antiperspirant Deodorant, for treating
  bee and wasp stings, 32
  insect bites, 204
  muscle pain, 239
Band-Aid Bandages
  for eyeglass repair, 132
  history of, 63
  for manicure and pedicure, 140–41
  removing, 95
  for treating
    acne, 1, 3
    bee and wasp stings, 32
    boils, 46
    calluses, 62
    chafing, 67
    snoring, 288
    warts, 326–27
Barbasol Shaving Cream
  for defogging eyeglasses, 132
  as hair gel, 177
  for treating
    cold sores, 76
    jellyfish stings, 213
Bar Keepers Friend, for milk stain removal, 50
Bathing tips
  humans, 26–27
  pets, 251–52
Bathtub rings, cleaning, 29
Bayer Aspirin
  history of, 186
  for treating
    backache, 20
    bee and wasp stings, 32
    calluses, 62
    green hair, 166
    insect bites, 204
    shingles, 284
    varicose veins, 320
    warts, 326
Bazooka Bubble Gum, history of, 171
Bed-wetting treatments, 30
Beer. See Budweiser beer

Bee sting treatments, 32–34
BenGay, for treating
    flu, 151
    headache, 184
    insect bites, 204
    knee pain, 217
    sore throat, 290
    stress, 296
Betty Crocker Potato Buds, for treating
    burns, 56
    insect bites, 204
Bioré Facial Cleansing Cloths, for defogging
        eyeglasses, 132
Black eye treatments, 37
Bleach. *See* Clorox bleach
Blister treatments, 40–41
Blistex, for treating warts, 326
Bloodstains, cleaning, 237
Body odor treatments, 42
Boil treatments, 46
Bounce dryer sheets
    as air freshener, 5
    for bathing and deodorizing pets, 251
    for cleaning eyeglasses, 131
    for deodorizing cat litter box, 253
    as insect repellent, 208, 253
    for manicure, 140
    for treating
        flyaway hair, 114
        foot ache, 158
        menstrual odors, 235
        smelly clothes, 43
        smelly diapers, 105
        smelly shoes and socks, 16
Bounty paper towels
    as baby wipes, 18
    with ice packs, 199
    for treating earache, 123
Breastfeeding tips, 48–49
Broken bone treatments, 51, 52
Bruise treatments, 54–55
Bubble Wrap
    history of, 53
    for treating
        arthritis, 11
        backache, 20
        broken bones, 51
        foot ache, 158
        knee pain, 217
        stress, 296
Budweiser beer
    as hair shampoo, 276
    as hair spray, 177
    history of, 115
    as insecticide, 35
    for treating dry hair, 112
Burn treatments, 56–58, 58

Burrs, removing from pets, 254
Bursitis treatments, 60–61
Butter. *See* Land O Lakes Butter

C

Callus treatments, 62
Campbell's Chicken Noodle Soup, for treating
    colds, 78
    diarrhea, 108
    flu, 151
    hangover, 182
    runny nose, 273
Campbell's Tomato Juice, for treating
    asthma, 13
    colds, 79
    flu, 153
    green hair, 166
    hangover, 182
    runny nose, 274
    skunk spray odor, 253–54, 286
    sore throat, 292
Canada Dry Club Soda
    for cleaning
        urine odors, 31, 255
        vomit stains, 324
    for treating green hair, 166
Canada Dry Ginger Ale, for treating
    flatulence, 146
    heartburn, 187
    indigestion, 201
    menstrual problems, 235
    morning sickness, 265
    nausea, 242, 265
    ulcers, 315
    vomiting, 322
Canker sore treatments, 65–66
Car-Freshner Pine Trees, as air freshener, 5
Carnation Condensed Milk, for treating
    burns, 56
    cold sores, 76
    dry hair, 112
    eczema, 129
    foot ache, 159
    pizza burn, 258
Carnation Evaporated Milk, as facial, 138
Carnation Nonfat Dry Milk
    for bathing and deodorizing pets, 251
    in baths, 26
    for bloodstain removal, 237
    as facial, 136
    for treating
        insect bites, 205
        menstrual problems, 235
        poison ivy, 261
        psoriasis, 268
        sunburn, 302

Cascade dishwasher detergent
  for cleaning
    bathtubs, 29
    milk stains, 50
    toilets, 111
  for treating poison ivy, 261
Cast itch treatments, 51
Castor oil, for treating
  breast inflammation, 48
  bursitis, 60
  calluses, 62
  herpes, 192
  warts, 326
  wrinkles, 329
Cat litter boxes, deodorizing, 253
Cellucotton, history of, 9
Chafing treatments, 67
Chapped lips treatments, 69–70
ChapStick lip balm
  for ring removal from finger, 298
  for skin protection while dyeing hair, 175
  for treating
    chafing, 67
    colds, 78
    corns, 87
    cuts and scrapes, 92
    dry cuticles, 140
    dry skin and windburn, 118
    flu, 151
    shaving nicks and cuts, 281
    sore nipples, 48
Cheerios breakfast cereal
  as facial, 136
  for treating
    chicken pox, 71
    dry skin and windburn, 118
    high cholesterol, 73
    poison ivy, 261–62
    sunburn, 302
Cheez Whiz
  for cleaning bloodstains, 237
  as shaving cream, 279
Chicken pox treatments, 71
Chigger bite treatments, 207
Chloroseptic, for treating premature ejaculation, 226
Cholesterol, treatments for high, 73–74
Clairol Herbal Essences Conditioner, as shaving cream, 279
Clairol Herbal Essences Shampoo
  in baths, 26
  for cleaning bathtubs, 29
Cleaning tips
  bathtubs, 29
  bloodstains, 237
  contact lenses, 85
  dentures and retainers, 102–3

eyeglasses, 131–32
food-coloring stains, 179
hair brushes, combs, and curling irons, 170
humidifier, 80
milk stains, 50
paint and grease, 179–80
pet stains and odors, 253, 255
toilets, 111
toothbrushes, 311
urine smell, 31
vomit stain, 324
Clean Shower
  for cleaning
    bathtubs, 29
    pet odors, 251
    razors, 279
    toilets, 111
    vomit stains, 324
Clorox bleach
  for cleaning
    dentures and retainers, 102
    humidifier, 80
    toilets, 111
  as insect repellent, 208
  for treating
    athlete's foot, 15
    jellyfish stings, 213
    lice, 221
    poison ivy, 262
    warts, 326
Close-Up Red Gel Toothpaste
  as hair gel, 177
  as shaving cream, 280
Coca-Cola
  for cleaning
    bathtubs, 29
    bloodstains, 237
    eyeglasses, 131
    milk stains, 50
    skunk spray odor, 286
    toilets, 111
  as hair gel, 177
  history of, 203
  for treating
    asthma, 13
    constipation, 83
    diarrhea, 108
    dry hair, 112
    flatulence, 146
    food poisoning, 156
    indigestion, 201
    jellyfish stings, 213
    nausea, 242
    sore throat, 290
    vomiting, 322
Coffee filters. See Mr. Coffee Filters
Colace Stool Softener, for earwax removal, 126

Cold sore treatments, 76–77
Cold treatments, 78–80
Colgate Toothpaste
  for cleaning
    eyeglasses, 131
    food-coloring stains on hands, 179
  for defogging eyeglasses, 132
  as facial, 136
  for manicure, 140
  for treating
    acne, 1
    burns, 56
    cold sores, 76
    hickey, 226
    insect bites, 205
    leech bites, 207
    toothache, 312
Comet cleansing powder, as hair shampoo, 276
ConAir Pro Style 1600 Hairdryer
  for bandage removal, 95
  for treating
    athlete's foot, 15
    bee and wasp stings, 32
    cast itches, 51
    diaper rash, 104
    earache, 123
    herpes, 192
    smelly shoes and socks, 16
    swimmer's ear, 306
    yeast infection, 331
Constipation treatments, 83–84
Contact lens tips, 85
Cool Whip Whipped Topping
  as facial, 136–37
  as sex enhancer, 226
  as shaving cream, 280
  for treating
    burns, 56
    cold sores, 76
    dry hair, 112
    foot ache, 158
    pizza burn, 258
    sunburn, 302
Coppertone sunscreen
  in baths, 26
  as hair gel, 177
  as insect repellent, 208
  for manicure, 140
  for treating
    cold sores, 76
    dry hair, 112
    dry skin and windburn, 118
    freckles and sunspots, 164
    insect bites, 205
    muscle pain, 239
    wrinkles, 329
Corn starch. See Kingsford's Corn Starch

Corn treatments, 87–88
Cortaid hydrocortisone cream
  for treating
    acne, 1
    dry skin and windburn, 119
Cosmetics, tips for removing, 224–25
Cotton balls. See Johnson & Johnson Cotton Balls
Cough treatments, 90
Country Time Lemonade
  for cleaning toilets, 111
  for hair coloring, 173
  as hair shampoo, 276
  for treating
    bad breath, 23
    kidney stones, 215
CoverGirl NailSlicks nail polish
  for identifying twins, 18
  as memory aid, 331
Crackers. See Krispy Original Saltine Crackers,
    for treating
Crayola Chalk, for treating warts, 326
Crayola Crayons, for treating stress, 296
Crest Toothpaste, for treating acne, 1
Crisco All-Vegetable Shortening
  for cleaning paint and grease on hands, 179–80
  for removal of
    ring stuck on finger, 298
    stickers and burrs from pets, 254
  for treating
    chafing, 67
    chapped lips, 69
    diaper rash, 104
    dry skin and windburn, 119
    eczema, 129
    foot ache, 158
    lice, 221
    psoriasis, 268
    sunburn, 302
    wrinkles, 329
Cutex Nail Polish Remover
  for cleaning hair brushes, combs, and curling
    irons, 170
  for treating
    poison ivy, 262
    shingles, 284
Cuts, treatments for, 92–93, 93
Cutty Sark Scots Whiskey, for treating sore
    throat, 290

D
Dandruff treatments, 96–97
Dannon Yogurt
  for calcium requirements, 233
  as facial, 137
  for treating
    allergies, 8
    canker sores, 65

Dannon Yogurt *(cont.)*
  for treating *(cont.)*
    cold sores, 76
    dandruff, 96
    diarrhea, 108
    dry skin and windburn, 119
    flatulence, 146
    flu, 151
    hemorrhoids, 189
    high cholesterol, 73
    lactose intolerance, 219
    menopausal symptoms, 233
    sunburn, 302
    ulcers, 315
    urinary tract infection, 317
    yeast infection, 331
  as vaginal lubricant, 226
DAP Caulk, for treating splinters, 294
Dawn dishwashing liquid
  for cleaning
    milk stains, 50
    paint and grease on hands, 180
    skunk spray odor, 286
  for defogging eyeglasses, 132
  as hair shampoo, 276
  as insecticide, 35
  for treating
    flea infestation, 147, 252
    lice, 222
    yeast infection, 331
Defogging eyeglasses, tips for, 132
Dehydration treatments, 99
Dental care
  dentures, 102–3
  plaque removal, 308–9
  retainers, 102–3
  tartar removal, 308–9
  toothache, 312–13, 313
Denture care tips, 102–3
Dentyne, for treating dental tartar and plaque,
    308
Desitin, for treating
  burns, 56
  hemorrhoids, 189
  sunburn, 303
Dial Soap
  history of, 45
  for treating
    body odor, 42
    colds, 78
    cuts and scrapes, 92
    flu, 152
    foot odor, 161
    smelly clothes, 43
    smelly shoes and socks, 16
Diaper rash treatments, 104–6
Diarrhea treatments, 108–9, 109

Dickinson's Witch Hazel, for treating
  acne, 1
  bruises, 54
  cold sores, 76
  cuts and scrapes, 92
  diaper rash, 104
  eczema, 129
  hemorrhoids, 189
  hives, 196
  poison ivy, 262
  shaving nicks and cuts, 281
  sunburn, 303
Dishwasher detergent. *See* Cascade dishwasher
    detergent
Dixie Cups, for treating earache, 123
Dr. Bronner's Peppermint Soap
  for cleaning dentures and retainers, 102
  as facial, 137
  for treating
    athlete's foot, 15
    bad breath, 23
    body odor, 42
Doctor's care for
  asthma, 13
  burns, 58
  cuts and scrapes, 93
  diarrhea, 109
  earache, 124
  food poisoning, 157
  fractures, 52
  headaches, 185
  heartburn, 187
  kidney stones, 215
  nosebleeds, 250
  poison ivy, 263
  pregnancy, 265
  shingles, 285
  sunburn, 304
  swimmer's ear, 307
  toothache, 313
  urinary tract infections, 317
  yeast infections, 332
Domino Sugar
  for cleaning paint and grease on hands,
    180
  as facial, 137
  as hair-setting lotion, 177
  for treating
    bee and wasp stings, 32
    dehydration, 99
    diarrhea, 108
    dry skin and windburn, 119
    food poisoning, 156
    hiccups, 194
    indigestion, 201
    pizza burn, 258
    vomiting, 322

Downy Liquid Fabric Softener
  as air freshener, 5
  for treating
    dry hair, 113
    flyaway hair, 114
Dry cuticle treatments, 140–42
Dryer sheets. *See* Bounce dryer sheets
Dry hair treatments, 112–14
Dry shampoos, 116
Dry skin treatments, 118–21

E

Earache treatments, 123–24, 124
Earwax removal, 126
Easy Cheese, for treating dental tartar and
    plaque, 308
Easy-Off Oven Cleaner, for cleaning
    bathtubs, 29
    milk stains, 50
Eczema treatments, 129–30
Efferdent denture cleanser
  for cleaning
    toilets, 111
    toothbrushes, 311
  for manicure, 140
  for treating smelly clothes, 43
Elmer's Glue-All
  as facial, 137
  as hair gel, 177–78
  for treating
    acne, 1
    splinters, 294
    warts, 327
Endust, for treating allergies, 8
Epsom Salt
  in baths, 26, 235, 239, 296
  as facial, 137
  as hair shampoo, 276
  for treating
    acne, 2
    corns, 87
    dry hair, 113
    flu, 151
    foot ache, 159
    insect bites, 205
    muscle pain, 239
    stress, 296
Eye care tips, 134
Eyeglasses
  cleaning, 131–32
  defogging, 132
  repairing, 132

F

Fabric softener. *See* Downy Liquid Fabric Softener
Facial treatments, 136–39

Fantastik, as hair lightener, 175
Febreze, for treating smelly shoes and socks,
    16
Fingernail treatments, 140–43
Flatulence treatments, 146
Flea treatments, 149, 252
Flex Free Horse Linament, for treating
    backache, 20
Flour. *See* Gold Medal Flour
Flu treatments, 151–54
Flyaway hair treatments, 114
Food-coloring stains on hands, removing, 179
Food poisoning treatments, 156, 157
Foot ache treatments, 158–60
Foot odor treatments, 161–62
Formula 409 All Purpose Cleaner, as insecticide,
    35
Forster Clothes Pins, as memory aid, 331
Forster Toothpicks
  for eyeglass repair, 132
  for manicure and pedicure, 140–41
Fractures, treating, 51, 52
Freckles, treating, 164
French's Mustard
  in baths, 26
  as facial, 137
  for treating
    arthritis, 11
    backache, 20
    bruises, 54
    colds, 78
    flu, 152
    foot ache, 159
    heartburn, 187
    knee pain, 217
    muscle pain, 239
    rashes, 271
    sore throat, 290
    sunburn, 303
Frito Company, history of, 238
Fruit of the Earth Aloe Vera Gel
  as facial, 137
  as hair gel, 178
  for treating
    blisters, 40
    burns, 57
    canker sores, 65
    chicken pox, 71
    cold sores, 77
    dental tartar and plaque, 308
    dry skin and windburn, 119
    herpes, 192
    insect bites, 205
    muscle pain, 239
    sunburn, 303
    toothache, 312
    warts, 327

G

Gatorade
  for cleaning toilets, <u>111</u>
  for treating
    chapped lips, 69
    colds, 78
    dehydration, 99
    diarrhea, 108
    flu, 152
    food poisoning, 156
    hangover, 182
    headache, 184
    menstrual problems, 235
    morning sickness, 265
    muscle pain, 240
    nausea, 242, 265
    runny nose, 273
    sore throat, 290
    vomiting, 322
Gelatin. *See* Jell-O gelatin
Gels, hair, 177–78
Gillette, history of, <u>283</u>
Glad Flexible Straws
  as eyedropper, 134
  for finding lost contact lens, 85
  for treating
    colds, 79
    earache, 123
    flu, 152–53
    swimmer's ear, 306
Glad Trash Bags
  for keeping casts dry during showers and
      baths, 51
  for treating
    allergies, 8
    asthma, 13
    bed-wetting, 30
    lice, 221
Gold Medal Flour
  as facial, 138
  as hair shampoo, 116
  for treating
    burns, 56
    stress, 296
Gold's Horseradish, for treating
  asthma, 13
  colds, 78
  flu, 152–53
  freckles and sunspots, 164
  muscle pain, 240
  runny nose, 273
  sore throat, 291
Grease on hands, removing,
    179–80
Green Giant Company, history of,
    38

Green Giant Sweet Peas
  for making ice pack, 198
  for treating black eyes, 37
Green hair treatments, 166, 168
Gum in hair, removing, 169–70

H

Hairballs in pets, treating, 252–53
Hair care tips
  coloring, 173–74, <u>175</u>
  dandruff, 96–97
  dry, 112–14
  flyaway, <u>114</u>
  gels, 177–78
  green hair, 166, 168
  gum removal, 169–70
Hairspray. *See* Aqua Net Hairspray
Halitosis treatments, 23–24
Halls Mentho-Lyptus lozenge, as sex enhancer,
    226
Hand cleansers, 179–80
Hangnail prevention and treatments, 141–42
Hangover treatments, 182–83
Hartz 2-in-1 Flea & Tick Collar, for treating flea
    infestation, 147
Headache treatments, 184, <u>185</u>, <u>186</u>
Heartburn treatments, 187–88, <u>187</u>
Heinz, history of, <u>167</u>
Heinz Apple Cider Vinegar
  as facial, 138
  as hair shampoo, 276–77
  as insect repellent, 253
  for treating
    arthritis, 11
    asthma, 13
    bad breath, 23
    colds, 79
    cough, 90
    dry hair, 113
    flu, 152
    freckles and sunspots, 164
    green hair, 166
    heartburn, 187
    hiccups, 194
    indigestion, 201
    muscle pain, 240
    psoriasis, 268
    rashes, 271
    sore throat, 291
    warts, 327
    wrinkles, 329
Heinz Ketchup, for treating green hair, 166
Heinz White Vinegar
  as air freshener, 5
  for cleaning
    bathtubs, <u>29</u>
    dentures and retainers, 102

eyeglasses, 131
food-coloring stains on hands, 179
humidifier, <u>80</u>
toilets, <u>111</u>
urine odors, <u>31</u>, <u>255</u>
vomit stains, <u>324</u>
for treating
   acne, 2
   athlete's foot, 15
   bee and wasp stings, 32
   brittle fingernails, 142
   bruises, 54
   burns, 57
   calluses, 62
   cold sores, 77
   corns, 87
   dandruff, 96
   diaper rash, 104
   dry cuticles, 141
   dry hair, 112
   dry skin and windburn, 119
   flatulence, 146
   foot ache, 159
   foot odor, 161
   insect bites, 205
   jellyfish stings, 213
   lice, 221–22
   nicotine withdrawal, 247
   nosebleed, 249
   poison ivy, 262
   smelly clothes, <u>43</u>
   smelly shoes and socks, <u>16</u>
   sunburn, 303
   swimmer's ear, 306
   yeast infection, 331–32
Hemorrhoid treatments, 189–90
Herpes treatments, 192
Hershey Foods, history of, <u>229</u>
Hershey's Milk Chocolate, for treating
  hangover, 182
  menstrual cravings, 236
Hershey's Shell topping, as sex enhancer, 226
Hershey's Syrup
  history of, <u>229</u>
  as sex enhancer, 226
  for treating sore throat, 291
Hiccups treatments, 194
Hickey treatments, 226
High cholesterol treatments, 73–74
Hives treatments, 196
Honey. *See* SueBee Honey
Horse care tips, 253
Hot flash treatment, 233
Huggies Baby Wipes
  for bandage removal, <u>95</u>
  for cleaning
    cat vomit, <u>255</u>

eyeglasses, 131
food-coloring stains on hands, 179
milk stains, <u>50</u>
toilets, <u>111</u>
vomit stains, <u>324</u>
after episiotomy, 265
for sponge bath, 26
for treating
   cuts and scrapes, 92
   hemorrhoids, 189
   hot flashes, 233
   menopausal symptoms, 233
Humidifier, cleaning, <u>80</u>
Hunt's Tomato Paste
  for hair coloring, 173
  for treating boils, 46
H.W. Lay & Company, history of, <u>238</u>
Hydrogen peroxide
  for cleaning
    bathtubs, <u>29</u>
    bloodstains, <u>237</u>
    skunk spray odor, 286
  for earwax removal, 126
  for treating
    acne, 2
    canker sores, 65
    dental tartar and plaque, 308
    sore throat, 291
    warts, 327

I

Ice packs, making, 34, 198–99. *See also* Ziploc
     Storage Bags, as ice pack for
Indigestion treatments, 201–2
Infections
  urinary tract, 317, <u>317</u>
  yeast, 331–32, <u>332</u>
Influenza treatments, 151–54
Ingrown toenail treatment, 142
Injuries, treating pet, 252
Insecticides, <u>35</u>
Insect repellents, 208–9
Insect sting and bite treatments, 32–34, 204–7
Insomnia treatments, 210
Intestinal gas treatments, 146
Ivory Soap, for treating insect bites, 205

J

Jell-O gelatin
  in baths, 226–27
  for hair coloring, 173
  as hair gel, 178
  for making ice pack, 198
  for treating
    black eyes, 37
    brittle fingernails, 141
    diarrhea, 108

Jell-O gelatin *(cont.)*
  for treating *(cont.)*
    foot odor, 161
    nosebleed, 249
    vomiting, 322
Jellyfish sting treatments, 213–14
Jet-Puffed Marshmallows, for pedicure, 141
Jif Peanut Butter
  for removal of
    bandages, 95
    gum from hair and dentures or retainers,
      102, 169
    ring stuck on finger, 298
  as shaving cream, 280
  for treating
    dry skin and windburn, 119
    hemorrhoids, 189
    hiccups, 194
Johnson & Johnson Cotton Balls
  for finding lost contact lens, 85
  for preventing fingernails from piercing
    gloves, 121
Johnson's Baby Oil
  for bandage removal, 95
  in baths, 26
  for cleaning paint and grease on hands, 180
  for earwax removal, 126
  as insect repellent, 208, 253
  for making baby wipes, 18
  for ring removal from finger, 298
  as shaving lubricant, 280
  for treating
    brittle fingernails, 141
    chapped lips, 69
    chicken pox, 71
    dry skin and windburn, 119–20
    earache, 123
    gum stuck in hair, 169
    lice, 222
    swimmer's ear, 306
Johnson's Baby Powder, for treating
  muscle pain, 240
  rashes, 271
Johnson's Baby Shampoo
  as facial, 137
  for making baby wipes, 18

K

Karo Corn Syrup
  history of, 89
  for treating corns, 87
Kellogg Company, history of, 191
Kellogg's Raisin Bran, for treating
  constipation, 83
  hemorrhoids, 189
  menstrual problems, 236

Kidney stone treatments, 215, 215
Kikkoman Soy Sauce, for treating burns,
  57
Kingsford Charcoal Briquets, for treating bad
  odors, 6
Kingsford's Corn Starch
  for bathing and deodorizing pets, 251
  as facial, 137
  as hair shampoo, 116
  for stopping bleeding nailbed of pets,
    254
  for treating
    acne, 2
    athlete's foot, 15
    blisters, 40
    body odor, 42
    chafing, 67
    chicken pox, 71
    diaper rash, 104
    dry skin and windburn, 119
    foot odor, 161–62
    rashes, 271
    shingles, 284
    smelly shoes and socks, 16
    sunburn, 303
Kiwi White Liquid Shoe Polish, for treating
  acne, 2
  poison ivy, 262
Kleenex Tissues
  history of, 9
  as nursing pad, 48
  as panty liner, 236
Knee pain treatments, 217–18
Kodak 35mm Film canisters, for treating
  earache, 123
  kidney stones, 215
Kool-Aid
  for cleaning toilets, 111
  for hair coloring, 173
  for treating
    chapped lips, 69
    green hair, 166
Kraft Real Mayonnaise, for treating lice, 222
Krazy Glue, for treating
  broken fingernails, 141
  calluses, 62
  cuts and scrapes, 92
  dislodged tooth from dentures, 102
Krispy Original Saltine Crackers, for treating
  bed-wetting, 30
  diarrhea, 109
  food poisoning, 156
  hangover, 183
  morning sickness, 265
  nausea, 242, 265
  vomiting, 322

L

Lactose intolerance treatments, 219
Land O Lakes Butter
  history of, _300_
  for paint and grease removal from hands, 180
  for ring removal of finger, 298
  as shaving cream, 280
  for treating
    dry hair, 113
    dry skin and windburn, 119
    foot ache, 159
    muscle pain, 240
Lay's Potato Chips
  history of, _238_
  for treating
    insect bites, 206
    menstrual problems, 236
Leech bite treatments, 207
L'eggs Sheer Energy Panty Hose
  for cast care, 51
  for finding lost contact lens, 85
  for herbal bath, 26–27
  with ice packs, 199
  as insect repellent, 208
  for polishing dentures, 102
  for treating
    bursitis, 60
    chicken pox, 71
    eczema, 129
    jellyfish stings, 213
    knee pain, 217
    lactose intolerance, 219
    muscle pain, 240
    neck pain, 245
    poison ivy, 263
    rashes, 271
    shingles, 284
    smelly shoes and socks, _16_
    sunburn, 303–4
    varicose veins, 320
Lemon juice. _See_ ReaLemon
Lice treatments, 221–22
Life Savers candy
  history of, _25_
  for treating
    colds, 79
    cough, 90
    earache, 124
    flu, 152
    sore throat, 291
Lip balm. _See_ Blistex; ChapStick
Lipton Tea Bags
  for hair coloring, 173
  for treating
    acne, 2
    baby inoculation pain, 18
    bee and wasp stings, 33
    blisters, 40
    boils, 46
    broken fingernails, 141
    burns, 57
    canker sores, 65
    colds, 79
    cold sores, 77
    cuts and scrapes, 92
    dental tartar and plaque, 308–9
    diarrhea, 109
    flu, 152
    foot odor, 162
    headache, 184
    high cholesterol, 73
    insect bites, 205
    nausea, 242
    runny nose, 273
    sore nipples, 48
    sore throat, 291
    sunburn, 303
    tired eyes, 134
    toothache, 312
    vomiting, 323
Listerine mouthwash
  for cleaning
    humidifier, _80_
    razors, 280
    skunk spray odor, 286
    toilets, _111_
  as hair shampoo, 277
  as insect repellent, 208
  for treating
    acne, 2
    athlete's foot, 15
    bee and wasp stings, 33
    blisters, 40
    body odor, 42
    canker sores, 65
    cuts and scrapes, 92
    dandruff, 96
    dental tartar and plaque, 309
    foot odor, 162
    hives, 196
    insect bites, 205
    lice, 222
    poison ivy, 262
    smelly shoes and socks, _16_
    toenail fungus, 141
    toothache, 312
Lubriderm moisturizing lotion
  for ring removal from finger, 298
  as shaving cream, 280
  for treating
    dry cuticles, 141

Lubriderm moisturizing lotion *(cont.)*
for treating *(cont.)*
dry skin and windburn, 119
eczema, 129
foot ache, 159
psoriasis, 268
sunburn, 303
Lysol disinfectant spray, for treating
flea infestation, 147
lice, 222
smelly shoes and socks, <u>16</u>
Lysol Tub and Tile Cleaner, for cleaning
eyeglasses, 131
hair brushes, combs, and curling irons,
<u>170</u>

M

Maalox, for treating cuts and scrapes, 92
Makeup, tips for removing, 224–25
Manicure tips, 140–43
Marital relations, 226–27
Massengill Disposable Douche, for cleaning
skunk spray odor, 286
MasterCard
for removal of
bee or wasp stinger, 33
jellyfish tentacle, 214
for scraping tongue, 23, 309
Maxwell House Coffee
grounds, baths and, 27
for hair coloring, 174
for preventing cats from digging houseplants,
254
for treating
asthma, 13
bad odors, 6, <u>16</u>
colds, 79
constipation, 83
flu, 152
hangover, 182
headache, 184
Maybelline Crystal Clear Nail Polish
for eyeglass repair, 132
for treating
allergies, 8
broken fingernails, 141
chigger bites, 207
warts, 327
Maybelline Moisture Whip Lipstick, for treating
chapped lips, 69
McCormick Alum, for treating
canker sores, 65
cuts and scrapes, 93
shaving nicks and cuts, <u>281</u>
McCormick Basil Leaves, for treating
headache, 184
insomnia, 210

McCormick Bay Leaves, for treating
arthritis, 11
backache, 20
dandruff, 96
varicose veins, 320
McCormick Black Pepper
for preventing pets digging in soil, 254
for treating
sore throat, 291
toothache, 312
McCormick Cinnamon, for treating yeast
infection, 331–32
McCormick Cream of Tartar
for cleaning bathtub, <u>29</u>
for treating
hives, 196
indigestion, 202
McCormick Curry Powder, for treating insect
bites, 205
McCormick Food Coloring
for making ice pack, 198–99
for treating
black eyes, 37
dental tartar and plaque, 309
McCormick Garlic Powder
breastfeeding and, 49
as insect repellent, 208
for treating
colds, 79
flea infestation, 252
flu, 152
runny nose, 273
sore throat, 291
yeast infection, 332
McCormick Ground (Cayenne) Red Pepper, for
treating cuts and scrapes, 93
McCormick Ground Cinnamon, for treating bad
breath, 24
McCormick Ground Cloves, for treating sore
throat, 291
McCormick Rosemary Leaves, for treating
dandruff, 97
McCormick Thyme Leaves, for treating
dandruff, 96
McCormick Vanilla Extract
as aphrodisiac, 227
for treating
bad odors, 6
burns, 57
indigestion, 201
stress, 296
toothache, 312
Memory aids, 231
Mennen Speed Stick deodorant, as air
freshener, 6
Menopause, treating symptoms of, 233
Menstrual problems, treating, 235–36

Milk-Bone, history of, <u>257</u>
Milk stains, cleaning, <u>50</u>
Miracle Whip salad dressing
   for cleaning paint and grease from hands,
      180
   as facial, 137–38
   for ring removal from finger, 299
   as shaving cream, 280
   for treating
      brittle fingernails, 141
      dry hair, 113
      dry skin and windburn, 120
      foot ache, 159
      insect bites, 205
      sunburn, 303
Mr. Coffee Filters
   for cleaning eyeglasses, 131
   for manicure, 141
   for treating
      allergies, 8
      arthritis, 11
      backache, 20–21
      bad breath, 24
      bad odors, 6
      dandruff, 96–97
      freckles and sunspots, 164
      headache, 184
      kidney stones, 215
      toothache, 312
      varicose veins, 320
Mrs. Stewart's Liquid Bluing
   for algae prevention in fish ponds, 252
   for bathing and deodorizing pets, 251
   for hair coloring, 174
   for treating
      bee and wasp stings, 33
      insect bites, 205–6
Morning sickness treatments, 265
Morton Salt
   in baths, 296
   for cleaning
      food-coloring stains on hands, 179
      paint and grease on hands, 180
      vomit stains, <u>324</u>
   for treating
      athlete's foot, 17
      body odor, 42
      colds, 79
      dandruff, 96–97
      dehydration, 99
      diarrhea, 108
      dry skin and windburn, 120
      flea infestation, 147
      flu, 152–53
      food poisoning, 156
      foot odor, 162
      insect bites, 205

      leech bites, 207
      pizza burn, 258
      poison ivy, 262
      runny nose, 273–74
      sore gums, 103
      sore throat, 291
      stress, 296
      toothache, 313
      vomiting, 322
      warts, 326
      yeast infection, 332
Mott's Apple Sauce
   as facial, 138
   for swallowing pills, 18
   for treating
      colds, 79
      diarrhea, 109
      flu, 153
      vomiting, 323
Mountain Dew carbonated beverage, as
      insecticide, <u>35</u>
Mousse, hairstyling 177–78
Mouthwash, 253. *See also* Listerine
      mouthwash
Murphy's Oil Soap, for cleaning
   milk stains, <u>50</u>
   vomit stains, <u>324</u>
Muscle pain treatments, 239–41, 265

N

Nailbiting treatments, 142
Nausea treatments, 242, 244
Neck pain treatments, 245
Neosporin, for treating
   acne, 2
   dry skin and windburn, 120
Nestea, for treating
   bad odors, 6
   burns, 57
   calluses, 62
   corns, 87
   dry hair, 113
   foot ache, 159
   poison ivy, 262
   sunburn, 303
Neutrogena Body Moisturizer, for treating
      rashes, 271
Newspaper, <u>16</u>, 99
Niagara Spray Starch, for treating sunburn, 303
Nicotine withdrawal treatments, 247
Nosebleed treatments, 249, <u>250</u>
Noxzema
   in baths, 27
   as shaving cream, 280
   for treating
      burns, 57
      chapped lips, 69

Noxzema *(cont.)*
  for treating *(cont.)*
    eczema, 129
    gum stuck in hair, 169
    hemorrhoids, 190

O

Oatmeal. *See* Quaker Oats
Ocean Spray Cranberry Juice Cocktail
  history of, 318
  for treating
    diaper rash, 104
    green hair, 168
    kidney stones, 215
    urinary tract infection, 317
Odor problems
  body, 42
  cat litter boxes, 253
  clothes, 43
  diapers, 105
  foot, 161–62
  humidifer, 80
  menstrual, 235
  pet, 251–52
  shoes and socks, 16
  skunk spray, 253–54, 286–87
Orajel, for treating
  bee and wasp stings, 33
  bruises, 54
  burns, 57
  hemorrhoids, 190
  ingrown toenail, 142
  insect bites, 206
  premature ejaculation, 227
  splinters, 294
Oral-B Mint Waxed Floss
  in eyeglass repair, 132
  as insecticide with beer, 35
  in ring removal from finger, 299
Oral-B Toothbrush
  for cleaning
    bloodstains, 237
    clothing stains, 43
    hair brushes, combs, and curling irons,
      170
    milk stains, 50
    razors, 280
  for manicure or pedicure, 142
Orville Redenbacher's Gourmet Popping
    Corn
  for making ice pack, 198
  for treating
    constipation, 83
    hemorrhoids, 190
    indigestion, 202

P

Paint on hands, removing, 179–80
Pain treatments
  foot, 158–60
  head, 184, 185, 186
  knee, 217–18
  muscle, 239–41
  neck, 245
  tooth, 312–13, 313
Palmolive, for treating diaper rash, 105
Pam Cooking Spray
  for cleaning paint and grease on hands, 180
  for removal of
    ring stuck on finger, 299
    stickers and burrs from pets, 254
  as shaving lubricant, 280
  for treating
    chafing, 67
    diaper rash, 105
    dry cuticles, 142
    dry skin and windburn, 120
    foot ache, 159
    gum stuck in hair, 169
    psoriasis, 268
    snoring, 288
Pampers
  for cleaning
    urine odors and stains, 31, 255
    vomit stains, 324
  history of, 107
  as nursing pad, 49
  for sponge bath, 27, 153
  for treating
    cuts and scrapes, 93
    dehydration, 99
    flu, 153
Panty hose. *See* L'eggs Sheer Energy Panty
    Hose
Paper towels. *See* Bounty paper towels
Parson's Ammonia
  for cleaning
    bloodstains, 237
    hair brushes, combs, and curling irons, 170
    vomit stains, 324
  as insecticide, 35
  as insect repellent, 208
  for treating
    bee and wasp stings, 33
    insect bites, 206
    jellyfish stings, 214
    poison ivy, 262
    smelly clothes, 43
    urine odors, 255
Paul Mitchell Tea Tree Shampoo, for treating
    lice, 222

Peanut Butter. *See* Jif Peanut Butter
Pedicure tips, 140–43
Peppermints. *See* Altoid Peppermints, for treating
Pepto-Bismol
  as facial, 138
  history of, <u>243</u>
  for treating
    bee and wasp stings, 33
    hives, 196
    ulcers, 315
Pet problems, treating, 251–54
Petroleum jelly. *See* Vaseline Petroleum Jelly
Phillips' Milk of Magnesia
  as facial, 138
  as hair gel, 178
  for treating
    acne, 2
    canker sores, 66
    chicken pox, 71
    cold sores, 77
    diaper rash, 105
    heartburn, 187
    hives, 196
    insect bites, 206
    poison ivy, 262
    shingles, 284
    sunburn, 303
    ulcers, 315
Pine-Sol
  for cleaning milk stains, <u>50</u>
  for treating
    athlete's foot, 17
    flea infestation, 147
Pizza burn treatments, 258
Plaque removal tips, dental, 308–9
Plastic wrap, 175, 254. *See also* Saran Wrap, for treating
Playtex Gentle Glide Odor Absorbing Tampons, for treating
  smelly diapers, <u>105</u>
  smelly shoes and socks, <u>16</u>
Playtex Living Gloves
  for cleaning skunk spray odor, 287
  for making ice pack, 37, 198
  for preventing dry hands, 120
Pledge, for defogging eyeglasses, 132
Poison ivy treatments, 260–62, <u>263</u>
Popsicle
  history of, <u>293</u>
  for treating
    bee and wasp stings, 33
    colds, 79
    flu, 153
    pizza burn, 258
    sore throat, 291
    toothache, 313

Post-it Notes
  for eye protection, 134
  as memory aid, 331
Powder. *See* Baby Magic Baby Powder;
    Johnson's Baby Powder, for treating
Pregnancy, treating symptoms of, 265–66, <u>265</u>
Premature ejaculation treatments, 226–27
Preparation H
  for ring removal from finger, 299
  for treating
    acne, 2
    athlete's foot, 17
    bee and wasp stings, 33
    blisters, 40
    bruises, 54
    burns, 57
    cold sores, 77
    cuts and scrapes, 93
    dry skin and windburn, 120
    insect bites, 206
    poison ivy, 263
    puffy eyes, 134
    sunburn, 303
    varicose veins, 320
    wrinkles, 329
Psoriasis treatments, 268–69
Purell, for treating
  body odor, 42
  cold sores, 77
  cuts and scrapes, 93

Q

Q-Tips Cotton Swabs
  for creating hair coloring streaks, 173
  history of, <u>127</u>
  as toothbrush, <u>311</u>
  for treating
    brittle fingernails, 141–42
    nosebleed, 249
    shaving nicks and cuts, <u>281</u>
    warts, 327
Quaker Oats
  as facial, 138
  as hair shampoo, 116
  for treating
    acne, 3
    arthritis, 11
    boils, 46
    chicken pox, 71
    constipation, 83
    dry skin and windburn, 120
    eczema, 129
    foot ache, 159
    high cholesterol, 73
    poison ivy, 263
    rashes, 271

Quaker Oats *(cont.)*
  for treating *(cont.)*
    shingles, 284
    sunburn, 303–4

R

Rash treatments, 271–72
ReaLemon
  for cleaning
    bathtubs, 29
    food-coloring stains on hands, 179
    humidifier, 80
    skunk spray odor, 287
  as facial, 136, 138
  for hair coloring, 174
  as hair shampoo, 277
  for stopping dog's barking, 254
  for treating
    acne, 2–3
    bad breath, 24
    bad odors, 6
    brittle fingernails, 142
    calluses, 62
    constipation, 83
    cough, 90
    cuts and scrapes, 93
    dandruff, 97
    dehydration, 99
    diarrhea, 108
    dry skin and windburn, 118, 120
    food poisoning, 156
    freckles and sunspots, 164
    green hair, 168
    hiccups, 194
    poison ivy, 263
    runny nose, 273
    sore throat, 290–91
    vomiting, 322
    warts, 327
Reddi-wip
  as facial, 138
  as sex enhancer, 227
  as shaving cream, 280
  for treating
    dry hair, 113
    pizza burn, 258
Repairing eyeglasses, tips for, 132
Resolve, for cleaning milk stains, 50
Retainer care tips, 102–3
Reynolds Wrap
  in keeping pets off furniture, 254
  in protecting eyeglasses while dyeing hair, 175
Rice. *See* Uncle Ben's Converted Brand Rice,
    for treating
Right Guard, for treating
  foot odor, 162
  poison ivy, 263

Rolaids, for treating insect bites, 206
Runny nose treatments, 273–74

S

Salt. *See* Morton Salt
Saran Wrap, for treating
  calluses, 62
  hangnails, 142
  knee pain, 217
  psoriasis, 268
Scope Cool Peppermint Mouthwash, as insect
    repellent, 253
Scotch-Brite Heavy Duty Scrub Sponge
  for making ice pack, 198
  for treating
    foot ache, 159
    knee pain, 217
Scotchgard, for treating
  bed-wetting, 30
  smelly clothes, 43
Scotch Packaging Tape
  for padding table corners, 18–19
  for treating
    allergies, 8
    arthritis, 11
    asthma, 13
    broken bones, 51
    cuts and scrapes, 93
    knee pain, 217
    splinters, 294
Scotch Transparent Tape
  for eyeglass repair, 132
  for finding lost contact lens, 85
  for treating hangnails, 142
Scrapes, treating, 92–93, 93
Selsun Blue Dandruff Shampoo, for treating
    chigger bites, 207
7-Up, as hair coloring, 174
Sex tips, 226–27
Shampoos, 18, 26, 29, 116, 137, 207, 222,
    276–77
Shaving cream. *See* Barbasol Shaving Cream
Shaving tips, 279–81, 281
Shingles treatments, 284–85, 285
Shout, for cleaning vomit stains, 324
Silly Putty
  as earplugs, 288
  for treating
    stress, 296
    swimmer's ear, 306
Skin care tips, 121
Skin-So-Soft
  for bandage removal, 95
  in baths, 27
  for cleaning bathtubs, 29
  as insect repellent, 209
  for manicure, 142

for treating
    dry skin and windburn, 120
    flea infestation, 252
    gum stuck in hair, 169
    insect bites, 206
    muscle pain, 240
Skunk spray odor, removing, 253–54, 286–87
Sleep problems, treating, 210
Slinky, for stress management, 297
Smirnoff Vodka
  for bandage removal, 95
  for cleaning
    bathtubs, 29
    eyeglasses, 131
    razors, 281
    vomit stains, 324
  as facial, 138
  as hair shampoo, 277
  history of, 155
  as insecticide, 35
  for making
    baby wipes, 18
    ice pack, 198–99
  for treating
    backache, 21
    bad breath, 24
    black eyes, 37
    blisters, 40
    cold sores, 77
    dandruff, 97
    earache, 124
    flu, 153
    foot ache, 159
    foot odor, 162
    jellyfish stings, 214
    nicotine withdrawal, 247
    poison ivy, 263
    sore throat, 292
    swimmer's ear, 306
    toothache, 313
Smith Brothers, history of, 84
Smucker's Concord Grape Jelly, for treating burns, 57
Soft drinks. See Canada Dry Club Soda; Canada Dry Ginger Ale; Coca-Cola
Snoring treatments, 288
Sore nipple treatments, 48
Sore throat treatments, 290–92
S.O.S Steel Wool Soap Pads, for cleaning hair brushes, combs, and curling irons, 170
Spic and Span, as hair lightener, 175
Splinters, removing, 294
Spray 'N Wash, for removing gum stuck in hair, 169

Star Olive Oil
  for cleaning paint and grease on hands, 180
  for treating
    arthritis, 11
    backache, 20
    bruises, 54
    bursitis, 60
    calluses, 62
    constipation, 83
    cough, 90
    dandruff, 97
    dry cuticles, 142
    dry hair, 113–14
    dry skin and windburn, 120
    earache, 124
    flu, 153
    high cholesterol, 74
    jellyfish stings, 214
    lice, 222
    muscle pain, 240
    psoriasis, 269
    sore throat, 292
    varicose veins, 320
    wrinkles, 329
Static Guard, for treating flyaway hair, 114
Stayfree Maxi Pads
  for making ice pack, 199
  as nursing pad, 49
  for padding table ends, 18
  for sponge bath, 153
  for treating
    blisters, 40–41
    bursitis, 60
    chafing, 67
    corns, 87
    flu, 153
    hemorrhoids, 189
    knee pain, 217
    smelly clothes, 43
Stayfree Ultra Thin Maxi Pads, as shoe insert pad, 162
Stickers, removing from pet, 254
STP Carb Spray Cleaner, for cleaning vomit stains, 324
Straws, drinking. See Glad Flexible Straws
Stress management tips, 296–97
Stuck ring, tips for removing, 298–99
SueBee Honey
  as facial, 136–38
  as sex enhancer, 227
  for treating
    acne, 3
    bed-wetting, 30
    bee and wasp stings, 33
    bruises, 54
    burns, 57
    colds, 79

SueBee Honey *(cont.)*
  for treating *(cont.)*
    constipation, 83
    cough, 90
    cuts and scrapes, 93
    diarrhea, 109
    dry hair, 112–14
    flu, 152–53
    foot ache, 159
    hangover, 183
    indigestion, 202
    insomnia, 210
    rashes, 272
    runny nose, 273
    sore throat, 290–92
Sugar. *See* Domino Sugar
Sunburn treatments, 302–4, 304
Sun-Maid Raisins, for treating constipation, 84
Sunspots, treating, 164
Sure-Jell, for treating cuts and scrapes, 93
Swimmer's ear treatments, 306, 307
Syrup, chocolate. *See* Hershey's Syrup
Syrup, pancake. *See* Aunt Jemima Original Syrup

T

Tabasco Pepper Sauce
  for preventing cats from scratching wood
      furniture, 255
  for treating
    arthritis, 11–12
    asthma, 13
    backache, 21
    bee and wasp stings, 33
    bruises, 54
    colds, 79
    cough, 90
    flu, 153
    foot ache, 159
    muscle pain, 240
    nailbiting, 142
    neck pain, 245
    runny nose, 274
    shingles, 284–85
    sore throat, 292
    toothache, 313
Tampax Tampons
  as earplugs, 288
  as eyeglass cleaner, 132
  as toothbrush, 311
  for treating cuts and scrapes, 93
Tang
  for cleaning toilets, 111
  as hair shampoo, 277
  for treating
    bad breath, 24
    hangover, 183

nicotine withdrawal, 247
    sore throat, 292
    warts, 327
Tartar removal tips, 308–9
Tea. *See* Lipton Tea Bags; Nestea, for treating
Therapeutic Mineral Ice, for treating muscle
      pain, 239
Tide
  for cleaning vomit stains, 324
  history of, 323
  for treating corns, 87
Tidy Cats cat litter
  as facial, 139
  for treating
    insect bites, 206
    smelly diapers, 105
    smelly shoes and socks, 16
Tissues, 9, 48, 236
Toenail treatments, 140–43
Toilets, cleaning, 111
Toothache treatments, 312–13, 313
Toothpaste, 1, 177, 280. *See also* Colgate
      Toothpaste
Training pets, 254–55
Trash bags. *See* Glad Trash Bags
Trojan Condoms, for making ice pack, 199
Tums
  for calcium requirements, 233, 236
  for treating
    lactose intolerance, 219
    menopausal symptoms, 233
    menstrual problems, 236
Turtle Wax, for cleaning bathtubs, 29
20 Mule Team Borax
  for cleaning
    bathtubs, 29
    humidifier, 80
    urine odors, 31, 255
    vomit stains, 324
  for deodorizing cat litter box, 253
  for treating
    flea infestation, 147
    smelly clothes, 43
    smelly diapers, 105
    smelly shoes and socks, 16
Twinkies
  history of, 212
  for treating insomnia, 210

U

Ulcer treatments, 315
Uncle Ben's Converted Brand Rice, for treating
  backache, 21
  bursitis, 60
  diarrhea, 109
  eye soreness, 134

food poisoning, 156
heartburn, 187
knee pain, 217
muscle pain, 240
vomiting, 323
Urinary tract infection treatments, 317, _317_
Urine smell removal, _31_
USA Today, for treating
    dehydration, 99
    smelly shoes and socks, _16_

V

Vaginal lubricant, 226
Varicose vein treatments, 320
Vaseline Petroleum Jelly
    as hair gel, 178
    for razor care, 281
    for ring removal from finger, 299
    for skin protection while dyeing hair, _175_
    for treating
        blisters, 40–41
        bruises, 54
        burns, 57
        chafing, 67
        chapped lips, 70
        colds, 80
        cold sores, 77
        corns, 88
        cuts and scrapes, 93
        diaper rash, 106
        dry cuticles, 142
        dry skin and windburn, 120–21
        flu, 153
        hemorrhoids, 190
        nosebleed, 249
        pets' hairballs, 253
        psoriasis, 269
        runny nose, 274
        warts, 327
Vegemite sandwich spread, for treating
    canker sores, 66
    dental tartar and plaque, 309
Vicks VapoRub
    history of, _144_
    as insect repellent, 209
    for treating
        acne, 3
        burns, 58
        calluses, 62
        foot ache, 160
        insect bites, 206
        toenail fungus, 142
Vinegar. *See* Heinz Apple Cider Vinegar; Heinz
    White Vinegar
Visine eyedrops, for treating acne, 3
Vomiting treatments, 322–23, 325

W

Wart treatments, 326–27
Wasp sting treatments, 32–34
WD-40
    for cleaning paint and grease on hands, 180
    as insecticide, _35_
    for razor care, 281
    for removal of
        gum from hair and dentures or retainers,
            103, 169
        ring stuck on finger, 299
        stickers and burrs from pets, 254
Wesson Corn Oil
    for bathing and deodorizing pets, 252
    for cleaning paint and grease on hands, 180
    for manicure, 143
    for treating
        dry hair, 114
        dry skin and windburn, 120
        earache, 124
        foot ache, 160
        gum stuck in hair, 170
        pets' ear mites, 252
        pets' hairballs, 253
        psoriasis, 269
        splinters, 294
Wilson Tennis Balls
    for padding table ends, 19
    for treating
        arthritis, 12
        backache, 21
        flu, 153
        foot ache, 160
        muscle pain, 240, 265
        snoring, 288
        stress, 297
Windburn treatments, 118–21
Windex
    for cleaning
        milk stains, _50_
        vomit stains, _324_
    as insecticide, _35_
    for ring removal from finger, 299
    for treating bee and wasp stings, 34
Wish-Bone Thousand Island Dressing
    for ring removal from finger, 299
    for treating insect bites, 206
Witch hazel. *See* Dickinson's Witch Hazel, for
    treating
Wonder Bread, for treating
    boils, 46
    corns, 87
    diarrhea, 109
    morning sickness, 265
    nausea, 242, 265

367

Woolite, as hair shampoo, 277
Wound treatments
  cuts and scrapes, 92–93, _93_
  pet, 252
  shaving nicks and cuts, _281_
Wrigley's Spearmint Gum
  for eyeglass repair, 132
  for treating
    earache, 124
    flatulence, 146
    heartburn, 188
Wrinkle treatments, 329

Y

Yeast infection treatments, 331–32, _332_
Yogurt. _See_ Dannon Yogurt
York Peppermint Pattie, for treating
  allergies, 9
  colds, 80
  cough, 90
  flatulence, 146
  flu, 154
  menstrual problems, 236
  nausea, 244

Z

Ziploc Freezer Bags
  for plugging bathtub drains, 27
  for bath pillow, 27
Ziploc Storage Bags
  for cleaning dentures or retainers, 103
  for diaper disposal, _105_
  as heat pack for
    backache, 21
    bursitis, 60
    earache, 124

for holding
  Huggies Baby Wipes, 233
  snacks, 247
  tampons, 236
as ice pack for
  backache, 21–22
  bee and wasp stings, 34
  black eyes, 37
  broken bones, 51
  bruises, 55
  bursitis, 60–61
  eczema, 130
  flu, 154
  foot ache, 160
  headache, 184
  hives, 196
  insect bites, 206
  knee pain, 218
  muscle pain, 241
  neck pain, 245
  nosebleed, 249
  psoriasis, 269
  rashes, 272
  shingles, 285
  sore breasts, 49
  sunburn, 304
  toothache, 313
for protecting hand from hot gels, 241
for tissue disposal, 80, 154, 274
for travel pillow, 21
for treating
  athlete's foot, 17
  chafing, 67
  colds, 80
  dry skin and windburn, 121, _121_
  foot odor, 162
as vomit bags, 266, 325

Joey Green—the author of *Polish Your Furniture with Panty Hose, Paint Your House with Powdered Milk, Wash Your Hair with Whipped Cream,* and *Clean Your Clothes with Cheez Whiz*—got Jay Leno to shave with Jif Peanut Butter on *The Tonight Show,* Rosie O'Donnell to mousse her hair with Jell-O on *The Rosie O'Donnell Show,* and Katie Couric to drop her diamond engagement ring in a glass of Efferdent on *Today.* He has been seen polishing furniture with Spam on *NBC Dateline,* cleaning a toilet with Coca-Cola in the *New York Times,* and washing his hair with Reddi-wip in *People.* Green, a former contributing editor to *National Lampoon* and a former advertising copywriter at J. Walter Thompson, is the author of more than twenty books, including *The Zen of Oz, Selling Out,* and *The Road to Success Is Paved with Failure.* A native of Miami, Florida, and a graduate of Cornell University, he wrote television commercials for Burger King and Walt Disney World and won a Clio Award for a print ad he created for Eastman Kodak. He backpacked around the world for two years on his honeymoon and lives in Los Angeles with his wife, Debbie, and their two daughters, Ashley and Julia.

Visit Joey Green on the Internet at www.wackyuses.com